Battlefield B

Siege, Surrender and Occupation, 1945

by

PETER SLOWE

and

RICHARD WOODS

ROBERT HALE · LONDON

© *Peter Slowe and Richard Woods 1988*
First published in Great Britain 1988

Robert Hale Limited
Clerkenwell House
Clerkenwell Green
London ECIR OHT

British Library Cataloguing in Publication Data
Slowe, Peter
Battlefield Berlin: siege, surrender
and occupation, 1945.
1. Germany, Berlin, 1945– Personal
observations
I. Title   II. Woods, Richard, *1964–*
943.1'55

ISBN 0-7090-3293-5

943. 155087

Photoset by Rowland Phototypesetting Limited
Printed in Great Britain by
St Edmundsbury Press Limited, Bury St Edmunds, Suffolk
and bound by WBC

Contents

List of Illustrations 7
Acknowledgements 9
Preface 11
Introduction 15

THE SIEGE OF BERLIN 19
Introduction 21
The End of Normal Life in Berlin: 1943 to 1944 22
The Non-Plot: 20 July 1944 26
The Decline and Fall of the Nazi Foreign Ministry:
  February 1945 30
Youth to the Fore: April 34
Albert Speer's Rebellion: March and April 37
The Last Social Call: 21 April 41
Last-Minute Vengeance of the Reich: 2 April 45

LAST BATTLE ON THE EASTERN FRONT 47
Introduction 49
The Battle of the Oder, Zhukov Slowed: 16–17 April 51
Defending Seelow: 16–17 April 54
The Battle of Lietzen: 16–20 April 58
Britische Freikorps: 18–19 April 62
Chuikov's Eight Guards Army – The Straight Road to
  Berlin: 16–23 April 64
From the Neisse to Berlin in Forty-Eight Hours:
  16–23 April 69
The Rise and Fall of the Ninth Army: March to May 74

THE REAL CASUALTIES 79
Introduction 81
'Speechless and Trembling', Landed Gentry in a Village
  Captured by the Red Army: 21–25 April 82
Punishment in the Workers' Suburb: 22 April 85
What the Gestapo Heard: 23 April 88
Out of Hiding: Christmas 1944 and Spring 1945 90
Liberation of a German Anti-Nazi Cell: 24–28 April 93
The Fall of the Wendl Family: Late April to Early June 97
A Diary of the End: 28 April to 2 May 101

The Story of a Berliner Boy and His Uncle: April 105
The Hotel Adlon, Number 1, Unter den Linden:
  March to May 108

WAR IN THE STREETS 113
Introduction 115
Escape to Berlin – and Fighting Back: 20 April 118
A Doctor is 'De-Nazified' and Meets Hitler: 23–30 April 125
The Last Flight from Berlin: 24–28 April 130
The Battle of Moabit: 26 and 27 April 133
Organizing the Defence of Berlin and Running Away:
  24–29 April 137
Toughness and Tenderness on the Potsdam Bridge:
  26–29 April 140
Iron Crosses: 28 April 144
Attacking the Reichstag: 30 April 147
Hitler Dispatches His Final Testament: 29 April to 1 May 150
Bluster and the Loss of the Reichstag: 28 April to 1 May 153
Hitler – The End and After: 30 April to 9 May 156
Joseph and Magda Goebbels – Infanticide and Death:
  January to May 159
The End of the French SS Volunteers: 30 April to 2 May 162
Bormann's Escape and Suicide: 1–2 May 166
The Surrender of Berlin: 1 and 2 May 169
Break-out and Capture: 2–3 May 172

AFTERMATH 177
Introduction 179
Nazis Don't Get Away with It: 20 May 181
A British Officer Explores – and Finds Japanese
  Aphrodisiacs: July to December 185
Churchill at the Potsdam Conference: 15 July to 2 August 188
Attlee at the Potsdam Conference: 15 July to 2 August 193
Survivors of the Destruction of Berlin: Christmas Eve 196
The German Communists: 15 January 1946 198
The Hitler Youth Returns: 1944 to 1946 201

Epilogue 205
Appendix: Berlin 1940–45 – Facts and Figures 207
Principal Sources and Select Bibliography 211
Index 213

List of Illustrations

Between pages 64 and 65
The ruins of the Gedächtniskirche
The Brandenburg Gate from Unter den Linden
Looking across the Wall towards the site of the Chancellery
The authors by the remains of Zhukov's command post
Falkenhagen Station
A 'Stalin Organ' in the museum at Seelow
A defender's view at Seelow
Lietzen manor house and church
The River Nieplitz at Salzbrunn
Entrance to the Horstmann estate at Kerzendorf
Ornamental lake where Lali Horstmann hid her jewellery
Remains of the Horstmanns' manor house at Kerzendorf
The Wendls' house in Kladow
Max Bock's flat in Meinekestrasse

Between pages 96 and 97
Heroic sculpture in Berlin's Treptow Park
The Olympic Stadium – scene of a bloody battle
The mass grave at Ruhleben
Water tower where Ruth Andreas-Friedrich assumed she would be
 shot
Berlin's East–West axis looking west from the Victory Column
The former headquarters of the Reich Labour Service
The Charlotte Bridge
Remains of the old Potsdam Bridge
No 2 Schulenburgring where General Weidling surrendered Berlin
Stadtmitte underground station
The ruins of Hitler's 'New Chancellery'
Timber-framed signalman's house at Salzkorn
Bullet holes from 1945 on Berlin's older buildings
Memorial to the Socialists

Photographs by Thomas Brendler and Richard Woods

Maps drawn by Diana M. Smith of the West Sussex Institute of
 Higher Education

Acknowledgements

The authors would like to thank all the many friends and colleagues who have helped them prepare this book.

In particular they are grateful to Brigitte and Thomas Brendler for their hospitality and for sharing their immense knowledge of Berlin. They would also like to thank Ian Crammond for help with sources and ideas, and the staffs of the libraries of the Imperial War Museum and the West Sussex Institute of Higher Education, who have been most helpful. Thomas Brendler has been a brilliant photographer, Gill Brady has been a marvellous typist, and Diana Smith has been an excellent cartographer: the authors are most grateful to each of them.

Peter Slowe
Richard Woods

This book is dedicated to Peter Slowe's brothers, Martin and Richard, and to Richard Woods' brothers, John and Robert.

Preface

Old Berlin crumbled in 1945. The best buildings were destroyed and many of the best people had died long before. Many more were killed or injured. The liberation from Nazism was violent and demanded terrible sacrifice. Berliners had been prisoners of Nazism, mostly willing prisoners, but still they were prisoners, kept within an ever more demanding prison system, terrified of the world beyond the walls.

The aim of this book is to take a look inside the prison, inside the minds of the prisoners, gaolers and liberators. Its method is to look at diaries and personal records carefully selected to reveal the whole story of the last stages of Nazi regime in Berlin and its replacement by Communist and Western control. It sets out to show what happened and how people behaved – and why.

There are personal records in English, French, German and Russian. The ones chosen tell the story as it happened from the last great battles of the Eastern Front to the immediate post-war politics in Berlin. The sources range from Joseph Goebbels to ordinary soldiers in the Red Army, from Nazi officials to Jews hiding in Berlin. They are set in landscapes which you can visit. You can see where the drama was enacted for real. This approach deepens understanding of the reality of what happened. The emphasis is on the words and feelings of the men and women themselves, their words, their buildings and their places.

Visiting Berlin Today

Berlin is still a front-line city. It is still technically a four-power city, divided into American, British, French and Soviet sectors. There is no sign of any kind of border when you cross from the American, British or French sectors, but when you cross into the Soviet sector you will come across the Wall. The American, British and French sectors make up West Berlin, and the Soviet sector is the capital of the German Democratic Republic, which also consists of the Soviet zone of Germany west of the Oder–Neisse line.

The area round Unter den Linden is again full of embassies, and the size of the Soviet one shows clearly the allegiance of the East

European state. The substantial NATO presence in West Berlin
shows clearly the allegiance of that part of the city to the Western
world.

There are heavily guarded border crossing points for foreigners on
the Potsdam side of West Berlin and also in Friedrichstrasse in the
city centre (Checkpoint Charlie). You can also cross from Lehrter to
Friedrichstrasse and back by train. Western visitors to east Berlin do
not need a visa in advance but there is the usual East European
rigmarole of money exchange. The German Democratic Republic
border police are not generally concerned about maps and photographs of the city and its surroundings. These days they are trained
to be friendly.

Most of the places on the maps in this book can be seen or touched.
In neither the east nor the west are they particularly sensitive about
the Wall, which is just as well, since many of the stories took place
very close to it, in the centre of Berlin and in Potsdam. Fortunately,
only Churchill's house in Potsdam, parts of Clara-Zetkin-Strasse
(formerly Dorotheenstrasse), Pariser Platz, Ebertstrasse (formerly
Hermann-Goering-Strasse), Potsdamer Platz and Leipziger Platz
are totally inaccessible, and all of these can be seen from the east in
the case of the first three and from the west in the case of the last
three. At Churchill's house, you can get out on the opposite side of
the road but the house and the pavement outside are rather too close
to the border for comfort. The world-famous Brandenburg Gate can
also be seen from both sides of the Wall but not actually approached.

The stories in this book and the maps that go with them should
provide a thorough and insightful history of a brief but crucial part of
the War. If you get a chance to visit them, you will find some of these
places evocative indeed. The atmosphere and feeling associated with
particular locations determine events as much as measurable facts
and calculations. That is why this book has concentrated on individuals, stories by individuals, experienced history and its geo-
graphical environment. As well as being an interesting way of
looking at events, it helps us understand them.

The end of the War in Berlin led to a sequence of events which no
one could have predicted. To understand what happened and why,
at such a dramatic time, you have to understand the people who were
there. Then you can grasp the nature of the extraordinary struggle of
people and ideologies, of great leaders and their followers. Then
there were ordinary men and women – perhaps just like many of you
– who were there in Berlin and took part in it all.

KEY FOR MAPS

(Owing to the use of different scales, some maps may vary slightly from this key.
The variations are self-explanatory.)

ᵀᵀᵀ	Brandenburg Gate		Reichstag
	Built-up Area		Bridge
	River or Canal		Church
	Woodland/Parkland	— — —	Army Front Line
—+—+—+—	Railway	—×—×—×—	The Wall
—+—■—+—	Railway Station		Lake
■	Building still standing		High Ground
⌐⌐	Building now demolished		Cutting

NOTES

1. Capital lettering on maps is used to show a feature which exists today or to indicate a modern name. Lower-case features are no longer in existence; lower-case names are no longer in use.

2. Dotted lines are used when a feature is no longer visible but its location is identified, for example a front line in battle or a demolished building.

Introduction

You're told you're worse than an ape. You are a Slav or an Oriental, maybe a Pole or even a Jew. You are told by the German Master Race that their conquest of your land was inevitable. You are their prisoner now and you will never escape.

A few years pass and those Slavs and Orientals, including Poles and Jews, are now the victorious army. They end the tyranny of the Master Race. They bring another ideology, Communism, under the leadership of Joseph Stalin.

You had seen with your own eyes unspeakable brutality, public hangings, mass murder carried out like military exercises, tortures, starvation and death. Men were killed; women were forced to serve their German masters in brothels; children were destined for slavery. Stalin's Communist troops who saved you maybe asked you to join them and fight the Master Race to destruction. Vengeance could be yours, although the aim was not vengeance except on a few of the leaders. The aim of the campaign was to free the ordinary people, including Germans, from the false ideology of Fascism and Hitler's particularly twisted interpretation of it, Nazism. The leaders of Stalin's Soviet state knew very well how ordinary people could be manipulated for good or bad ends, and they wanted to win such people to their side and not to wreak vengeance on them. Not even when they at last reached their capital, Berlin.

By 1945, Stalin's Army, the Red Army, had practically won. Ordinary Germans thought of 'The War' mainly as the war in the east, against the Red Army, because that was where most of their sons, brothers and fathers were dying. Huge unmarked, unremembered mass graves signified Hitler's defeat in the east, the defeat that mattered more than any other. It was that defeat which disposed of the Master Race theory and proved wrong all Hitler's military and political strategies. The Soviet Union had not collapsed in three months or six months, but $3\frac{1}{2}$ years after Operation Barbarossa had launched the Nazi armies into Russia, the Red Army were less than eighty kilometres from Berlin.

Contrary to what Hitler had hoped for and still may have expected, the Allies had not split up. Churchill, Roosevelt and Stalin had planned at Yalta for the future of Europe with no role for Germany, and they were sticking to it. The Western Allies had

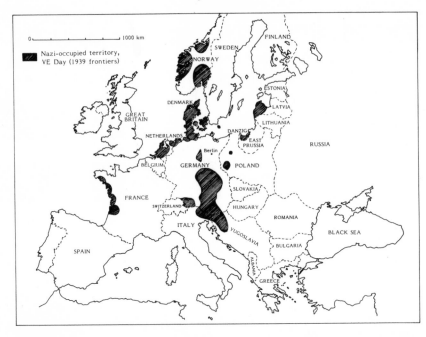

stopped on the Elbe, as they had agreed at Yalta. They left Berlin to
the Red Army. For Stalin, Berlin was 'the Lair of the Fascist Beast' to
be taken as its ultimate prize by the victorious Red Army. It was
intended by Hitler and Goebbels to be the scene of a *Götterdämmerung* in which the earth would shake at their downfall.

It did not really happen as either Hitler or Stalin wanted.

Berlin, the imperial capital, was severely damaged in advance in
massive air raids by the Americans and British. The buildings and
population were reduced and battered, and a great city scarcely
remained to be defended or conquered. The older children of Berlin –
sixteen- and seventeen-year-olds – were sent to ward off the siege by
land, to defend Berlin on the Oder and Neisse; the younger ones,
including ten- and eleven-year-olds, were kept back to defend the
city streets themselves from Red Army tanks. Then the Red Army
won – with some difficulty – the Battles of the Oder and Neisse and in
a few days encircled Berlin, which was now at their mercy.

There was still the prospect of street fighting in a city with 2½
million civilians. Some of the fighting was vicious and costly, especially in the city centre, but most German soldiers and civilians knew
the war was over and wanted only to escape to surrender to the
Western Allies instead of to the Red Army or else at least to get the
front line past their homes as quickly as possible and then to endure
whatever had to be endured.

Berlin was conquered by an army motivated by the desire to liberate and the urge to punish. The desire to liberate was fulfilled over the years as a showpiece Communist city developed in the east and as capitalist democracy flourished in the west. The urge to punish was gratified quickly and painfully, by forced labour and rape. The city divided by the Wall reminds each generation of Berliners of the consequences of following a psychopath down the Nazi road to Hell.

THE SIEGE OF BERLIN

Introduction

The destructive power of two air forces damaged Berlin beyond repair. It would never again be the imperial capital of Germany. It would never again be a city on a grand scale.

Berlin was a battlefield long before the Red Army reached it. The bombers had hit Hitler's capital back in September 1940. At that time they could not hit it hard. Spandau was slightly damaged and that was about all. Gradually the bombing increased in frequency and intensity, culminating in the Royal Air Force's thousand-bomber raids in November 1943 and in January and February 1944. From then on, Berlin suffered by day from American bombers and by night from the Royal Air Force. There was hardly a let-up. One home in three was destroyed and 150,000 people were seriously injured or killed.

The people suffered worse than the industry which was often the ostensible target. At the end of 1944, two-thirds of industry still worked at full production, but the people who worked in it were exhausted and terrified.

Berlin responded fiercely to the treatment it received from its enemies. Six concrete forts – 'flak towers' – the size of twelve-storey office blocks were built in the major open spaces and parks. These hideous structures were built so solidly that they were almost indestructible from the air. They provided stable platforms for whole batteries of high-velocity 105 mm and 88 mm anti-aircraft guns. The largest of these structures, the G Tower in the north-west corner of the zoo, contained barracks, a hospital, a storeroom for art treasures and an air-raid shelter for an incredible 15,000 people.

Berlin also depended on Luftwaffe fighter squadrons, including the specially equipped night fighter units. But as the war closed in on Germany, there was just not enough fuel to carry on, and American Mustang and Lightning fighters soon dominated the air. Only solitary Luftwaffe night fighters mingled with the vast columns of bombers destroying Berlin and all the other German cities. Sometimes they caused damage, but it was really the last gasp.

The physical destruction of Berlin was equalled by its moral self-destruction. Its people readily inflicted upon themselves a Nazi regime which brought with it a brutal police state. A police state must always have new victims. Even with their city being blown to pieces around them, the Gestapo watched assiduously for signs of dissent: they read letters, they listened to telephone calls, they paid midnight calls on their victims, and the Propaganda Ministry controlled the press and broadcasting as thoroughly as ever.

The 20 July Bomb Plot in 1944 gave all these sinister forces of the Nazi state another chance for a violent purge. In the aftermath of the plot, every imaginable opponent of the regime disappeared.

When the Propaganda Ministry had exhausted its venom on plotters, conspirators, traitors, cowards, defeatists and so on, it turned its attention to proving that life, though hard, was normal and jolly. By January 1945 the Red Army was less than eighty kilometres east of Berlin, in the Oder Valley, but Berliners and soldiers and airmen on leave could have a good time in the Kurfürstendamm. Sometimes they were forced into shelters and cellars, but concerts and plays, restaurants and brothels all kept resolutely going. Partly it was because individuals had to find ways to escape the horrors. Partly it was because if you did not appear to enjoy yourself you could be seen as defeatist, and such behaviour could well attract the attention of the Gestapo.

Young teenagers were sent out to the Front in 1945, torn away from families, often already bereaved, who had hoped their youngsters would be spared the full horrors. The old Wehrmacht had been destroyed. There was no way of holding off the Red Army, and Berlin was encircled by 24 April. Shells replaced bombs. Berlin was in the front line.

In this last stage, the final physical siege, Nazism waxed and waned. Hitler raged that after him there could be no Germany. He ordered that all the bridges and factories should be destroyed rather than be allowed to fall to the enemy. Armaments Minister Speer managed to stop most of this purposeless destruction. People, however, were not always as lucky as the bridges and factories. The Gestapo and the SS were active up to the last few hours.

Berlin was surely at the limit of moral degradation, and perhaps also at the limit of physical endurance, when the Red Army reached it. It was called the Fall of Berlin, but it was really the Relief of Berlin or even the Liberation of Berlin.

The End of Normal Life in Berlin:
1943 to 1944

British bombers brought the war to Berlin and to Ursula von Kardorff of 21 Rankestrasse in the city centre.

'Klaus and I could not stand it any longer and, since the bombing had stopped, we ran up to the flat. It looked as though all the furies had been let loose on it. All the doors were off their hinges, only splinters of broken glass remained in the windows and the rest lay on the floor, the furniture had been tossed around as if by a tornado, the plaster had fallen from the walls and the whole scene was bathed in a horrid blood-red light. In the drawing-room stood a terrifying stranger in a flapping cloak, and only when I came close did I realise that it was a tailor's dummy which Papa had dressed up in scarlet robes for the portrait of the Rector of the University which he is painting. Every time we saw that ghostly figure in the light of the fires it made us jump.'

'Papa' had already lost sixty paintings, much of his life's work.

The outskirts of Berlin were not so much affected by the raid after raid after raid which hit the centre. As late as March 1945, Berlin's factories ran at seventy per cent capacity. Even in the centre, shattered night after night, morale stayed high throughout all the heavy early raids; it even improved as everyone 'got stuck in' together, helping and comforting each other, Nazi and anti-Nazi alike, facing with a new-found comradeship the constant threat of injury and death from bombs and mines, phosphorus fires and collapsing buildings.

Things really started to change in the catastrophic raid of 22 November 1943.

The 'heavy' warning for a major raid was early that night. Ursula von Kardorff, her brother Klaus and their parents swallowed what they could of some braised rabbit and made for the cellars.

The nearby explosions and distant thuds started almost at once. Bombs were landing terrifyingly close. Ursula knew that the cellar was not particularly strong and that any kind of bomb or mine landing too close could have appalling consequences – burst lungs or deep shell-shock. She also knew that any direct hit would kill the whole family.

The raid seemed endless, twice as long as usual. How could a city take this sort of thing? Shops and cafés along the Kurfürstendamm, full half an hour earlier of revellers taking a night off from the war, exploded into oblivion. When the zoo was hit, lions and tigers and poisonous snakes escaped into the streets, where for the most part they died quickly. The monumental Gedächtniskirche, Kaiser Wilhelm Memorial Church, was wiped out of the centre of Berlin by burning sheets of phosphorus.

As the raid at last came to an end, Klaus von Kardorff's girlfriend, Jutta Sorge, turned up, having cycled in from the suburbs. Her sister and brother-in-law up from Cologne had gone for an evening on the

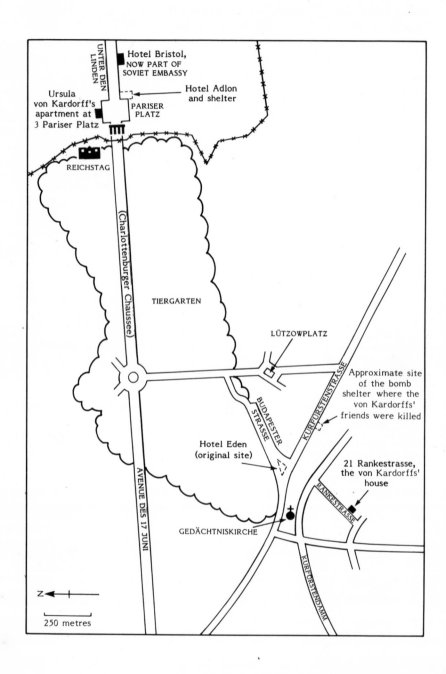

town. From out of town, Jutta had witnessed the massive raid. Ursula and Klaus set out to help her search.

The way was blocked at the Hotel Eden. Beyond lay an inferno of fire and ruin. Ursula never forgot Jutta's look that night. She could not persuade her to come back with them. She just wanted to stay and stare, alone.

The rumour was that a public air-raid shelter in Kurfürstenstrasse had been hit direct. By the end of the night, it was proved right.

'Her sister and brother-in-law actually were in the wrecked shelter. A woman, who was nearer to the front wall and who had been dug out, had seen them there. They had been on their way home. When the bombing started, they turned back. The temperature in the shelter is said to have been 150 degrees Fahrenheit. The corpses were all unrecognisable – all quite black.'

21 Rankestrasse was now virtually uninhabitable. The main iron front door had gone and in their apartment the von Kardorffs had wrecked furniture, crumbling walls, collapsing ceilings and no windows. The parents moved out of town. Klaus, a journalist like Ursula, went off to the Italian Front. Ursula rescued a few bits and pieces both from her flat and from her burnt-out office and found a new place for herself at 3 Pariser Platz.

The new flat was near the Hotel Adlon, which had the advantage of one of the most secure air-raid shelters in Berlin. To get to it there was at times an orderly queue. At other times there was a scrum – Ursula's sex meant little or nothing. Apart from a growing community of prostitutes servicing the men whose families had been evacuated, women seemed to have lost their femininity under the new conditions:

'The creature who wears trousers and extinguishes incendiary bombs like a regular fireman, who hacks her way through into buried shelters with a pickaxe, who fire-watches on the roofs in a steel helmet, who lugs furniture out of burning rooms, who can plot the bursts of anti-aircraft shells or the falling of a stick of bombs like a trained gunner – can this sexless, brave, tough creature really be a woman?'

Right through 1944, Berliners made determined, if sometimes pathetic, efforts to do normal things. Ursula made herself attend concerts given in half-ruined halls to packed audiences usually mid-morning when air raids were least likely, and she spent fortunes on good food and new clothes: there might well be no tomorrow, so why not 200 marks for a dress, 14 marks for mushrooms?

Nazism carried on as normal. Ursula found herself in a heated discussion with a colleague who could see nothing wrong with pressing half-Jews into the Army but then denying them promotion as a matter of course. She then found herself worrying about the possible consequences if the Gestapo got to hear about her side of the discussion. The Gestapo and SS at least were carrying on as if nothing was happening.

Ursula even had some social life. There were now so few upper-class girls left in Berlin that she kept finding herself at important social and diplomatic functions. She could usually succeed in wiping out the horrors of everyday life and the ghastly sights from her mind and with an effort of will enjoy good food and interesting conversation. On one such occasion, she was engaged in conversation with Anfuso, the Italian Ambassador. Gradually, she found it difficult to swallow her food and to concentrate. She started to remember . . .

She remembered the knocking sound she had heard as she passed the Hotel Bristol. She remembered her friends. The Hotel Bristol had been destroyed the night before; in fact, the raging fire had kept Ursula awake. In the morning loud tapping could be heard from where the shelter had been – thousands of tons of masonry had fallen on top of it. Rescue attempts were half-hearted and it was expected to take several more days to penetrate as far as the heavily protected shelter. By the evening the tapping was weaker. Ursula realized with horror that the previous night's guests at the Hotel Bristol would finally suffocate at about the time that coffee was served to her and the Italian Ambassador at the Hotel Adlon.

The world was collapsing inwards on Nazi Berlin.

Source
U. von Kardorff, *Diary of a Nightmare*

The Non-Plot: 20 July 1944

The famous July Bomb Plot lasted only for an afternoon. In Berlin there were a few signs of excitement but they soon died down.

It was true that the Bomb Plot was daring, even heroic. If it had been successful, it could well have ended the War, ended the Holocaust and stopped the destruction of Berlin. But the plotters showed that they were not even capable of blowing up Hitler. 'They were too civilized, too respectable, and most of them far too old and lacking the unrelenting and spontaneous zest for action without which no forceful overthrow of an established government can succeed.' As the Danish journalist Paul Stemann noticed, they never thought to tell the people of Berlin what was going on. Hardly anyone found out about the Bomb Plot till it was all over.

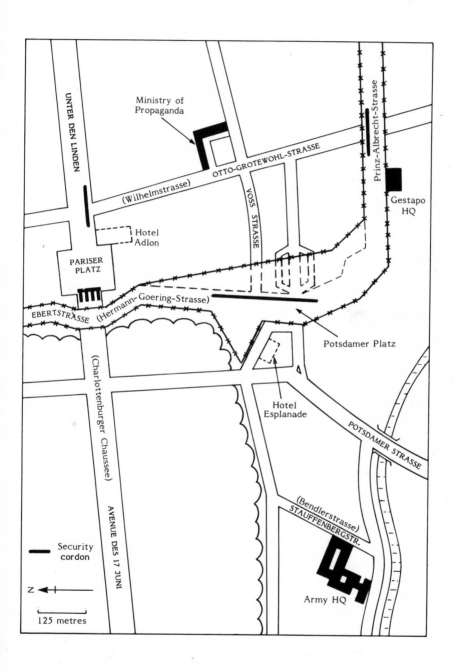

UNTER DEN LINDEN

Ministry of
Propaganda

OTTO-GROTEWOHL-STRASSE

Prinz-Albrecht-Strasse

(Wilhelmstrasse)

VOSS STRASSE

Gestapo
HQ

Hotel
Adlon

PARISER
PLATZ

EBERTSTRASSE (Hermann-Goering-Strasse)

Potsdamer Platz

(Charlottenburger Chaussee)

Hotel
Esplanade

POTSDAMER STRASSE

(Bendlerstrasse)
STAUFFENBERGSTR.

AVENUE DES 17 JUNI

Security
cordon

N

125 metres

Army HQ

The bomb blew at the Wolf's Lair in East Prussia at 12.30 p.m. At 4 p.m. Stemann received a telephone call in his room at the Esplanade Hotel from a colleague across the Potsdamer Platz at the Press Club telling him an attempt had been made on the Führer's life. Stemann hurried out and ran towards the Press Club.

A few wild rumours circulated among the journalists, but they seemed to be the only ones in Berlin who had the slightest idea there was anything wrong. The Ministry of Propaganda reacted so lackadaisically that for over an hour they could not even find an official to announce the fact that Hitler was alive and not in danger.

Stemann missed such excitement as there was because he was stuck on the wrong side of Potsdamer Platz and could not get to the Ministry of Propaganda briefings or discuss the matter with his colleagues. He had encountered a cordon of soldiers down Hermann-Goering-Strasse and across the Potsdamer Platz who blocked his way but had no idea why they were there.

'There were only few people about and no excitement. Apparently the Government quarter had been cordoned off. At intervals, there were machine-gun positions and the soldiers had fixed bayonets. There were police in steel helmets. On both sides of the cordon were queues of trams which were not allowed through and in the square people were lying down on the grass seemingly uninterested in what was going on and passively waiting to be let through. They were not even curious what it was all about.

'Not how I imagined a revolution,' Stemann thought. He went back to his hotel, scribbled a message to his paper in Copenhagen and phoned the Press Club. A Swedish journalist friend, Herje Granberg, came up to the cordon and took the notes for relaying when Stemann's expected phone call came in from Copenhagen. The soldiers with bayonets and machine-guns did not mind pieces of paper passing through. It was people they had to watch, not paper.

By the evening, only the main Government buildings were guarded, so Stemann and Granberg went off to dine at the smart Hotel Adlon. There, for the first time, Stemann noticed tension. The Adlon routine was the same as ever. High-up guests handed over their ration cards, and the waiter solemnly cut off tokens for five grams of fat with the scissors hanging on a string around his neck. But there was an atmosphere behind the small-talk and polite conversation.

A few yards away, in the garden of the Ministry of Propaganda, the first rumblings of Nazi vengeance were under way. Goebbels and Himmler worked out their most brutal purge yet. Anyone related to or friendly with a conspirator would die. Anyone whom Goebbels and Himmler had wanted to get rid of for some time would die.

There were several in the Hotel Adlon restaurant that night who knew in their bones that they had gambled and lost.

On his way back to the Esplanade Hotel, Stemann heard rifle shots from the military headquarters in Bendlerstrasse. The first four plotters had died.

In the days that followed, others disappeared. Faces that had become familiar about town were seen no more. Names were whispered. The Gestapo was rarely mentioned but it was implied time and again.

'Although they all knew that arrest meant torture and likely execution by hanging, no one offered any resistance. Only a few went underground and tried to escape but with an odd exception they were duly denounced and picked up in an almost leisurely way by the police and sent back to the Gestapo in Berlin.

'The Gestapo's operation was incredibly childlike in its simplicity. Mostly they just sent a couple of men in a small car to someone's home or office and quietly collected their victim who would invariably have a small bag ready with such essentials as would be useful in prison. Often the Gestapo did not even go to this trouble but would just telephone the suspect and say that they wished to see him next day at a given time in the Gestapo headquarters – office number so-and-so. The poor soul would then spend a sleepless night and next day with a bag in hand miserably trot through the ruins to Prinz-Albrecht-Strasse, careful not to be late and, sheeplike, walk through that fateful door which, when it closed behind him, was not to open again.

'For the Gestapo it was easier to gather their prey than it is for a shepherd to get his sheep into a pen. They didn't even need the help of a dog.'

Even for Stemann himself, the times were dangerous. Everyone was under suspicion. As a foreign journalist, he was always tailed now. As a journalist from a Nazi-occupied country, there could be no escape if someone in a high place was after him.

The fear was stepped up on the Home Front.

Source
P. E. v. Stemann, unpublished diary

The Decline and Fall of the
Nazi Foreign Ministry: February 1945

Hans Georg von Studnitz, a press officer at the Foreign Ministry,
writing in his diary on Monday 5 February 1945, considered himself
a virtual prisoner in a doomed city.

'The State Defence Council has decided that the Government
must remain in Berlin, and there await either a miracle or annihila-
tion. The decision was taken because the evacuation of millions of
Berliners was seen to be technically impossible and it was felt that
the population could not be compelled to resist to the end if the
Government deserted them. If the Russians thrust into Berlin itself,
the City defences are to be organised in three rings, the innermost of
which will be the Government district. Local Home Guard units are
to set up an organised defence of their own sectors of the City.

'In this way the hopes of many that they will be able to escape to
the West have come to naught. Anyone who attempts to leave risks
being picked up in the provinces, where the machinery of the regime
is still functioning, and shot as a deserter. Those who remain here
have the choice between death and capture by the Russians.'

Back at his desk in the main Foreign Ministry building, 73–4
Wilhelmstrasse, Studnitz reflected how, when a nation is rich and
powerful, diplomacy is easy. Much of the world wants you as a friend
and ally. When a nation is like Nazi Germany in 1945, bombed to
pieces and about to lose an apocalyptic war, only those who cannot
avoid remaining friends and allies stay. So it was in Berlin. The
Spanish, Swiss, Irish and Swedes were there in small numbers, but it
was really only the Japanese, Croats, Slovaks and other representatives of Nazi-dependent states who stayed in force.

Although diplomatic papers were worth thousands of marks on
the black market, they provided no immunity from the daily destruction from the air in February 1945. The daylight attack on Saturday
3 February was devastating. As Berlin was smashed a few feet above
him, Studnitz found himself sharing with a number of diplomats and
fellow Foreign Ministry officials the shelter under the Hotel Adlon:

'The attack began at 10.45 a.m. and ended at 12.30. The Adlon
shelter is a foot deep in water which has leaked through from the
melting snow above. Many people had to wade about underground
for two hours in icy water. Under the heavy explosions the massive
shelter swayed and shivered like the cellar of an ordinary house.
Finally all the lights went out and we felt that we had been buried
alive.'

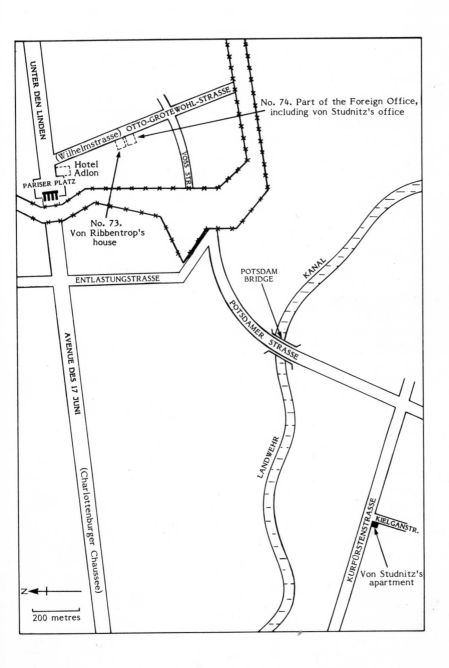

UNTER DEN LINDEN

(Wilhelmstrasse) OTTO-GROTEWOHL-STRASSE

VOSS STR.

No. 74. Part of the Foreign Office, including von Studnitz's office

Hotel Adlon

PARISER PLATZ

No. 73. Von Ribbentrop's house

ENTLASTUNGSTRASSE

POTSDAM BRIDGE

KANAL

POTSDAMER STRASSE

AVENUE DES 17 JUNI

(Charlottenburger Chaussee)

LANDWEHR

KURFÜRSTENSTRASSE

KIELGANSTR.

Von Studnitz's apartment

N

200 metres

They had not been buried alive but, when they emerged, heavy clouds of smoke hung over the whole city. The part of the Foreign Ministry building at 74 Wilhelmstrasse, where Studnitz had his office, was still standing, but 73 had gone, including Ribbentrop's rooms – the Foreign Minister and the Japanese Ambassador wandered about among the ruins.

Studnitz could not get to his office because of unexploded bombs but he struggled over half a mile of debris and through gigantic puddles fed by burst water mains to his favourite hotel, the Esplanade, in Bellevuestrasse. It had been hit seven times but not destroyed. He helped clear up; the top two storeys would never be habitable again, but the rest struggled back to working order within twenty-four hours. A cinema opposite was now a heap of rubble.

A few days later, Studnitz discovered that among those killed in the big raid was Dr Freisler, President of the People's Court, and most of his colleagues. 'Freisler's death has aroused considerable excitement in Berlin and is regarded as an act of just retribution for the revolting manner in which he conducted the case against the July 20th accused.' Studnitz was secretly delighted by the news of the end of the torturers and persecutors of the heroes of the Bomb Plot. Even the dense war-clouds over Berlin had a thin silver lining.

Air raids continued and barricades were set up for the defence of Berlin. 'The barricades, they say, will save Berlin because, when the Russians see them, they'll die of laughter.'

Massive delayed-action bombs brought additional terror to everyday life. Studnitz's flat in Kielganstrasse was severely damaged by a large bomb exploding an hour after the 'all clear' had sounded – rain poured through the roof, the windows were all broken and there were cracks everywhere.

Some attempts at normal life continued – for example, Ribbentrop continued to play host at luncheons and diplomatic teas. Studnitz found these as boring as ever, but at least these meals were better than pancakes and pea soup made from potato starch and then coloured, the staples of most of the restaurants.

To Studnitz it seemed that the Croat Legation's motto was, 'Eat, drink and be merry for tomorrow we die.' Alfred Rukavina, the chargé d'affaires, had managed to get twenty cars to evacuate his ninety staff; but where should they go? Croatia was to be part of a Communist Yugoslavia for the foreseeable future, and a former Croat diplomat would be unwelcome almost everywhere in the world, so they made the best of things while they could. Every night they threw an uproarious party.

'Each banquet is followed by a drinking bout, in which strong spirits flow freely. At about midnight, a Croat choir appears and sings folk-songs. When the "all clear" sounds, the gunners of a Croat anti-aircraft battery stationed nearby for the protection of the Legation come in and give a jazz concert. During these festivities the revellers frequently fire off their revolvers into the air. The porter of the Croat Legation lost three of his fingers as a result of such horseplay. Participants in these "farewell parties", in addition to the Legation staff, include Germans drawn from every walk of life, stars of stage and screen, representatives of the regime and foreign diplomats. Not infrequently, distinguished but hopelessly intoxicated gentlemen have to be carried away.'

The next morning, a terrible jolt back to reality: 'Dresden destroyed from the air. Although people have now become accustomed to the horrors of war, the destruction of Dresden has given rise to greater consternation than perhaps any other event in recent times. As the town had so far not been attacked, people had come to presume that it would be spared – an illusion that has been shattered in the most brutal manner.'

Studnitz was as horrified by the destruction of Dresden as everyone else in Berlin, but he was even more horrified by the proposal that reprisals should be taken against British and American prisoners of war. What would happen to the millions of German prisoners of war in Britain and America? Would gas be used in the final attack on Germany? The idea, which originated with Goebbels and was opposed by Ribbentrop, was in the end turned down by Hitler.

A blunder almost as bad – which Studnitz had no idea was coming or he might have been able to help stop it – was the press statement by General Guderian, Chief of the General Staff: 'I have myself fought in the Soviet Union, but I have never seen any trace of those fiendish ovens, gas chambers and other phenomena which are the product of a diseased imagination. The object is obvious: barefaced lies of this nature are being spread in order to kindle hatred in the heart of the primitive Soviet soldier.'

The effect on foreign journalists and foreign governments, which this statement was designed to impress, was completely negative. They all knew what had gone on in the occupied territories, and they all knew that Guderian knew.

The bombs kept falling. The Esplanade Hotel was hit again. In anticipation of final collapse, false papers and military passes changed hands for staggering prices. Now even the yellow star was at a premium. All the male employees of the Foreign Ministry, from the end of February onwards, had to spend one day a week labouring, shovelling debris. 'I was detailed to shovel debris lying in the Wilhelmstrasse into iron trucks and transport it into the courtyard of the Ministry, where others were engaged in strengthening the side-walls of the air-raid shelter. While we were at work, ankle-deep in muck, hundreds of Russian prisoners of war watched us derisively.'

It was a taste of things to come.

Source
H.-G. von Studnitz, *While Berlin Burns*

Youth to the Fore: April

Helmuth Altner had been trained to be a Nazi soldier almost all his life. He had been four years old when Hitler came to power. His Nazi upbringing gave him complete faith in the Führer, reinforced in the Jungvolk, the Hitler Youth and the National Labour Service. Now he was seventeen.

In March 1945 Altner was shifted from the National Labour Service to the Wehrmacht. A little cursory training in Berlin and he was on his way to the Eastern Front. But not before his training had included loading the corpses of executed deserters into coffins. This was intended to instil fear and to make him and his pals used to the sight and feel of death.

At Fürstenwalde, Altner had found Gisela, and his friend Stroschn had found Ilona. They had only a few hours to spend there, and Altner thought it sad that it might be a long time before he saw Gisela again – after all, he was off to march victoriously across Russia now. No time to lose. The girls' parents were away and it was not long before Ilona took Stroschn off into another room, leaving Altner alone with Gisela. For Altner it had been love at first sight, and his thoughts and memories of this brief encounter were to remain with him throughout the difficult time ahead.

From love to chivalry. Altner and Stroschn joined a group of soldiers at the station defending civilians, mostly women, against the SS men who were trying to confiscate some food they had foraged from the countryside.

Their narrow-gauge train soon took them slowly to Falkenhagen, where they had to dismount and make their way warily to a deserted V-weapon assembly plant a few miles away. 'Sitting down, leaning against a tree, Altner could see searchlights probing the sky only twelve kilometres away on the Front. Whenever a flare was fired, it would be followed by another and the occasional noise of a rifle shot or burst of machine-gun fire would disturb the silence of the night.'

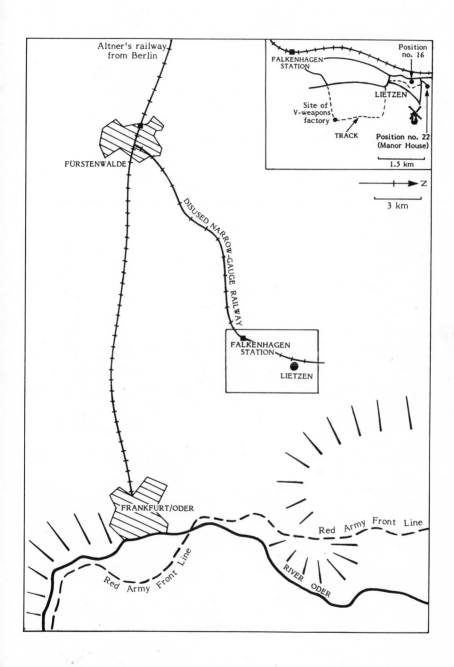

Next morning, on to Lietzen. They passed a great many tanks abandoned for want of fuel. They passed the SS men who chased deserters in the area – they were playing peacefully with their bloodhounds when Altner saw them. They passed a field hospital smelling unpleasantly of blood and antiseptic. They were finally inspected by an officer who told them that the 'Class of 1928' was Germany's last hope: 'The Führer is depending on you.'

Lietzen was just a normal Prussian village. The church bells rang for matins, and fat cows lazed in the fields. It had been lightly shelled and there was a lot of military activity, but it was still a normal village in the spring sunshine.

Altner and the boys with him got big helpings of pea soup at the village command post and trudged off to their quarters, which were some dug-outs in a field. 'Position 16', Altner's, was in a field across a small flooded valley from the village – on the far side from the Front. They could see across to the windmill on the other side of the village, and from the windmill it was possible to see the range of hills which made up the front line itself.

There was a whole system of trenches and cramped dug-outs in the field which Altner and his pals explored. They even ventured into a nearby field for some potatoes which were gratefully boiled for supper. The steaming pot made a cheerful fug in the dug-out, which consisted of a passage-way so dark, narrow and low that they almost had to crawl between the rows of narrow bunks on either side.

Between them, Altner's section had only one rifle, so guard duty needed only one person. Altner took ten-to-midnight on the first night, 8 April.

They discovered the next day that the absence of weapons did not save them from 'training'. Drill. 'The Staff Sergeant took them off to use the time for foot-drill in the meadows where the water soon seeped into their boots as the drill orders were given in quick succession. Dissatisfied with their performance, he made them go further into the water until it was well above their toe-caps and splashing knee-high. Then he ordered them to lie down in the cold mud and water and began a fresh series of commands that had them up, doubling, down and swivelling on their belt-buckles. All the time they sank deeper into the water as he stood there smoking and laughing beside a solemn-faced sergeant.'

The boys were told that evening that Vienna and Hanover had fallen. Stroschn expressed some doubts as to whether Germany would ever win the war. This irritated everybody. Altner just wondered if he would be allowed back to Germany as soon as the war was won or whether he would have to remain with the garrison troops in Russia.

Altner's section was shifted on 11 April to 'Position 22', next to the old manor house. It was a welcome move. It relieved them of the depressing view of the new military cemetery that had been set up by the windmill. It was filling up fast. Nor had they been encouraged by a handful of veterans, aged eighteen, telling them they were the only survivors of 800 who had set out for the Front a month before – they had been occupying the position next door.

The war started to encroach more and more directly on Lietzen. On guard at night, Altner noticed a red glow in the direction of Berlin – another enormous raid – was his mother safe? Some Russian shells from the east landed uncomfortably close and killed some old Home Guardsmen in a nearby dug-out. Altner's first encounter with death in battle.

He started to feel uneasy, but he and his friends were cheered up by a film at the village 'cinema' called *Viennese Blood* (a rather unpromising title under the circumstances but it turned out to be escapist).

Sunday 15 April. Orders to move to new trenches to the east of Lietzen – the dangerous side. Continuous strafing by Russian planes.

Monday 16 April, 4 a.m. 'The air was filled with the horrendous din of shells exploding or hurtling overhead to targets further back; the shapes of bombers could be seen briefly against the black clouds. . . .'

The waiting was over. Nazi Germany was fighting for its life. The front line would soon reach Helmuth Altner.

Source
H. Altner (ed. T. Le Tissier), *Totentanz Berlin*

Albert Speer's Rebellion: March and April

Goebbels' diary entry for 14 March 1944:

'Speer arrives for an interview. He gives a gloomy report. Speer's view is that economically the War is more or less lost. At the present rate the German economy can hold out for another four weeks and then it will gradually disintegrate. Speer deplores the fact that he can get no decisions on vital problems from the Führer. He thinks that, owing to his physical disabilities, the Führer has become far less active. Speer is right in his views about maintenance of the German people's basis of existence. He is very much opposed to the scorched-earth idea. He says that if the lifelines of our food supply and our economy are to be snapped, it is not for us but for our enemies to do it.'

On 19 March, however, Goebbels went along with Hitler's 'demolition order', and Speer was left isolated, thinking he was the only voice of reason left.

Speer, Minister of Munitions, had the power to go where he wanted in a motor car filled with petrol. In Germany, in 1945, you had to be a top Nazi, a minister or a general to do that and even then you had of course to stay in the rapidly dwindling bit of Germany that was still Nazi. Speer was certainly such a top Nazi, one of Hitler's few real friends; an architect in the imperial Nazi style, Hitler saw him as a fellow-artist and a visionary.

On 15 April Speer drove to General Heinrici's headquarters near Prenzlau. There he also met General Reymann, Commander of Berlin, for the moment answerable to Heinrici, Commander of Army Group Vistula. It turned out that Heinrici shared Speer's opposition to Hitler's scorched-earth policy. Privately they both argued that Germany would inevitably be conquered now, so why make it so she could never rise again? Reymann disagreed:

Reymann: 'I must fight and therefore I must be able to destroy bridges.'
Heinrici: 'But only in the direction of the main blow?'
Reymann: 'No, wherever there is fighting.'
Speer: 'Are all bridges in the centre of the city also to be destroyed if the fighting comes down to street battles?'
Reymann: 'Yes.'
Speer: 'Are you going to fight because you believe in victory?'
Reymann: 'Yes.'
Speer: 'If Berlin is thoroughly destroyed, then industry would be wiped out for the foreseeable future. And without industry all war is lost.'

It was enough for Heinrici. He snapped an order that all the charges were to be removed. At that moment, the bridges of Berlin were saved. Even in the height of battle, hardly one bridge in ten was blown up.

Heinrici had intimated to Speer that the big Russian attack on the Oder was expected the next day, 16 April. Speer went to the village of Wrietzen and climbed a hill overlooking the Oder valley to watch.

With dawn came a terrifying din but nothing to see at first because of the mist and then because of the smoke of battle. At about 10 a.m. a forester came and told Speer and his companions that they had

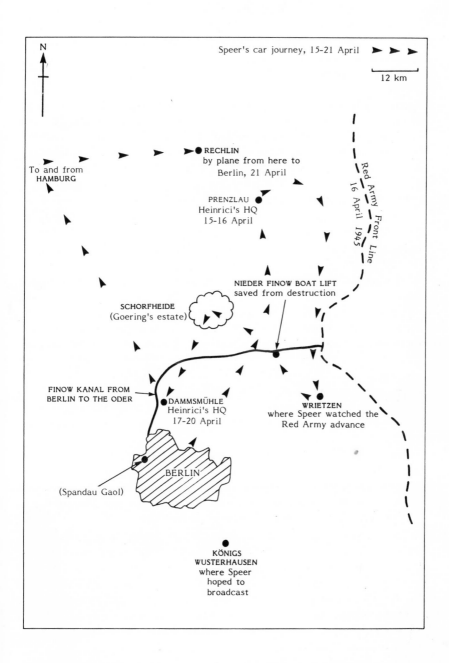

N

Speer's car journey, 15–21 April ► ► ►

12 km

► ► ► ► ►● RECHLIN
To and from   by plane from here to
HAMBURG   Berlin, 21 April

PRENZLAU ●
Heinrici's HQ
15–16 April

Red Army Front Line
16 April 1945

NIEDER FINOW BOAT LIFT
saved from destruction

SCHORFHEIDE
(Goering's estate)

FINOW KANAL FROM
BERLIN TO THE ODER → ● DAMMSMÜHLE
Heinrici's HQ
17–20 April

WRIETZEN
where Speer watched the
Red Army advance

BERLIN

(Spandau Gaol)

●
KÖNIGS
WUSTERHAUSEN
where Speer
hoped to
broadcast

better go at once. The Russians had broken through and were just around the corner.

It was all happening too fast now for Speer. He had reckoned on a longer battle on the Oder and having more time to save the bridges and factories between the Oder and Berlin.

He sped to one of the most remarkable pieces of engineering in the area, '. . . the great ship elevator of Nieder-Finow, a technical marvel of the thirties and the key to shipping from the Oder to Berlin. Everywhere along the 120 foot [36 metres] high iron framework, demolition charges had been skilfully placed. We could already hear artillery fire some distance away. A lieutenant of the Engineers reported that all preparations for demolition had been completed . . . acting on Hitler's demolition order of 19th March. . . .'

Speer used all his persuasive power, and the ship elevator survived the war, but he was deeply depressed. He could with great effort save a piece here and a piece there, but much of what was left of Germany was now doomed.

He drove on to Schorfheide, Goering's country park (Goering had long since gone). He resolved to be a rebel.

It must go without saying that to rebel against a regime which is almost dead, exposed to the world as uniquely evil and totally incapable of defending itself effectively, was hardly a great act of bravery. Anyway, Speer sat down in Goering's forest and laboriously penned a speech: 'I wanted to issue a call for resistance, bluntly to forbid any damage to factories, bridges, waterways, railways, and communications, and to instruct the soldiers of the Wehrmacht and the militia to prevent demolitions with all possible means, if necessary with the use of firearms.' The speech also called for surrendering political prisoners, which included the Jews, unharmed to the occupying troops, and stipulated that prisoners of war and foreign workers not be prevented from making their way back to their native lands. It prohibited Werewolf (guerrilla) activity and appealed to the cities and villages to surrender without a fight.

Speer conspired with Heinrici at his temporary headquarters at Dammsmühle to broadcast on Germany's most powerful radio station at Königs Wusterhausen. At that time, it was centrally controlled and broadcast Goebbels' propaganda and instructions to the Werewolf resistance in occupied Germany. As the radio station came inevitably into the front line, however, it came under Army control. This was to be Speer's moment. Then it was conquered by the Russians. The moment was lost.

Speer claimed afterwards that it was because the radio station was overrun so quickly, and certainly it would have been difficult for him to get there at the right time, but if he had really had the courage of his convictions he could have broadcast even if it had not been from the powerful transmitters at Königs Wusterhausen.

He drove off to Hamburg and played a part in helping the local Gauleiter save the docks from being blown up. Then he flew back to Berlin where he took part in plans to kidnap Himmler, Bormann and Goebbels, because he thought they should face trial and not commit suicide, but nothing came of it. He also tried to persuade Magda Goebbels to save herself and her children, but he failed in that too. He even started planning to gas Hitler in his bunker, but Hitler fixed anti-gas devices before Speer was ready. Hitler almost certainly did not know about the gassing plan but he knew about the rest; he knew his friend was restive; the intelligence service was still quite sound, and Speer was not a clever conspirator. Many had been executed for less, but Hitler wanted to spare one of the few men he felt shared his creative vision of the Germany of the New Age.

No one took Speer seriously any more. He undoubtedly helped save some important places that would otherwise have been destroyed. Basically, though, he was floundering in a swamp of defeat. Although he sometimes liked to think of himself as such, he could never really be a rebel against his Führer. He was captured after the German surrender and served twenty years in Spandau gaol for war crimes.

Source
A. Speer, *Inside the Third Reich*

The Last Social Call: 21 April

'One can hang four Nazis from one lamp-post.' In the last few years this had become a popular comment on the beautiful four-armed lamp-posts on Charlottenburger Chaussee. Albert Speer's view in designing them had been somewhat different. He had wanted them to be part of the new Berlin which he believed he would have to design. Now, in circumstances never envisaged in Speer's nightmares, they were removed to make way for an escape runway, which never really worked because Hitler had forbidden the removal of some withered, obstructive trees.

Max Bock recorded the dismantling of Speer's lamp-posts in his diary. He was a Jew. He had survived in hiding in Berlin throughout the war.

Max Bock had promised to return the key of his friend's country house. He had used the house as a store for his belongings, and it was

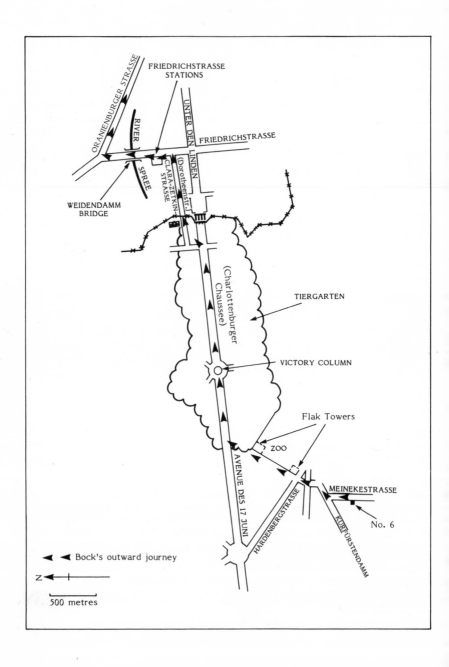

a point of honour to return the key. True, under the circumstances, on 21 April 1945, he could be forgiven for not returning the key, but he also wanted to see his friends, perhaps for the last time for a very long while.

Bock left his house in Meinekestrasse and headed for the zoo, which was dominated by two gigantic flak towers. These concrete monstrosities, fifty metres high, had come to symbolize Berlin's last gasp, its last hard fist. Gaunt, with steel-shuttered windows, topped by deafening anti-aircraft guns, well-nigh impregnable, containing hospitals and living-quarters for all ranks, these flak towers were hideous fortresses. Slogans were painted on the walls: 'Better dead than slaves' and 'Our honour is our faith'. In the end the flak towers were pathetic – Bock saw soldiers driving a herd of cows towards them, getting in stores for a siege.

Past the Victory Column and the Brandenburg Gate – and past huddles of refugees – the route became more dangerous than expected. On his way down a side road, Dorotheenstrasse, Bock was told about the dead and injured in Unter den Linden. Friedrichstrasse street-level station was under fire, and the streets around, including Unter den Linden, were unsafe. Bock quite suddenly found himself amid falling masonry, flying glass and stray shells, and dived into the tunnels of Friedrichstrasse underground station. Carrying on towards the north, he emerged at the somewhat quieter Weidendamm Bridge and made his way to his friend's shop in Oranienburger Strasse.

'I find the shop shut and my friend and his wife in the air raid shelter. A great welcome, handing over of keys, and then a fond farewell as all of us are thinking of what may lie ahead of us. Then I hurry home as fast as my feet will carry me. . . .'

Events were moving fast. The Russian bombardment got heavier and more damaging and injured and killed more people fleeing hopelessly and vaguely westwards. Bock survived by sheltering in the underground station and, when he was outside, by chance he picked up Nazi Berlin's last-remaining newspaper:

'The *Nachtausgabe* . . . is on sale, probably for the last time and announces a worsening of the situation in eastern Berlin. The dimmest schoolboy must be aware of that, so that it has become impossible for Dr Otto Kriegk to pull the wool over the Berliners' eyes any longer. Dr Ley's well-known editorial appears once again and holds forth about the Führer's holy mission. This article, as most of its predecessors, reaches its height of absurdity with its assertion that no one should imagine that National Socialism and the Führer are finished. "If we were corrupt and mean enough to deliver the German people and their life and freedom to the Bolshevik and

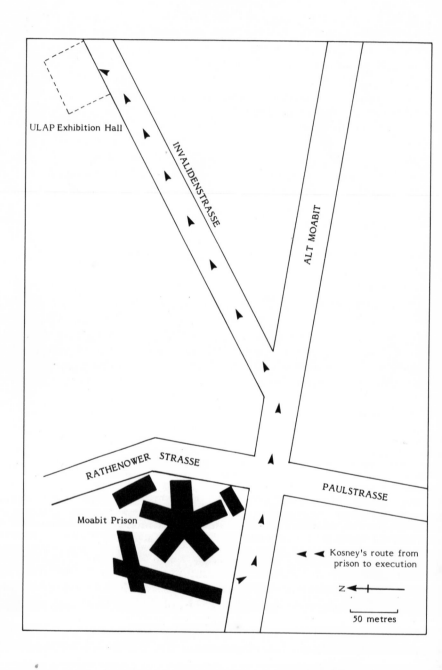

ULAP Exhibition Hall

INVALIDENSTRASSE

ALT MOABIT

RATHENOWER STRASSE

PAULSTRASSE

Moabit Prison

◀ ◀ Kosney's route from prison to execution

Z

50 metres

plutocratic hangmen, the Jews in Moscow and New York would accept us the same as any other traitors." As if any decent people in the rest of the world would consider talking to these political criminals. They have lost that privilege for ever – the Allies made that quite clear.'

Source
M. Bock, unpublished diary

Last-Minute Vengeance of the Reich: 2 April

As the Third Reich collapsed, it took some good people with it in simple acts of vengeance. The anarchy of the last days of Nazi Berlin allowed every bully and criminal in uniform to satisfy his sadistic lust or to settle old scores. One thug who fell into this category was SS Gruppenführer Heinrich Müller, in charge of B Wing in gloomy Moabit Prison.

Müller's charges included sixteen prisoners who had been condemned but, for one reason or another, had not yet been executed. They had all been implicated in the plot to kill Hitler in 1944. Some of the links were extremely tenuous. There was the servant of a man who knew Stauffenberg, who planted the bomb at Hitler's conference in East Prussia; there was an old Communist who had somehow avoided being picked up before this last 'purge', and there were Corporal Herbert Kosney and his brother Kurt, old opponents of the Nazis.

With Russian guns clearly audible in the suburbs of Berlin, most of the guards, with an eye to the probable future, started to smile at the prisoners, to do them little favours, even run errands. Then the conscientious objectors, mostly Jehovah's Witnesses, were freed – Kurt Kosney escaped pretending to be a Witness. No one seemed to care any more.

But there was a handful of guards who were really fanatical, led by Müller himself. They had certain special prisoners with whom they wished to deal personally. Their names were called; Herbert Kosney's was among them. At first he was pleased. They were all pleased. Like the Jehovah's Witnesses, they were all surely destined for freedom now – or at least to be allowed to take their chance in the chaos of Berlin in 1945.

'The prisoners were marched off in the direction of Invalidenstrasse. It was raining; Herbert Kosney turned up his jacket collar and tied a towel he was using as a scarf tighter around his throat. Half way down the street, the men were stopped and searched, and their personal effects, which had been returned to them a short while earlier, were taken from them again. The column set off once more, each prisoner flanked by an SS man with a machine pistol on his back and a gun in his hand. As they reached Invalidenstrasse an SS sergeant suggested taking a short cut through the bombed-out ULAP Exhibition Hall. They marched through the rubble and entered the ruins of a massive building with its skeletal concrete pillars. Suddenly each prisoner was grabbed by the collar by his SS guard. One group of prisoners went to the left, the other to the right. They were marched right up to the wall of the building and positioned six to seven feet apart. And they all knew what was going to happen.'

Herbert Kosney was the only survivor. When he regained consciousness, the wound in his neck and throat caused him indescribable pain, but he had survived because by chance he had moved his head at the vital moment. He could still walk. He made it to his home in the east of the city.

'His wife Hedwig opened the door. The man who stood there was unrecognisable. His face was a mass of blood, as was the front of his coat. Horrified, she said, "Who are you?" Just before he collapsed, Kosney managed to say, "I'm Herbert." '

He lived to tell the world about the Moabit Prison massacre.

Source
C. Ryan, *The Last Battle*

LAST BATTLE ON THE EASTERN FRONT

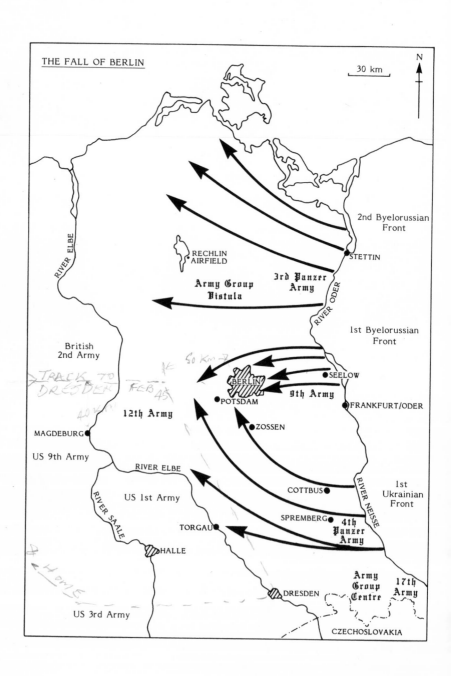

THE FALL OF BERLIN

30 km

N

2nd Byelorussian
Front

STETTIN

RIVER ELBE

RECHLIN
AIRFIELD

𝔄rmy 𝔊roup
𝔙istula

3rd 𝔓anzer
𝔄rmy

RIVER ODER

1st Byelorussian
Front

British
2nd Army

50 Km

BERLIN

SEELOW

POTSDAM

9th 𝔄rmy

FRANKFURT/ODER

12th 𝔄rmy

TRACK TO
DRESDEN

FEB 45

40 Km

ZOSSEN

MAGDEBURG

US 9th Army

RIVER ELBE

US 1st Army

COTTBUS

RIVER NEISSE

1st
Ukrainian
Front

RIVER SAALE

SPREMBERG

TORGAU

4th
𝔓anzer
𝔄rmy

HALLE

HOME

DRESDEN

𝔄rmy
𝔊roup
ℭentre

17th
𝔄rmy

US 3rd Army

CZECHOSLOVAKIA

Introduction

The Germany Army on the Oder and Neisse rivers prepared the best defence it could and then waited. It was not as they would have liked it but they were now so inferior to the Red Army that any thought of counter-attack or of dictating the terms of the battle to come was out of the question. They could only wait and hope that their final collapse would be as painless as possible.

Hitler had put Himmler, with no combat experience, in charge of Army Group Vistula in time for the big January battles in Poland. He was pitted against the most successful commander of the war, Zhukov. In three weeks, Zhukov's first Byelorussian Front had advanced from just west of Warsaw to within eighty kilometres of Berlin. Himmler then gave way to Heinrici. By that time it was certainly too late.

The Red Army had overwhelming superiority in both men and machinery when it faced the Germans across the Oder and the Neisse at the end of January. It could deploy 40,000 artillery pieces, 6,000 tanks and 7,500 aircraft. In response, the Wehrmacht could muster 10,000 artillery pieces, 1,500 tanks and 3,000 aircraft.

In the past on the Eastern Front, the Wehrmacht had rarely had actual superior numbers but had still enjoyed considerable success. But now the quality argument that had so often been in their favour in the past had turned against them too. The Red Army's equipment was now better designed. It sometimes lacked German refinement, but on the other hand it could often be more easily repaired; additionally, replacement parts were easier to supply because there were fewer basic models. For the Germans, with a war economy totally disrupted, obtaining spare parts became a nightmare, and a good deal of equipment had to be abandoned or destroyed. Even more serious for the Germans was their shortage of ammunition, which terribly limited the capacity of their artillery and infantry to hold off any Red Army offensive, let alone to counter-attack. Anyway, counter-attack would have required motorized units well supplied with fuel, and Luftwaffe air support consuming thousands of litres an hour, all impossible in Germany in 1945. So serious was the fuel situation with the Luftwaffe that airmen and ground crew were for the most part drafted into the infantry, otherwise they would have had nothing to do.

It was not just the equipment that was no good any more in the

Wehrmacht. It was also the men. The nucleus of highly trained and experienced troops that had built the Nazi empire between 1939 and 1942 was wounded, dead or captured at Stalingrad, Kursk, the Crimea, Normandy, the Ardennes, Königsberg. . . . Inexperienced sixteen- and seventeen-year-olds, policemen, elderly volunteers and grounded air crew could make up numbers, but they could never make up an army.

The Red Army soldier was by now a very different type from his or her Wehrmacht opposite number. He or she was war-hardened and determined to destroy Nazism and avenge what it had done to the Soviet Union. The Red Army was now for the most part experienced from fighting across thousands of kilometres of eastern Europe; its soldiers were capable of great cunning and subtle improvisation.

On 16 April 1945 the Red Army attacked across the Oder and the Neisse. This was the inevitable blow to fell Nazi Germany once and for all. Berlin would be taken and the Red Army would meet the Western Allies on the Elbe. They were checked only temporarily. That they were checked at all under the circumstances was a tribute to the exceptional generalship of Heinrici and also a comment on Zhukov's over-confidence.

Heinrici knew how to cope with an inferior army. He had had that experience outside Moscow in the winter of 1941–2, when his command had held its position for several weeks against odds as great as twelve to one and prevented the collapse of the German Front. A repeat performance in front of Berlin would have been miraculous indeed. He was under no illusions about his task. He stripped Berlin itself of most of its defences with the intention of holding the Red Army as long as possible on the Seelow Heights and at the river crossings to the north and south. He hoped that there would be enough time for the Western Allies to decide to cross the Elbe and take Berlin; he was not at all concerned about the Western Allies, only with the fate of Germany ruled by the Soviet Union; this he feared above all. He anticipated a gradual withdrawal north and south of Berlin, ultimately surrendering in the west. He wanted to avoid if at all possible street-fighting in Berlin itself with all the appalling consequences that it would have for the population of about 2½ million.

At first, Heinrici's plan went well. He anticipated the time of the initial attack and withdrew his front-line troops, rendering the Red Army barrage mainly ineffective. His defence on the Seelow Heights held firm and, as far south as Frankfurt/Oder, the first Byelo-russian Front got virtually nowhere in the first twenty-four hours. Making the enemy waste most of the energy he puts into his assault had been one of Heinrici's techniques right through the eastern campaign; it involved skilfully second-guessing people like Zhukov. Heinrici had got it right uncannily often, and Zhukov was becoming predictable.

Even Heinrici could not have hoped to hold on for more than three days. But it took a full three days for the Red Army to overcome the Seelow Heights. Then there followed a massive breakthrough to the outskirts of Berlin between 20 and 22 April. This part of the advance was so quick that reports reaching Berlin were out of date before they were read. Orders were dispatched to the SS to defend towns and villages which were now several kilometres behind Red Army lines.

Everything was breaking up for Heinrici. The Western Allies had stopped firmly on the Elbe, west of Berlin. The Red Army's first Ukrainian Front had advanced so quickly from the Neisse in the Cottbus region south of Berlin that Stalin had given its commander, Marshal Koniev, permission to turn north to Berlin, a second fatal threat to the City.

Berlin was quickly encircled. The armies that had been supposed to defend it dispersed. About 200,000 were trapped in the marshy area north of the Spreewald, of whom some 30,000 eventually escaped to the west.

Joseph Goebbels, Gauleiter of Berlin, found he had only about 90,000 men, women and children to fight house-to-house. This was enough, however, to make sure that the very thing Heinrici and many others had striven to avoid would happen. Street-fighting in Berlin was now inevitable.

The Battle of the Oder, Zhukov Slowed: 16–17 April

The Red Army had been hardened by the experience of the German Occupation, by imprisonment and torture and by siege. It had a fanaticism which had enabled its soldiers defending Soviet Russia to hurl themselves under German tanks to explode their grenades shouting 'Stalin'. Now, certain victory and the liberation of its own land had reduced the Red Army's blind ferocity, but it had added a hatred and a thirst for revenge that curdled the blood.

The Red Army had a massive superiority of men and machinery at the start of the Battle of the Oder at 4 a.m. on 16 April 1945. It stormed the Seelow Heights successfully on 17 April. By then, it had cost thousands of lives too many and taken a day too long.

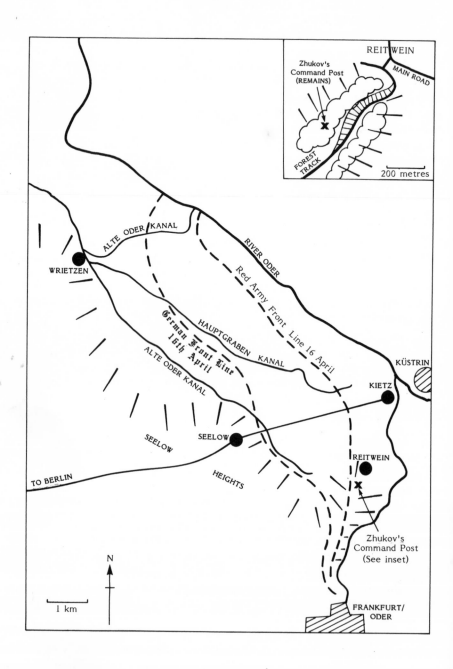

Inset labels: REITWEIN, MAIN ROAD, Zhukov's Command Post (REMAINS), FOREST TRACK, 200 metres

Map labels: ALTE ODER KANAL, RIVER ODER, WRIETZEN, Red Army Front Line 16 April, HAUPTGRABEN KANAL, German Front Line 15th April, ALTE ODER KANAL, KÜSTRIN, KIETZ, SEELOW, SEELOW, REITWEIN, TO BERLIN, HEIGHTS, Zhukov's Command Post (See inset), N, 1 km, FRANKFURT/ODER

Marshal Georgi Konstantinovich Zhukov's 'Byelorussian Front' had a wide bridgehead over the Oder extending some fifteen kilometres north and south of Kietz. The whole front waited in the Oder valley until everything was ready to attack on 16 April. Zhukov and his commanders waited for 4 a.m. in their command post built into the top of the sandy hill above the village of Reitwein.

At 4 a.m. sharp, 140 massive searchlights were directed onto the Oder Valley and the German-occupied Seelow Heights, Zhukov's objective which overlooked it. Then the artillery started: 'The whole valley of the Oder rocked: 20,000 guns had opened fire. 20,000. An avalanche of fire descended on the Seelow Heights. The earth reared up in what seemed an unbroken wall reaching up to the sky itself. On its far side, over there, the darkness remained; here, in the East, the dawn had broken in fire. The artillery bombardment, using every gun and mortar and reinforced by bombers and dive-bombers, lasted twenty-five minutes.' The noise was so tremendous, so painful, that blood flowed from some soldiers' ears.

The Byelorussian Front started its advance.

Very soon, things started to go wrong: Zhukov's searchlights were not much use. He had hoped to blind or madden the German defenders in the early morning darkness but in the event, if anything, they lit up his own troops as targets for the German artillery which started up about an hour after his bombardment finished; they also created light-and-shade effects which advancing troops found disorientating and confusing, as the contrast ruined their night vision.

The enemy was soon fighting back. The Germans were still on the Seelow Heights. They had suffered few casualties in the bombardment because Zhukov was now too predictable. A very high proportion of the shells had fallen on open country because the Germans had withdrawn from the front in time for the offensive. Their intelligence had found out the exact time of the offensive in advance, and their experience of Zhukov's bombardments told them how far they should withdraw and for how long. The Stalin organs played; their rows of destructive *katyusha* rockets tore into the Seelow Heights, but 'forewarned is forearmed' and German defences largely survived intact.

Still, the Byelorussian Front flowed over the Oder, and some units even reached the hamlets below the Seelow Heights. Not that it was easy. Tanks were bogged down and destroyed by artillery. The Hauptgraben–Alte Oder waterways proved formidable obstacles: they were wide and deep; the bridges were all destroyed; thousands died trying to cross them; almost everything had to crowd onto the few main roads, where temporary bridges became hopelessly congested and provided more sitting targets for German artillery. Tanks and infantry were dangerously separated in a terrifying confusion of noise, smoke and death on a large scale. By mid-morning the whole massive attack had virtually ground to a halt.

Zhukov was humiliated. His failure on that one day, 16 April 1945, meant that he would not be the first into Berlin. Now it would be his rival, Koniev, from the south, who had broken through; it would be Koniev, Stalin's man, who would be first in Berlin.

The atmosphere in the command post above Reitwein was not pleasant. Zhukov flew into a rage when he heard that the advance in some places was barely a thousand metres. The generals started blaming everyone but themselves – the searchlights, the predictability of the artillery barrage, inadequate reconnaissance of the terrain. Zhukov decided to bludgeon his way into the Seelow Heights no matter what the cost. He ordered more bombing raids on German artillery positions and more tanks in from the east. General Katukov, commander of the reserve tanks, was in the command post and protested that it would only make more congestion: his tanks and men would be wasted. Still hot with rage, Zhukov stormed out of the command post. Katukov hesitated momentarily before giving the necessary orders. Zhukov barked at him like a sergeant-major at a recruit – 'Well. Get moving.'

Vast superiority in the air and in numbers of artillery and men ensured that, reinforced, the Red Army on the Byelorussian Front overcame the Seelow Heights the next day. The defending remnants of the German Army in the end had no hope. Bad planning had nevertheless allowed them one more chance to kill Russians.

Source
J. Toland, *The Last 100 Days*

Defending Seelow: 16–17 April

The west hardly mattered any more. Compared with the imminence of death from the east in April 1945, the Germans almost welcomed the British and Americans. The threat of the *Untermensch*, the orientals of the Steppes, was overwhelming. Every inch of territory had to be defended against them. Every village was to be a barrier on the road to Berlin.

This opinion put Seelow on the map. It was the dominating strongpoint on the Seelow Heights, a range of low hills overlooking the Oder Valley where the Red Army had a bridgehead. So it happened that the 9th Parachute Division of Army Group Vistula, airmen and ground crew, hastily converted to infantrymen, including eighteen-year-old Gerhard Cordes, found themselves in Seelow with the job of holding it in the face of the Red Army's planned assault now expected on 16 April.

Right along the Front the warning went out – the attack was due in the small hours of 16 April. The night before, the main force was pulled back from the front line, a tactical manœuvre which saved thousands of German lives from the predictable bombardment of the front line which was bound to precede the push forwards. A few men were kept out in front just to give the appearance of a force if scouts were sent out, a show of strength. Although he did not realize it, Cordes was one of the few out in front.

Cordes was ordered to dig into a foxhole in the mud, as deep as possible, and await the attack. His position was about half a kilometre from the bottom of Seelow Ridge just by the main road to Küstrin. His chances of survival were slim.

At 4 a.m. on 16 April, 20,000 Red Army artillery pieces fired. The noise of the explosions was terrifying. It was the softening-up before the attack along the whole front and the advance to Berlin. Hardly a square metre of earth was left unchurned. Cordes dug himself deeper with his hands. When he looked up, he saw neighbouring foxholes being blown to pieces with his friends inside them, but he survived, and the artillery stopped firing after about twenty-five minutes.

A blaze of light from powerful Red Army searchlights. 'The Russians are coming!'

There was a rumble then a roar of T-34 tanks, mixed in with a few fearsome 'Joseph Stalins', the most gigantic tanks Cordes had ever seen, and there was a crash of artillery from the German flak guns behind. Tanks and self-propelled artillery seemed to stretch as far as the eye could see, to the north and south; the first wave was tanks alone, but the second wave contained the infantry, men riding on tanks and sheltering behind them – thousands of men. To the north and south of the Seelow Heights, the Red Army mostly broke through, but the survival of the bulk of German men and equipment in the bombardment and the concentration of German artillery on the Heights and the slow business of crossing the marshes either side of the Küstrin road, the one main road across the Oder Valley, gave the German defenders a chance. Tanks were blown up by hand-held disposable anti-tank Panzerfaust shells, and infantrymen were shot as they approached the foxholes. Even the most heavily armoured T-34s and Joseph Stalins reached the bottom of the ridge at only one or two points to the north of the village.

The survivors of the foxholes were ordered back to defend Seelow

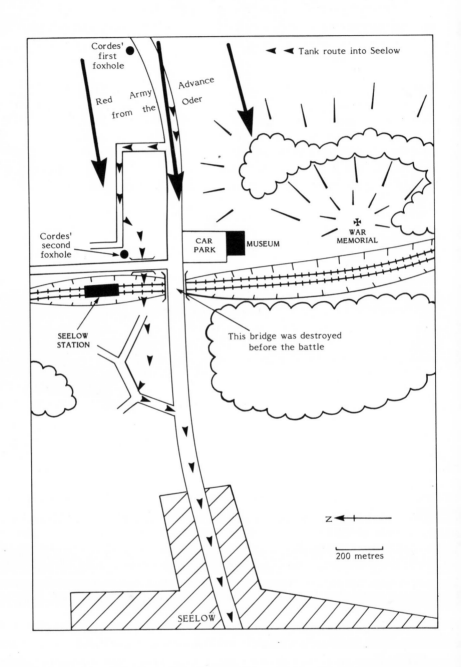

Cordes'
first
foxhole

Red Army
from the

Advance
Oder

◄ ◄ Tank route into Seelow

Cordes'
second
foxhole

CAR
PARK

MUSEUM

✠
WAR
MEMORIAL

SEELOW
STATION

This bridge was destroyed
before the battle

Z

200 metres

SEELOW

itself from the next attack. Cordes was to be one of the defenders of the Küstrin road where it had led straight uphill into the village before the main railway bridge was destroyed. He was allocated a rough foxhole just below the railway line, so he overlooked the alternative road, which led under the side road leading to the station and across the railway line, from its left-hand side looking down towards the Russians in the valley plain.

While battles raged north and south, it became quite quiet for an hour or two on the Küstrin road while the Red Army regrouped to have another go at the Seelow Heights and above all on the strongpoint of Seelow itself.

One tank eventually nosed round the corner on the road up to Seelow. It was alone. Cordes wanted it to be blown up. One tank could easily be destroyed with a single Panzerfaust. The tank rumbled closer. No shot was fired. One tank could not conquer Germany, so why give away any position? When it was so close to Cordes that he could see an unfriendly expression on the tank commander's face, an 88 mm flak gun fired. The tank was put out of action, and the crew scurried straight down the hill.

A few minutes later, before he could see anything approaching, Cordes suddenly heard one of the gun crew behind him cry, 'I want those bastards in front of my guns before the first round is fired.' No giving away of any position. 'Don't do anything unless they get up to us.'

Then everything started to happen at once. 'The din of motors and clank of treads was tremendous. The earth trembled.' Cordes picked up a Panzerfaust. 'From behind came an abrupt, heavy-throated chorus; 88 mm shells screeched overhead and smashed into the first tanks. Flames shot up, parts of metal and shell fragments rained over the foxholes. At least six tanks were on fire, but others kept coming on and on. In the reddish glare they stood out with clarity and were helpless before the withering fire of big guns. Red Army infantrymen began erupting from the middle of this massive conflagration. There must have been 800, and they scrambled up the hill shouting.' There was an appalling slaughter. A third of Cordes' companions were killed in the first hour and probably twice as many Russians.

A wounded Russian hurtled into Cordes' foxhole – 'His eyes were wild and blood gushed out of a great hole that had once been his chin.' Cordes lost concentration and soon found himself surrounded by advancing infantry. Tanks still ground up the hill towards him and past him. He pulled himself together and shot the commander of one with his carbine; a shot from his Panzerfaust slammed into the turret of another, exploding the ammunition inside. Still there were enough tanks to rumble on almost to the top of the ridge in places but they could not overcome the well-entrenched German armour, especially lethal heavy self-propelled guns; they finally forced a Russian retreat.

By midday, the attack on the Seelow Heights had been called off. The Heights had become a powerful salient. Even though it was almost impossible for the Germans to get any reinforcements through, it took the best part of a day for the second attack, on 17 April, to succeed. Outnumbered and massively outequipped, the defenders still took a huge toll of Russian lives. Waves of tanks and infantry finally overcame Seelow in the late morning, and the rest of the Heights fell during the afternoon and evening. By the time the attack came, on the morning of 17 April, there was no German artillery to resist. What little remained from the previous day had been abandoned or destroyed.

Cordes and his friends took to their heels and fled through the forests to the west.

Source
J. Toland, *The Last 100 Days*

The Battle of Lietzen: 16–20 April

The seventeen-year-old on guard was Helmuth Altner. He had been in the Wehrmacht three weeks. He found himself on the road into the village of Lietzen from the east. The time was dawn on 16 April 1945. The Red Army was attacking along the Oder front twelve kilometres away.

As Altner stood guard, he gazed at the evidence of battle in the east, the clouds of black smoke reaching right up to the clouds. He listened to the continuous roar of guns. In Lietzen village, behind him, the shelling had stopped for the time being, but everything seemed to be burning. In front of him, supply wagons pulled by terrified, uncontrollable horses hurtled towards him and passed into the village. Knots of refugees trudged past him with a handful of belongings.

Altner had been left on guard with his friend Stroschn while the rest of the company went to pick up some weapons from headquarters in the village. They returned in extended order unhurt, and it was Altner's and Boy's turn to run through the village. 'It had been damaged beyond all recognition. Some farmers were trying to rescue cattle from the blazing sheds, while other distraught villagers sought missing relations. The smell of scorched flesh hung heavily over the shattered buildings.'

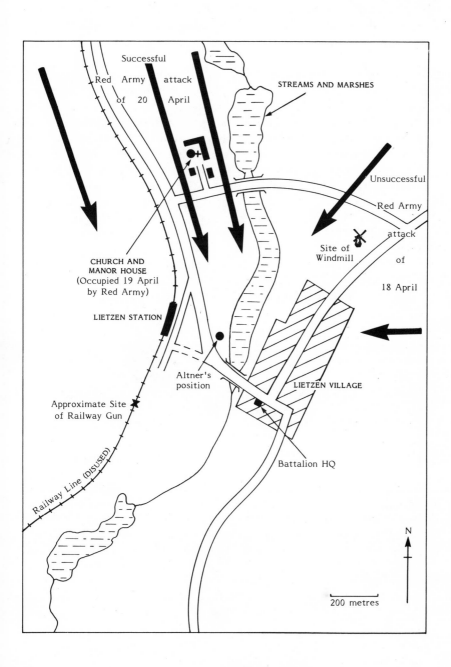

Successful

Red Army attack

of 20 April

STREAMS AND MARSHES

Unsuccessful

Red Army

attack

Site of
Windmill

of

18 April

**CHURCH AND
MANOR HOUSE**
(Occupied 19 April
by Red Army)

LIETZEN STATION

Altner's
position

LIETZEN VILLAGE

Approximate Site
of Railway Gun

Battalion HQ

Railway Line (DISUSED)

N

200 metres

The new weapons were handed out and Altner was very pleased. However, he only discovered how to use his Italian submachine-gun when he nearly shot his foot. Submachine-guns had not featured in his brief training.

As Altner and Stroschn ran back through the village, they were nearly startled out of their wits by a massive explosion from a gigantic gun mounted on a railway wagon on the line west of the village. Altner wondered for a moment if that was the famous Secret Weapon, but it was shortly to be blown to pieces in a bombing raid.

By lunchtime, the bombing and shelling had brought about the first casualties in Altner's company, three elderly men crushed in a shellhole they were using for shelter. As the men were buried and the destruction went on, Altner's belief in the final inevitability of German victory wavered, but he and his friends were stiffened by the new Führer Order:

'Berlin stays German, Vienna will be German again and Europe will never become Russian. Form yourselves into sworn brotherhoods to defend not only the concept of fatherland, but your homes, your wives, your children and, with them, our future. In these hours the entire German people look to you, my Eastern warriors, and only hope that by your resolve, your determination, your weapons and under your leadership, the Bolshevik onslaught will be drowned in a sea of blood. The turning point of the War will be decided by you.'

The night was quiet but next morning the Soviets attacked again from the air. A fortified windmill at the end of the village was blown up by Germans now serving in the Soviet Air Force, part of the so-called 'Seydlitz' forces (named after a Nazi general who had been captured, changed sides and had raised a force of prisoners-of-war to fight for the Red Army). 'Soldiers could be seen jumping out of the burning building as the attacking aircraft began to rake them with machine-gun fire. A runner arrived with a message to beware of Seydlitz aircraft and then they realized that the Messerschmidt 109s lacked the normal Maltese Cross and Swastika insignia.'

For the rest of the day there was peace in Lietzen. A copious meal gleaned from abandoned farms provided an unaccustomed rich diet which kept Altner and several of his pals awake for what otherwise might have been a restful night.

Wednesday 18 April started with rumours. Was the Red Army outflanking Lietzen? Was Lietzen the last isolated pocket of resistance? It certainly seemed quiet enough now. Artillery boomed in the distance but Altner's company filled in the time deepening dug-outs and improving camouflage.

'Suddenly, a barrage of Stalin-Organ rockets descended on their position. They dived for cover on the bottom of the trenches as a hail of metal churned up the earth all around them in an unending petrifying din.' It stopped. A few minutes passed. For a moment the world seemed unrecognizable. Then alarm – ' "Stand to. The Russians are coming." They grabbed their weapons and took up their allotted firing positions. German soldiers with Weimar armbands were running towards them. "Seydlitz troops." They aimed and fired steadily as they had been taught, aiming at the body.'

The enemy faltered, then fled. They had misjudged the terrain, which was favourable to the defenders of Lietzen, and consequently suffered heavy casualties. They had misjudged the numbers of defenders, and Altner thought in the first moments of victory that they had misjudged the quality of the defenders and their determination to fight for Hitler. But he started to feel exhausted rather than exhilarated. He was distressed at the carnage all around him. He was distressed by his dead friends. He was distressed at having to shoot at the living bodies of his own countrymen attacking him. In short, young Helmuth Altner went into shock, and it was only his first battle.

One in five of Altner's company were killed. He and Stroschn were unhurt. They pulled themselves together and helped bury those who could be identified. They, the living, now in the front line, stood by for the next assault. The Waffen SS moved up to the village to make sure the front line stayed put.

On Thursday 19 April the Red Army quietly occupied the manor house a few hundred metres north of Altner's position. So when night fell, a raid was organized and a prisoner captured. He was made to wait outside while Altner and his friends celebrated. Then he was interrogated and shot.

The Soviet attack in the early dawn of Friday 20 April proved irresistible. The numbers of soldiers and the ferocity meant one thing only – flight.

'Outside with all your kit. The Russians are here.' The Russians were everywhere. Machine-gun and rifle fire tore through the night. Altner and his friends careered back through the village, which was in flames again – more fiercely than ever, threatening to engulf them as they ran but it did not stop them. One of Altner's pals, sixteen-year-old Kohler, was not even stopped by a large metal shrapnel splinter embedded in his leg. He just ran on till he collapsed.

It was Hitler's birthday, and Altner had expected a turn-around. The battalion commander had announced that a peace treaty had been concluded with the British and Americans the night before. He had told the youngsters that they just had to stick it out for another twenty-four hours and help would come, and they believed him. Now Altner and Stroschn no longer knew what to believe.

Dawn broke. The reality was full-scale rout. Battalion headquarters was deserted. Blood and injury were all around. The Russians were some 200 metres behind and moving fast. A long, dangerous trail back to Berlin lay ahead.

Source
H. Altner (ed. T. Le Tissier), *Totentanz Berlin*

Britische Freikorps: 18–19 April

John Amery was a Nazi. So were Oberscharführer Butcher and the New Zealander Unterscharführer Montgomery. The Britische Freikorps were mostly recruited from British prisoners of war. It had been John Amery's idea and, even though he was Cabinet Minister Leo Amery's son and intelligence hero Julian Amery's brother, he was hanged for it in December 1945. The thirty or so others who fought on the Oder or in Berlin either died or disappeared.

The British were part of the Nordland Division of foreign SS troops setting out for the Eastern Front on 16 April. That was the day the Russians attacked at dawn. The whole of the Eastern Front was under intolerable pressure. Reinforcements were desperately needed. The muddle was horrendous. The Nordland men had no idea where to go now. Previous orders were out of date. Villages which they should be defending were already in Russian hands.

By evening, they had arrived at the village of Hohenstein and had managed to get a message back to Berlin that they were awaiting further orders.

'The Third German Corps is going to attack from Strausberg. Join them at once.'

The road back to Strausberg was a revelation, even to hardened soldiers, of what it was like to see not just an army in rout but a nation in rout: refugees mixed with fleeing soldiers in the chaos of the night, made worse by constant bombing and machine-gunning from the air. The British found themselves in a storm of Germans with the Red Army in hot pursuit.

The counter-attack at Strausberg never materialized. The British and the others in the Nordland Division made it back to the Berliner Ring *autobahn*, where they joined Danish volunteers, also part of the same division, under Sturmbannführer Per Sørensen. They marched with them to the suburb of Friedersdorf and waited for orders at a temporary command post by the motorway junction.

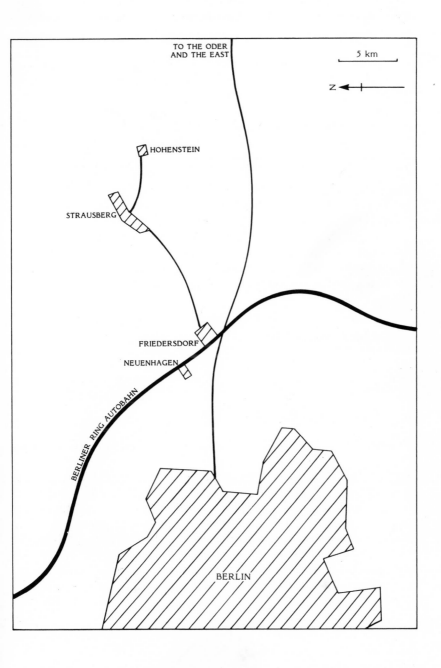

TO THE ODER
AND THE EAST

5 km

Z

HOHENSTEIN

STRAUSBERG

FRIEDERSDORF

NEUENHAGEN

BERLINER RING AUTOBAHN

BERLIN

During the night the message came through that the Russians had reached Neuenhagen, which had previously been thought to be well within German lines. The breach had to be repaired at once. Sørensen split his command into small assault groups made up of men used to working with each other, including the Britische Freikorps volunteers. Each assault group had a few light vehicles and some Panzerfausts.

The Russians had advanced even further than Neuenhagen. Within minutes, before even reaching the next motorway junction, the British ran into four advanced T34 tanks. They took up positions on the embankment and destroyed two of them.

It was a bright night. Four tanks had been stopped on the motorway but the British SS men could see the countryside was overrun with Soviet armour. The advance was unstoppable.

They fled.

Some finished up in Berlin to fight to the last and to die there. Others changed identity and tried their luck, first moving west and then to Spain or South America. An audacious few faced their compatriots head on and returned to Britain. Only Amery was tried and executed.

Source
J. Mabire, *La Division Nordland*

Chuikov's Eighth Guards Army – The Straight Road to Berlin: 16–23 April

The muffled thunder of the massive artillery barrage on the Oder at 4 a.m. on 16 April could be heard in the eastern suburbs of Berlin nearly eighty kilometres away. General Vasily Ivanovich Chuikov's Eighth Guards Army was on its way straight down the road from Küstrin to Berlin, part of Marshal Zhukov's First Byelorussian Front. Chuikov and his men, some of whom had fought from the Volga to the Oder, were proud to be in the lead in the assault on Berlin, the enemy's heart.

By breakfast time on 16 April, east Berlin could just smell the scent of burning pines as the distant forests were put in flames by Red Army artillery.

The Red Army's winter advance across what is now Poland had been dramatic. Then in February and March the Front was virtually stationary on the Oder, consolidating for the attack on the German heartland in April.

The ruins of the Gedächtniskirche, or Kaiser Wilhelm Memorial Church,
standing in the midst of Berlin's shops and entertainments

The Brandenburg Gate from Unter den Linden, first stage on the journey west. In the foreground is Pariser Platz. The Adlon Hotel was on the near left corner and Ursula von Kardorff took a flat on the far right

Looking across the Wall from the west side of Potsdamer Platz towards the heart of Nazi Germany. *Far left*, Goebbels' Ministry of Propaganda; *centre right*, Goering's Air Ministry; *far right*, Gestapo HQ

The authors, Peter Slowe (right) and Richard Woods (left), discover the remains of Zhukov's command post for the Battle of the Oder

Falkenhagen Station, where Helmuth Altner disembarked and was marched into battle

A fearsome 'Stalin Organ' stand the courtyard of the museum at Seelow, on the site of some of the fiercest fighting in the Battle of t] Oder

A defender's view at Seelow – tanks entering Seelow had to come under this bridge and over the railway. Gerhard Cordes was defending the far side of the bridge when the tanks got through

Lietzen manor house and church – the Red Army launched its successful attack from here at dawn on Friday 20 April 1945

The River Nieplitz at Salzbrunn where Büsse's 9th Army met up with Wenck's 12th, enabling 30,000 men to escape capture by the Red Army

Entrance to the Horstmann estate at Kerzendorf

The ornamental lake where Lali Horstmann and her maid hid her jewellery

All that now remains of the Horstmanns' manor house at Kerzendorf

The Wendls' house in Kladow – a tranquil setting for destruction and death

Max Bock's flat in Meinekestrasse (2nd floor of the white building in the centre). The Battle of Berlin moved down the street from left to right; bodies were buried where cars now park

Despite the period of consolidation and reorganization, the Byelorussian Front, the middle section opposite Berlin commanded by Marshal Zhukov, was in some ways ill-prepared for the assault it launched on 16 April. Chuikov and Zhukov were surprised by the effectiveness and strength of German defences on the Seelow Heights and of the SS brought up to stiffen the outer defences of the Berlin region. They miscalculated the problems offered by the marshy land of the Oder Bruch, the flat valley before the Seelow Heights criss-crossed by deep canals, swamped with lakes and bogs. Zhukov's technique of shining searchlights on the enemy was also of little use since it mainly disorientated his own troops. A good deal of the progress of the first few days of the campaign was the result of the bravery of individual field commanders and their units. It owed little to the Marshal or his generals.

One occasion where the advance might have been halted, if not reversed, was saved by Colonel Yefin Gritsenko. At Diedersdorf, on the strategic main road to Berlin from the east, the SS mounted fierce counter-attacks. 'Gritsenko used his own methods to fight these enemy tactics. He refrained from making frontal attacks upon inhabited points and centres of resistance; the battalions of his regiment by platoons or even by sections with mortars and light arms made their way by roundabout routes to take inhabited points from the rear, and force the enemy formations to give battle under disadvantageous conditions, attacking them from the flanks.' He sustained heavy losses in and around Diedersdorf but ended by clearing the road.

Further south, where progress was especially slow and fighting was still going on around the Seelow Heights village of Dolgelin late on 17 April, there would have been disaster but for the personal initiative of Colonel Alexander Semikov, who personally led small units to destroy an enemy position at the intersection of the railway with the main road from Seelow southwards. 'In the regiment's path were five "Tiger" tanks dug into the ground. Neither heavy guns nor salvoes from the "Katyushi" mobile multiple rocket launchers or "Stalin Organs" could cope with them. The armour of these tanks was shielded by whole piles of road cobbles, making them absolutely invulnerable. Semikov found the way out. Experienced sappers with "Faustpatronen" [single-firing tank destroyers] and explosives were sent round to take them in the rear. After a few hits from there the "Tigers" ceased fire and their crews ran for it. Soon a powerful artillery blow descended on Semikov's regiment. . . .' Again there were heavy losses, and Semikov himself was injured by a bomb which shattered his right hip and broke his arm and shoulder.

A few individual Heroes of the Soviet Union could not substitute

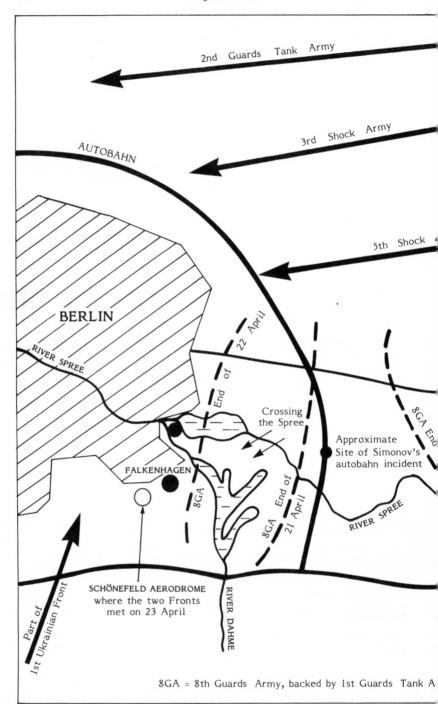

SCHÖNEFELD AERODROME
where the two Fronts
met on 23 April

8GA = 8th Guards Army, backed by 1st Guards Tank A

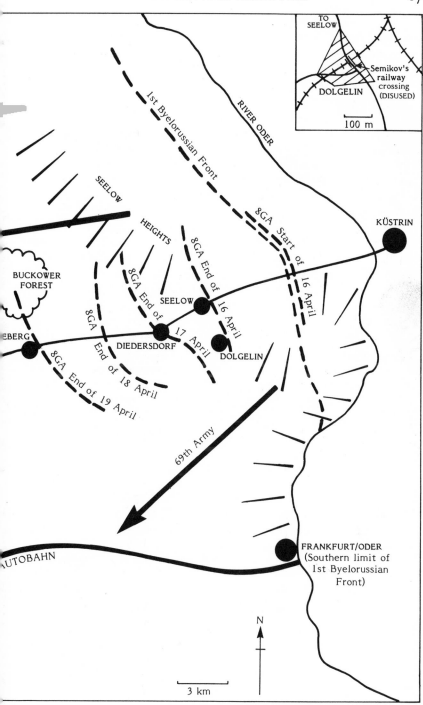

TO SEELOW

Semikov's railway crossing (DISUSED)

DOLGELIN

100 m

1st Byelorussian Front

RIVER ODER

SEELOW

HEIGHTS

8GA Start of 16 April

KÜSTRIN

BUCKOWER FOREST

8GA End of 16 April

8GA End of

SEELOW

8GA End of 17 April

DIEDERSDORF

DOLGELIN

EBERG

8GA

8GA End of 18 April

8GA End of 19 April

69th Army

AUTOBAHN

FRANKFURT/ODER
(Southern limit of
1st Byelorussian
Front)

N

3 km

for an effective attack. Zhukov, who was by now under direct pressure from Stalin, issued an absurd and panicky order: 'All officers who have shown themselves incapable of carrying out assignments and have displayed lack of resolution will be replaced by able and courageous officers.'

Chuikov, among others, ignored it. He did not feel he could identify poor junior officers after two days of badly generalled battle. He did, however, work with Zhukov on getting things operating effectively again, sorting out transport, supplies and rear services and co-ordinating all the complex work of an attacking army which simply had not been worked out properly in advance.

At the same time, the Germans had to release some of the pressure they were applying to Chuikov and Zhukov to meet the now more serious threat from Koniev's First Ukrainian Front advancing on Berlin from the south. Things started to run more according to plan. Nowhere was this more apparent than in the taking of Müncheberg, the main town on the Berlin–Oder highway, on Chuikov's route.

Müncheberg was attacked from the Buckower Forest to the north-west. This was made possible by a series of fast infantry manœuvres through the woods north of Müncheberg co-ordinated with diversionary artillery fire and a feigned frontal retreat. When Müncheberg was attacked from the north-west, escape routes were cut off and confusion was effectively sown among the defenders. 'The enemy lost about four hundred soldiers and officers, eight tanks, seven "Ferdinand" self-propelled guns, and twelve armoured carriers. Our men captured 137 motor vehicles loaded with ammunition and 150 railway waggons of military supplies.'

Now the whole Byelorussian Front was unstoppable and working like a well-oiled machine. Chuikov's Eighth Guards Army repelled a German attempt to cut off the Berliner Ring *autobahn*, the results of which were witnessed by the journalist Konstantin Simonov:

'The *autobahn* cut through a dense forest divided by a long clearing and disappeared into the far distance. The German troops had tried to break through to the *autobahn* along this clearing, and at the intersection of the two, which they reached that morning, they had suffered a devastating defeat – evidently before daybreak. This was the picture we saw: in front of us lay Berlin, and to our right a forest clearing now a chaos of jumbled tanks, cars, armoured cars, trucks, special vehicles and ambulances. They had uprooted hundreds of trees, probably in an attempt to turn round and escape in this black, charred confusion of steel, timber, guns, cases and papers, a bloody mass of mutilated corpses lay strewn along the clearing as far as the eye could see. Then I noticed a host of wounded men lying on greatcoats and blankets or leaning against tree trunks; some of them bandaged and others covered in blood, with no one to tend them. The broad concrete ribbon of the *autobahn*, already cleared and open to traffic, ran straight past this grisly scene.'

Chuikov's men were soon at the River Spree where it enters Berlin. They swam and rafted across the river, taking the suburbs of Falkenhagen and the whole area of Köpenick by surprise. There were very few losses – and when some Germans opened up behind Chuikov's lines, they were often resented and even forced to surrender by the local population, who wanted no more of it.

Chuikov's and Zhukov's rivals, Koniev's men, were already in the southern suburbs of Berlin, and the two conquering armies met at Schönefeld aerodrome. The scene was set for destruction, conquest and occupation. There were many Germans now in Berlin who wished fervently that they or their compatriots had behaved rather differently when the boot had been on the other foot about three years earlier.

Source
V. Chuikov, *The End of the Third Reich*

From the Neisse to Berlin in Forty-Eight Hours: 16–23 April

Stalin and two of his marshals in the field, Koniev and Zhukov, were convinced the British and Americans wanted to be first in Berlin. Despite the understanding at Yalta, it did go through the minds of some of the American generals, including supremo Eisenhower, who thought about an airborne attack. In the end the British and Americans held back – they were exhausted anyway, and supplies were getting to be a problem in Central Europe.

What was left was the friendly rivalry between the two Soviet marshals. The famous Zhukov was on the Oder, and the quiet, intellectual and much less well-known Ivan Stepanovich Koniev was further south, on the Neisse. Both had been in the Tsarist Army and had changed sides after the Revolution, but then their careers had taken different turns. Zhukov continued to rise through the ranks as an ordinary soldier; Koniev became a political commissar, a powerful representative in the Army of the Communist Party. Political commissars were not always popular, but Koniev was popular where it mattered more than ever – with the Party and with its General Secretary, Joseph Stalin.

Zhukov and Koniev both had excellent records in the field. In Moscow, Stalin had allocated the sector of the Front opposite Berlin to Zhukov. The crossroads at Lübben was the end of the southern boundary between his area of responsibility and Koniev's in the south; after Lübben, they would have to wait and see how the land lay.

On 16 April it was time for attack. Zhukov's 'Byelorussian Front' took on the Seelow Heights in the north. Koniev's 'First Ukrainian Front' took on the crossing of the Neisse in the south.

Koniev was nearly killed by a sniper in the first few minutes of the 4 a.m. attack – though he did not realize it at the time – when a bullet slammed into the tripod of his fieldglasses. He soon withdrew from the River Neisse to his command post to watch the attack from a distance. He could get a better view further back anyway, because he had ordered a thick smokescreen along the whole of the river, and from the bank he could hardly see anything of what was going on.

By 8.30 a.m., 4½ hours after the start of the attack, 133 out of the 150 planned bridgeheads over the Neisse had been established. Tanks and infantry poured across, destroying German defences as they went. Paths had been cleared by a massive but carefully directed artillery barrage; the only problem was that some of the woods had caught fire, which tended to slow tank and infantry advances. Stormovik dive-bombers harried retreating German units and caused havoc to defensive positions. The Luftwaffe had virtually no planes left with which to oppose them.

Koniev's policy was to avoid centres of resistance and to press on, avoiding isolated villages and even machine-gun nests until they had been well and truly flattened by artillery as well as completely surrounded. The crucial morale-boosting objective was to cover distance securely. Cottbus and Spremberg were both important towns resisting but between them ran the river which ultimately flowed through Berlin, the upper reaches of the Spree. Koniev had wanted his armies to cross the Spree on the second day of the attack.

'When I reached the river Spree, I gathered from the reports of our scouts and from my own observations that, in general, things were turning out rather well. But since we had to fight all the way there, we had been unable to forestall the enemy. The Hitlerites had managed to deploy some units on the west bank of the Spree and were able to open fire. But I could feel that the fighting was unco-ordinated and poorly organised. In other words, we did not face a system of concentrated and heavy fire. We did not face one as yet. To give the Germans time to organise it would have been an unpardonable mistake on our part.'

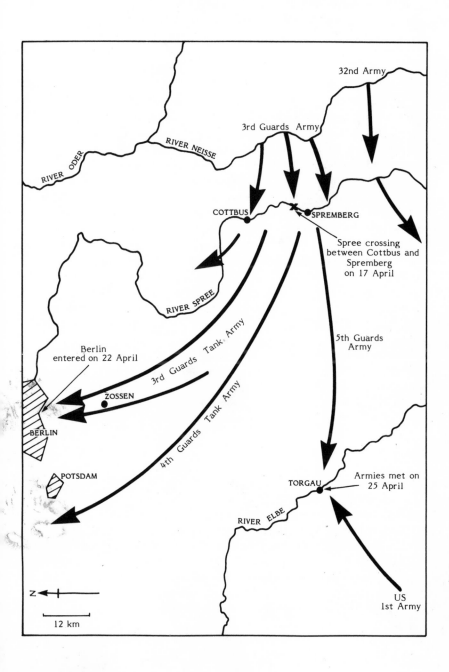

Koniev consulted the Commander of his Third Guards Tank Army, Colonel-General Rybalko:

'The desire to win time at all costs dictated the following decision to us: without waiting for bridges, we should try to ford the river in tanks, especially since they were proof against the machine-gun and submachine-gun fire which the Germans were delivering from the Western banks. In the advance detachment, we picked the best, bravest and best-trained crew and ordered it to ford the river.

'At this point the river was forty to sixty metres wide. Before our eyes, the tank rushed ahead and crossed the river which turned out to be only about one metre deep.'

By the end of 18 April, a bare sixty hours after opening fire on the Neisse, Koniev's tanks had advanced forty-five kilometres beyond the Spree, level with Lübben. His success meant decision-time for Stalin. Zhukov had been held up on the Seelow Heights.

'Comrade Stalin, the situation at our Front is developing favourably, we have enough forces and we can turn both our tank armies north.'

'Very good. I agree. Turn the tank armies towards Berlin.'

Before Berlin lay the extraordinary village of Zossen. Major Boris Polevoi, political commissar at Koniev's headquarters, recalled the scene as he entered Zossen:

'To the casual eye, this village looks no different from many others in the neighbourhood of Berlin; brick cottages, each one a replica of the next; red brick church; sickly trees entwined with wild grape, and the inevitable pigeons nesting in the eaves.

'The only thing that might strike one as rather odd is the untidiness of the usual back yard. And there is a curious absence of paraphernalia outside the sheds and barns.

'The village stretches into a wood. The trees are densely planted. The ground under them looks as though someone has been over it with a vacuum cleaner. You stroll a few yards – then. . . . What in the world is this?

'In a clearing stand twenty-four concrete buildings, camouflaged with excessive care and nearly invisible under the young pines. The concrete paths running between the buildings are overhung with netting. The compound is surrounded by a barbed wire fence through which a high-tension current could be run.

'By the side of the road are pillboxes splashed with dull yellow paint almost invisible even a few yards away.

'It was here, in this tiny village, or rather deep under it, that Hitler, all through the War, had his thieves' kitchen. To be more precise, it was the real HQ of the German General Staff – which officially, of course, was supposed to be in the centre of Berlin.

'Over the General Staff Building in the capital a flag always waved and gorgeously attired porters glided about, noiselessly opening doors, shutting doors. . . . But in the village of Zossen there were neither porters nor flags.

'The creatures who loosed the tide of blood through all Europe, lurked here deep underground like moles.'

Zossen was evacuated quickly and overrun virtually without a fight.

'Hans Beltau, the German engineer who had charge of the complex electrical installations, willingly showed us over the place. He had been only too glad to remain discreetly behind when his masters were getting out.

'The lifts were not working so we had to descend by means of a spiral staircase. At last we reached the bottom. Corridors branched in every direction. They were lined with numbered doors.

'Everything in this devil's kitchen testified that the Red Army's blow had been so staggering and unexpected that it caught even the German General Staff unprepared. The floors were strewn with documents, maps and reference books. In the office of the Chief of Staff a dressing gown lay flung over a writing desk; on the floor lay a pair of bedroom slippers.

'The bed in the adjoining room was unmade. On a small table stood a bottle of wine, a couple of glasses half-full, and a dish of apples. Underwear and family photographs spilled out of a half-open suitcase.'

Poveloi also noticed records of some last-minute communications, desperate attempts to get some military or personal messages out to Oslo or Prague. The last message from the apparatus for running a far-flung Nazi empire ended with the words – 'Ivan is literally at the door.'

'Ivan', in the form of Koniev's First Ukrainian Front, spearheaded by the Third and Fourth Guards Tank Armies, had more or less forgotten about Zossen by the time Poveloi found the message. The southern suburbs of Berlin were falling.

Koniev had won the race to Berlin.

Source
I. S. Koniev, *Year of Victory*

The Rise and Fall of the Ninth Army: March to May

Germany was already doomed when the Ninth Army rose to its brief prominence. It stood full square between the Red Army and Berlin.

Küstrin, a German stronghold east of the Oder almost surrounded by the Russians, was kept German for two months by the Ninth Army at enormous cost. The corridor to Küstrin across the flat, marshy Oder Bruch was kept open by a pincered army burnt and bruised. Then it was lost. The attempts to relieve Küstrin which followed, the massacres of 23 and 27 March, showed that even a well-generalled, disciplined army never had a realistic chance of carrying out impossible orders from the Führer's bunker. In the bunker, divisions were flags bearing the Swastika. In the field, there was by now insufficient ammunition, poor equipment, not enough tanks and inexperienced troops – at least in the case of the Ninth Army.

General Theodor Büsse, Commander of the Ninth Army, never questioned the people who gave him orders, though he grieved for the men who died because of them. His sheer competence as a general was shown on 16 April, when the Red Army attacked in earnest. It swarmed over the Oder and the Neisse. It broke through to the north. It stormed across the Neisse in the south. It got a bloody nose when it came up against the Ninth Army in the centre. From the Seelow Heights to Frankfurt/Oder, the line held against the mass attack on the opening day of the last phase of the war. In Frankfurt/Oder, the Ninth Army actually stopped the Red Army advance.

Whatever the bravery, however good the generalship, the flood could be stopped for at most only a few days. In some places, units of the Ninth Army were outnumbered twenty or thirty to one. Everywhere they lacked adequate support from artillery and from the air. Soon Zhukov's army had swept them from the main road to Berlin, and Koniev's army had swept them from the south. So chaotic was the northern zone between Küstrin and Berlin that General Weidling, in charge of the 56th Panzer Corps, decorated in battle in Russia and later to be entrusted with the defence of Berlin, had to shift his headquarters four times in an afternoon. He lost contact with Büsse and was condemned to death in his absence for desertion. He was let off later.

The town of Beeskow, in the lake district north of the Spreewald, had largely escaped the war. Its citizens knew about the terrible bombing

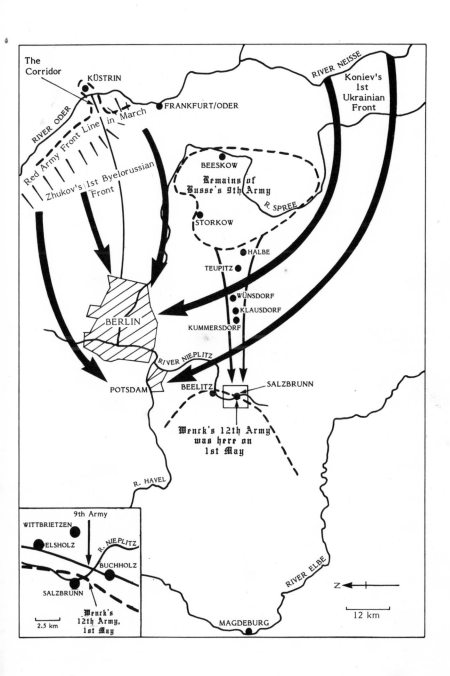

raids in Berlin and all the other cities, but Beeskow was a sleepy market town.

Troops started pouring into Beeskow, as Zhukov's and Koniev's armies advanced and the local people came out into the streets to watch as half the Ninth Army wound its way through, nearly 100,000 men, some apparently in good order and good heart, most in rapid retreat mixed up with civilian refugees.

From the east of the town, they suddenly heard a loud whining noise. There were no planes, and it was not a bombing raid. Some soldiers who were in the know dived for cover. For a moment the locals seemed mesmerized, staring in the direction of the noise. All at once it was too late. Thousands upon thousands of shells exploded in Beeskow. Crowds of townspeople became piles of torn flesh and flowing blood as they were blown up. A cattle shed was hit, and the scene was made more hideous as the maddened beasts, some of them on fire, charged through the exploding streets. The whining noise had been the music of the Stalin organs, Katyusha rockets playing on the retreating Ninth Army. Beeskow had become a front-line town.

The Red Army had broken through to the outskirts of Berlin on the Küstrin road in the north and moved through Cottbus and the southern part of the Spreewald and was driving into Berlin from the south. Büsse's Ninth Army had been partly destroyed and totally disorganized. Part of it, under Weidling, had withdrawn into Berlin itself, but Büsse's most successful front was now in the greatest danger. Effective resistance on the Oder front south of Frankfurt and Büsse's strict obedience to Hitler's command never to withdraw had created a pocket of some 150,000 men in the lakes, marshes and forests in the Beeskow–Storkow district. By 25 April this number had increased to 200,000 as the remains of routed divisions from north and south moved into this last corner of German-held territory in the area outside Berlin itself.

Zhukov's and Koniev's advance to Berlin to the north and south bypassed these 200,000 men. They had no supplies – one attempted air-drop was a fiasco – and for the most part they lacked the will to fight on. They did, however, have a strong desire to escape to the west rather than to surrender to the Russians. Their opportunity came when Hitler ordered General Wenck's Twelfth Army to stop fighting the Americans – they looked like stopping at the Elbe anyway – and to relieve Berlin. He was to do this by joining up with Büsse and entering the capital from the south. Büsse was ordered to send his best divisions, led by the SS Panzer Grenadier Kurmark Division to link up with Wenck.

To the men holed up by the lakes and in the forests, it was obvious that they could contribute nothing at all to the relief of Berlin, but if they could obey part of the order and just link up with the Twelfth Army they could perhaps reach the Elbe, and the comparative luxury of surrender to the Americans. The drive westwards began.

While the Russians had been prepared to tolerate temporarily a static German-occupied pocket which posed no threat, the move to the west looked like an attempt to cut Berlin off from the south. It looked like a counter-attack. They fought it hard, and the Kurmark Division – and the rest of the raggle-taggle army which followed it – lost an average of 1,000 men every kilometre.

The Russians first knew about the drive westwards when the Kurmark attacked their garrison at Halbe. The Kurmark wanted to avoid contact with the Russians as much as possible on the way to reach Wenck but the only road out to the west was through Halbe. The Russians pulled out to the surrounding countryside, taken by surprise, but they were soon firing back on Halbe, using artillery from their own garrison and stopping some of the movement on the nearby motorway on its way to Berlin and using extra guns from that source. Halbe was flattened in a couple of hours. The Kurmark suffered heavy losses, but at least they had something with which to fight back. The thousands with little or no ammunition who followed them just ran the gauntlet of Russian shells, and their losses were terrible.

Almost every village was the same. Teupitz, Wünsdorf, Klaus-dorf, Kummersdorf . . . by the time the remnants of the Kurmark and the rest of the Ninth Army had sighted the Twelfth Army near Beelitz on the morning of 1 May, there were about 30,000 men, two tanks fuelled for the last time from abandoned vehicles, and almost no ammunition. The trudging army and trudging civilians supported each other, totally exhausted, with the thought that, whatever the horrors, some might just reach the West. No one thought any more of Berlin or Germany, just the chimera of 'the West'.

The moving mass of half-hearted soldiers and civilians across his supply lines to Berlin was never a threat to Koniev, just sometimes a diversion or inconvenience. But as the Twelfth Army moved slowly east to meet them, a force might be formed which conceivably could do some damage.

The decision was taken rather late to make a serious effort to prevent the link-up. It fell to Major-General Yermakov's Fifth Mechanized Corps to get between Wenck and Büsse. Wenck was still quite well equipped with tanks and artillery; Büsse's army was little more than a mass of refugees.

Yermakov deployed his corps along the road south of Beelitz between the villages of Elsholz and Buchholz. Wenck had reached Salzbrunn, a kilometre to the west. Büsse had reached Wittbrietzen a kilometre to the east. Wenck fought his way over the Nieplitz Stream which actually crossed the road by an old mill at Buchholz. In the fields east of the stream, he deployed the advance guard of the Twelfth Army in defensive positions only a couple of hundred metres from Büsse's two remaining Tiger tanks.

Whatever the losses – they were appalling – the two German armies would inevitably meet now. Yermakov realized it. He kept his distance. It was enough to rake the two German armies with artillery fire from north and south; there was no need to risk the loss of infantry. While the Nieplitz reddened with blood, 30,000 of Büsse's men escaped, including less than a quarter of the Kurmark Division and a higgledy-piggledy stream of refugees behind, utterly exhausted and hardly even trying to dodge the shells any more.

This was the link-up of the two armies planned by Hitler to turn on the Russians and relieve Berlin. They struggled west to the Elbe, and a surprisingly large number crossed over to surrender to the Americans on 5, 6 and 7 May.

Sources
T. Büsse, *The Last Battle of the Ninth German Army*
I. S. Koniev, *Year of Victory*

THE REAL CASUALTIES

Introduction

The war came first to the villages around Berlin and then to the streets of Berlin itself. The citizens had already had the bombs. Then they had had the shells. For months they lived in cellars and basements. For a week, as the front line grew nearer, they hardly dared set foot outside. Getting food and drink, combating suicide and hysteria, were real problems for the cellar 'tribes'. In the end they just wanted the front line to pass them by as soon as possible, to get the present carnage over with and to face whatever had to be faced.

It was frightening indeed when your street, where you bought your newspaper and chatted to the neighbours, became a battleground. There was certainly an element of curiosity in looking out of your window and seeing the Red Army, although the shells and bullets quickly took the shine off the experience. There was a sinking feeling in the pit of your stomach when you had to answer that first bang on the door. Questions came thick and fast – Who lives here? – Hiding any soldiers? – What weapons have you got? Then a search.

When they first met the Red Army, German civilians almost invariably got a pleasant surprise. They had expected monsters, but soldiers in the combat zone, even if they had felt so inclined, were not concerned with anything other than the battle. They were up front and rarely risked their or their comrades' lives for the sake of rape and pillage.

The second wave was nastier for civilians. The supply troops and back-up services took very little notice of Stalin's instruction to treat the German worker as a fellow to be liberated. Instead, they raped and looted at will. Some of the treatment endured by the civilian population from this second wave of troops during the first four or five days of occupation was violent and degrading in every way. On the whole it was less vile than Goebbels' wild predictions and a great deal milder than earlier German treatment of Soviet civilians. But it was bad. Some soldiers were disciplined, but generally there was little attempt to uphold Stalin's instruction as far as debasing civilians in and around Berlin was concerned.

The Red Army allowed itself – just for a week – to be the unruly horde from the East, the German myth.

Armies are, of course, made up of individuals with wide differences in attitudes and also in education. Some officers – army doctors, for example – tried to take steps to avoid the worst excesses, and all front-line officers had instructions to sort out the handful of anti-Nazis from the rest and to ensure that they suffered no more.

Within a fortnight, the great multi-national army of Russians, Poles, Armenians, Azerbaijanis, Estonians, Georgians, Jews, Kazakhs, Latvians, Lithuanians, Mongols, Tadjiks, Ukrainians and a hundred other races, had settled down to the life of a strictly disciplined army of occupation.

'Speechless and Trembling', Landed Gentry in a Village Captured by the Red Army: 21–25 April

Their splendid manor house was in ruins, bombed by the RAF, and they had been obliged to move into the summer house. Now Lali and Freddy Horstmann even had to share their summer house with crowds of strangers – with refugees and terrified villagers, and also with their farm workers.

Things could hardly get worse.

They had hoped the British and Americans would make it to Kerzendorf village first, but no. It was to be the Russians, with all the frightening stories of ill-treatment and rape.

Things might well get worse.

'Try to get away from them, by all means, but if they do catch you just shut your eyes and pretend that it is your husband. How often does he fail to ask you if you want his love and force you to it when you do not want it? If you think of it in that way, you will be able to stand it, and it will be over quickly.'

Kerzendorf was well and truly cut off. The Red Army's advance to Berlin had bypassed the village to the east, and its advance towards Potsdam had bypassed to the west. There was no electricity and no telephone. Lali and her maid Ida had taken some of the most valuable things in the house and buried them by the lake in the grounds. Freddy had refused to part with his watch: 'I hold on to the only thing still working in a disrupted world.'

Machine-gun fire could clearly be heard in the late afternoon of

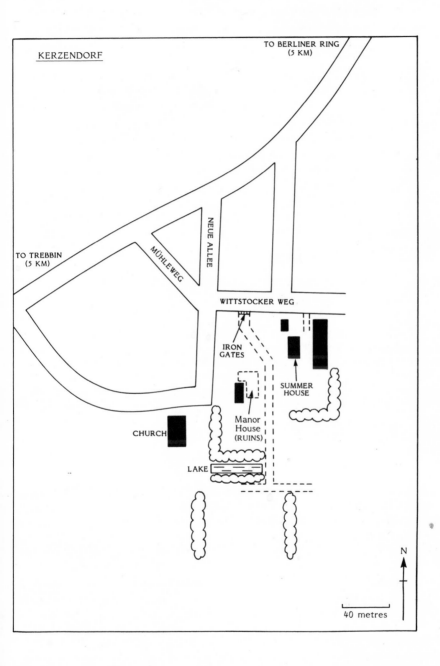

KERZENDORF

TO BERLINER RING
(5 KM)

TO TREBBIN
(5 KM)

NEUE ALLEE

MÜHLEWEG

WITTSTOCKER WEG

IRON
GATES

SUMMER
HOUSE

CHURCH

Manor
House
(RUINS)

LAKE

N

40 metres

19 April. Tanks were rumbling and there was a massive explosion as a nearby railway bridge exploded. The gun-fire drew nearer, but still no Russians arrived. Lali and Freddy talked about architecture and holidays.

'As soon as it is feasible,' Freddy declared, 'we will go off on a holiday to Lisbon. Soon it may be possible to travel there by boat.'

'There was a loud hammering on the door, which echoed through the house. When my husband opened the door a tall, fair-haired officer in a uniform we recognised as Russian, although as yet we had never seen one, stood on the doorstep. It was the conqueror present in flesh and blood. When he entered the room, the Russian Army itself was in our home, taking possession. As always, reality differed from anticipation, for it was not he that was violent, but Bibi who flew at his legs before we could stop her, while the soldier made a friendly gesture towards the outraged little dog. . . . He talked in the serious tones of a kindly grown-up soothing frightened children and, helpless though we were, we had a mutual respect for each other's unalterable position.' He searched the house, found no German deserters and left with a crisp salute.

It was 1.30 the following morning when the drunk, pistol-waving Russian infantrymen arrived. They were not the least interested in a letter in Russian which a Serb slave-worker had written saying the Horstmanns were nice people. They certainly were not interested in Ida's Nazi protestation that she was of superior race and therefore not to be touched, although it did appear to put them off her in particular. Half a dozen women were huddled there – Lali Horstmann and her staff. The soldiers chose Ulla Zarn, pretty teenaged daughter of Rudolph Zarn, one of the servants, who had last been heard of somewhere on the Eastern Front.

Freddy Horstmann was pushed up into the attic. His watch, 'the only thing still working', was taken from him. No one dared to move. Ulla suffered and sobbed.

'We were witnessing the logical conclusions of defeat. It was the rape of the Sabines all over again, a repetition of the wars of Rome and Greece and ancient Asiatic feuds. It was a symbol of defeat that men should no longer be able to defend their women, to suffer the shame of seeing them become part of the conquerors' loot.'

They knew, with horror, that this was going to happen again and again. Was there any possibility of escape to the West? Freddy and Lali studied a map and realized escape was impossible. More Russian soldiers came. More rapes. Lali and her immediate entourage were protected for a while by a fifteen-year-old Ukrainian servant boy they called 'Gabriel' for his angelic features – he was taken for a girl on several occasions by some quickly disappointed would-be rapists. 'Gabriel' spoke Russian and managed to direct truckloads of soldiers away from his mistress and her staff towards a barn crowded with helpless refugees from the East.

Lali took her Fabergé paper-knife to protect herself, and she tried to make herself as ugly as possible to put off rapists – until Freddy objected. She and Freddy eventually left the summer house and went to live in the remotest possible barn.

No end was in sight.

A brigade of tanks waiting to be thrown into the Berlin battle drew into Kerzendorf. Lali and Freddy watched, too frightened to move, as tank crews poured into the summer house. Lali could hardly bear it. Through a continuation of a strength of will and a feeling that there was nothing more she could lose, she braved it out in the open and sought out the general among the hundreds of Russians in her former home. She was told by an adjutant she would have to leave in an hour and could take some belongings with her.

Lali made her way, somehow to the general. She explained that she understood the military necessity of the take-over of her summer house by the Red Army. She only wished to ask the general to look after some paintings and books which were very old and precious; they had survived so many wars before. Could he save them for their own sake? The general replied: 'Houses have been destroyed all over the Ukraine, where I come from. I have lost all trace of my wife and children. . . .'

But the Red Army general was not like a Nazi general. Lali and Freddy were allowed to live in a corner of the summer house after all. They wondered what their fate would be in Communist Germany.

Source
L. Horstmann, *Nothing for Tears*

Punishment in the Workers' Suburb: 22 April

Ernst Brandt was neither a capitalist nor a Nazi. He had been quiet, and his quietness could have been taken for support for the Nazis and their atrocities.

A handful of Germans had quit Germany, through either necessity or desire, and had gone to neutral countries. Some committed anti-Nazis had even joined the Red Army. A few had resisted the Nazis within Germany, but they were very few indeed. Ernst Brandt had been in none of these categories; he was just ordinary. Soviet propaganda could not possibly distinguish between people like Ernst Brandt and enthusiastic Nazis. His was part of the collective guilt, so he deserved part of the collective punishment.

The troops that freed Lichtenrade, a working-class suburb of Berlin, from the Nazis were from Mongolia and Central Asia. They had heard the propaganda about what the Nazis had done and they had seen the evidence – of Auschwitz, of Treblinka, of the Ukraine – with their own eyes. They aimed to conquer and to punish.

'*Privetstvuitye*,' Ernst Brandt repeated to himself again and again. 'Welcome.' This was how he planned to greet the Red Army, whose arrival was now inevitable. The shells had stopped falling. The remains of the Wehrmacht had withdrawn nearer to the centre of Berlin. For a moment Lichtenrade was in no man's land. Soon it would be taken.

Ernst Brandt was in charge of an air-raid shelter in Hohenzollernstrasse containing over 400 civilians, mostly women and children. They left the steel door slightly open and prepared acorn coffee and several hundred cigarettes as peace-offerings.

'He came suddenly, with a crash of horses' hooves – a rider wearing a white fur jacket, one hand gripping the reins of his rearing horse, the other slashing at the dust-filled air with a long broad-bladed sword. As horse and rider danced crazily in the doorway, bullets from machine pistols streaked whistling past him into the bunker, sawing off chunks of plaster from the ceiling. A woman screamed and the child next to her along the wall looked curiously at the liquid red spot forming on her thigh.'

A whole platoon of the Red Army was soon in the shelter. The few men were flattened and the rape of all the women was soon under way. Coffee, cigarettes and '*Privetstvuitye*' were soon forgotten.

'He poked one foot behind the woman's legs and pushed her over on to the floor and fell on her, sword in hand. But the sword was too unwieldy; he tossed it aside and plucked a knife from his belt. Then he used the knife to cut through the woman's dress and brassiere and panties with one long slash. He fumbled with the front of his trousers while forcing himself between the woman's thighs with his own legs.'

For maybe an hour the women of the Hohenzollernstrasse air-raid shelter paid for the crimes of their husbands, fathers and children against the women and land of the Soviet Union. They paid an old price which the women of conquered states had paid for a thousand generations.

Ernst Brandt, who had been knocked out, woke an hour later with his mouth filled with blood and broken teeth. The whole shelter

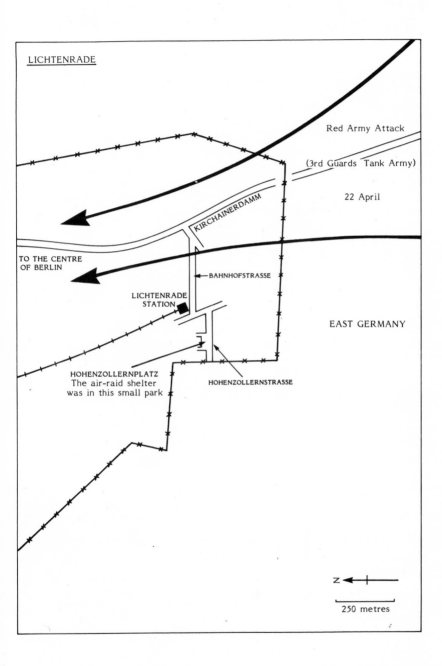

LICHTENRADE

Red Army Attack

(3rd Guards Tank Army)

22 April

KIRCHAINERDAMM

TO THE CENTRE
OF BERLIN

BAHNHOFSTRASSE

LICHTENRADE
STATION

EAST GERMANY

HOHENZOLLERNPLATZ
The air-raid shelter
was in this small park

HOHENZOLLERNSTRASSE

Z

250 metres

stank of sweat and urine. Most of the raping was over and some looting was going on.

'Me Communist,' pleaded one local worker, probably truthfully. He was kicked hard again and again. His cries could hardly be heard above 'Watches' and 'Woman, come.'

When the shaken and broken inhabitants of the shelter were allowed out into the sunlight, they saw their little park looking quite peaceful. There was a camp fire with woman soldiers preparing meals for the others. There was a Sherman tank delivered a year or so before by the Americans for the Soviet war effort. Next to the tank was a camel nursing its foal, all the way from Mongolia.

The punishment of the people of Lichtenrade was over for the time being.

Source
A. Tully, *Berlin: Story of a Battle, April–May 1945*

What the Gestapo Heard: 23 April

Even as late as 23 April, the Gestapo were still, unbelievably, listening in to phone calls:

'What? Haven't you burnt your picture of Hitler yet?' Or an old man to his lawyer: 'Destroy my records immediately – you know which ones. . . .'

There was nothing they could do. They could not get around the city any more. They had lost their power to arrest, terrify and torture. However, they noted the numbers just in case. One of the numbers they noted was that of Fritz Liedtke, who had an interesting little story to tell.

Some Wehrmacht soldiers came to Fritz Liedtke's flat that day, 23 April. Liedtke lived at 52 Silbersteinstrasse in Berlin-Neukölln. He was sixty-eight years old and sprightly, although he had managed to get himself discharged from the Volkssturm, the Home Guard, on account of his age.

The Wehrmacht soldiers asked him if they could mount their machine-gun on one of his windows which overlooked the deep railway cutting behind the block.

'Are you crazy? I don't want to die before my time. Go somewhere else, where the people are tired of living.'

To give such an answer would have been a capital offence a week ago. Now the soldiers just shrugged and left.

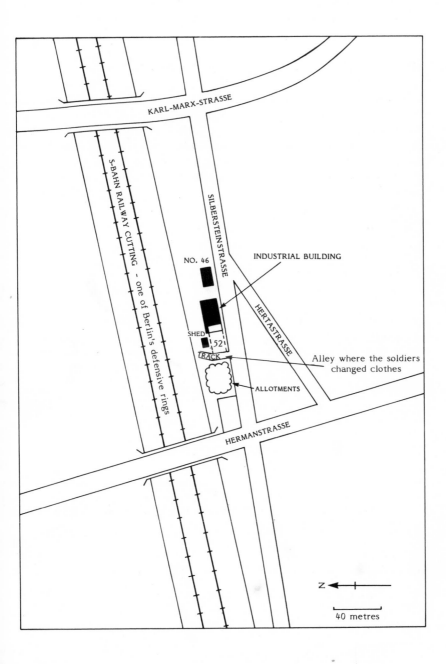

KARL-MARX-STRASSE

S-BAHN RAILWAY CUTTING - one of Berlin's defensive rings

SILBERSTEINSTRASSE

NO. 46

INDUSTRIAL BUILDING

HERTASTRASSE

SHED

52

TRACK

Alley where the soldiers changed clothes

ALLOTMENTS

HERMANSTRASSE

N

40 metres

Liedtke was rather surprised to see that they walked off down a
blind alley next to his house. There they put down the machine-gun,
opened up the haversack and slipped into civilian clothes.

'Goodbye, soldiers – welcome, civilians,' said Liedtke. They
grinned at him, and one of them bowed from the waist.

The machine-gun was tossed away.

Liedtke realized the Red Army would arrive very soon indeed. He
decided to make himself useful by gathering a number of women he
knew in the neighbourhood and hiding them in the cellar of his
house. When the Red Army eventually arrived, they found the
women almost immediately and took their watches and jewellery,
but they did not rape them or maltreat them as Liedtke and the
women themselves had expected.

Liedtke was also pleasantly surprised when he found himself
taking cognac with a Red Army major:

'I tell you I'm a factory worker.'

'Look. You have electric lights and water in your house. You're no
worker, you're a director, a capitalist.'

Liedtke poured the major a second – larger – cognac.

The telephone still worked, so when the major had left, Liedtke
rang a friend in the centre of Berlin and told him that the Russians
were quite decent.

'We've already been conquered.' The Gestapo wearily wrote
down Liedtke's number. 'The Russkies aren't so bad if you handle
'em right. . . .'

Source
A. Tully, *Berlin: Story of a Battle, April–May 1945*

Out of Hiding: Christmas 1944 and Spring 1945

'Fritz Croner could only wonder, as he completed his second year of
life underground, if there were another Jew in Germany in a more
anomalous position. He could hardly be accused of living luxuri-
ously, but the truth was that, thanks to his prosperous jewellery
trade, he, his wife Marlitt and his daughter Lane had all the food
they needed in a country where food was now gold. For Lane there
was even hot chocolate when she wanted it, and for Fritz, each
evening, if he wished, a fine after-dinner cigar. And yet the taste that
prevailed in their mouths each day was fear.'

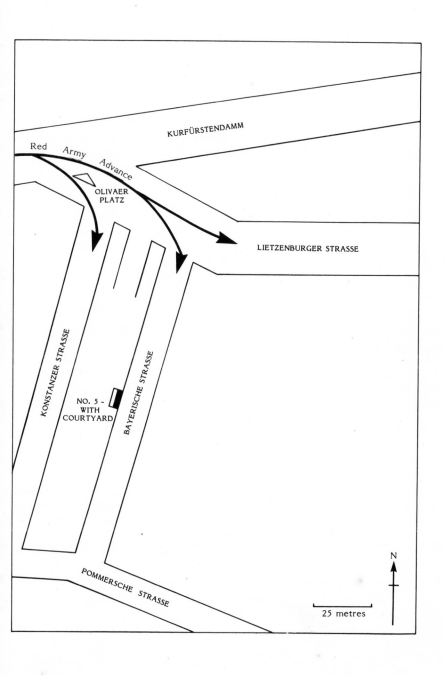

Fritz Croner and his family were Jews in hiding. They lived at 5 Bayerische Strasse, not far from the centre of Berlin. The constant fear of being found, picked up by the Gestapo, tortured and killed was oppressive, and the Gestapo became more and more fanatical as defeat in battle followed defeat. Fritz and Marlitt had a three-year-old daughter, Lane, and the trouble with her was she was starting to talk. Three-year-olds are indiscreet, and a Jew in Berlin in 1944 had to be very discreet.

Lane was the darling of their corner of Bayerische Strasse. She did not know she was Jewish, but Fritz and Marlitt realized that it was coming up to Christmas and that they would have to pretend to be Christian so that Lane would say the right things to the neighbours. With a feeling of treachery in their hearts, they bought their first Christmas tree, the *Tannenbaum*, lit the candles and found a toy for Lane for a present. Now when Lane was tickled under the chin by a neighbour in the air-raid shelter at night she could talk about her Christmas present, the tree and Christmas.

Fritz and Marlitt were sad. Had they survived for this? When Lane was asleep, they discreetly lit each night from one to eight candles on the tree. Thus their Christmas tree suddenly became host to the Jewish winter festival of Channukah, the Festival of Lights, celebrating the victory of the Jewish forces in Palestine over 2,000 years before. Their Hebrew prayers were silent, but one of their prayers was that they would be able to tell Lane soon that she was Jewish.

The Western Front collapsed, then the Eastern, and the Russians were in Berlin. Now, for a week, the Croner family lived on tinned food and boiled water in the storage room in their cellar. The overwhelming mood in that week was fear – terrible fear of the SS and Gestapo in their death throes, who would round up all and sundry on the slightest pretext; terrible fear of the Russians, who were hardly likely to wait to find out whether Croner were Jew or Gentile before shooting or deporting him to slave labour; terrible fear of the shells and bombs – the Second World War was now being fought round the corner in Olivaer Platz and in the back yards of Bayerische Strasse.

The Croners spent all day in the cellar. At night the Russians tended to bivouac, and it went much quieter. The Croners would creep out into the courtyard. Lane hardly noticed the twelve dead Germans there one day, for, at three years old, she was used to the sight of death in Berlin.

Then it went quiet. The war in Berlin was over. Fritz ventured into the street for the first time in over a week. Immediately he was confronted by a Russian officer:

'Soldier?' (In bad German.)

'No. I am a Jew. I want to thank you.' (In German.) Incomprehension. 'I am a Jew.' (In bad Russian.)

'No Jew. Germany. Dead.' (In bad German.)

Fritz Croner found the yellow-star identity card he had kept for this moment.

'You're really a Jew?' (In joyful Yiddish.)

'I told you so.' (In astonished Yiddish.)

The Russian Jewish officer grinned from ear to ear. He only wanted to help but could not think of anything. Then suddenly (still in Yiddish): 'Here. Have a watch.'

Fritz was suddenly the owner of a looted gold watch. The officer hurried away.

The Croners were free now. They could do little to help some of their benefactors of their years in hiding. The Swedish Lutherans were burnt out; the White Russians were deported. And the Croners learnt with horror the full extent of the Holocaust.

Still, at least one Jewish family had survived the entire war in the heart of the Nazi capital. It was a small victory over evil.

Source
O. Gross, *The Last Jew in Berlin*

Liberation of a German Anti-Nazi Cell: 24–28 April

The basement in Steglitz, a suburb of Berlin, was crowded and stuffy but relatively safe. It had run out of food and water but an irrepressible teenaged girl called Heike who had lived there for some months braved the bombs and shells to get to the nearest well (where three deserters from the Home Guard were hanging from makeshift gallows with placards around their necks stating their crime) and to a butcher who suddenly got some meat and let the populace have it off ration. Obviously Nazi ration cards would not matter for long now.

There was one very special feature of this basement in Steglitz. Its occupants were long-standing anti-Nazis. They hid deserters and Jews. They genuinely longed for liberation by the Red Army.

These anti-Nazis shared one deep fear. It was that they would be caught and shot in the last few hours of war. The SS were on the prowl and more vicious than ever in their death throes . . . look what had happened to those three Home Guardsmen.

The door of the basement flew open. A man in uniform rushed in. Only one? Dishevelled.

The man on watch barred his way. Everyone almost stopped breathing with fear and apprehension.

'Stop. Where are you going?'

'Anywhere – anywhere but – out there – you have no idea what's going on – out there.'

'Suppose you calm down, for a start. Do you want water?'

'Not water, clothes. Civilian clothes. If they find me like this . . . .'

Panzergrenadier Stolzburg was soon plain Herr Stolzburg, the carpenter he had been until he was called to be Hitler's cannon-fodder eighteen months earlier.

Ironically, within a few minutes, shells stopped falling and Stolzburg's 'out there' became rather more peaceful. By the evening, Ruth Andreas-Friedrich thought she would take a breath of fresh air with another leading member of the anti-Nazi cell, Frank. They strolled arm in arm up to the cemetery on the hill. It smelt of spring flowers and leafy hedges in the gathering gloom of an April evening.

It was not, however, just any April evening. It was the evening of 24 April 1945, and it was Berlin. Russian fighters and dive-bombers appeared over the watertower on top of the cemetery hill. Then the shelling began again.

'A harsh whistling overhead. I feel a blow in the back, stagger forward, and plunge deep into the hedge. Another whistling howl. Not 20 yards away the earth bursts open. Bits of tombstone fly through the air, broken wreaths, rotten planks. The dead. Merciful heaven. The dead. Something dangles eerily in the branches of a weeping willow before me. War has snatched the dead from their tombs. In torment I dig my face deep into the ground.'

They waited for a momentary lull and scrambled desperately the couple of hundred metres back to their basement. They swore not to leave it again until peacetime, and sat and listened instead to a cracked version of *The Beggars' Opera* on an old phonograph. Outside, shells gave way to bullets and the front line crept closer.

'Open up! OPEN UP!'

SS. A shudder.

'What is it?'

An SS man screams: 'WATER! WATER! We have no water.'

'Where's the front?'

'Along the canal. They've broken through. Over on the Priester-weg too.'

It was so near that all was plainly lost as far as the SS were concerned. They would be caught and executed. That much was

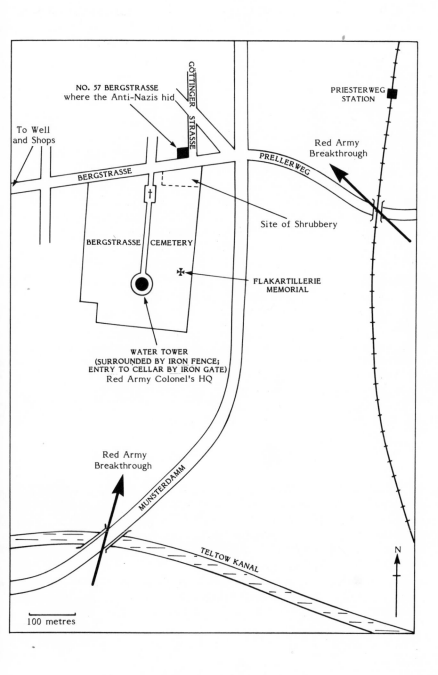

certain. Now, after twelve long years, Ruth Andreas-Friedrich had the upper hand over the Nazi masters of violence.

'Be off with you.'

'Where to? We're bottled up. We've lost our squad leader. They'll shoot us if we come without a leader.'

'My heart bleeds for you.'

A touch of old Nazi arrogance from the youngest SS boy: 'Watch yourself, Miss. Things haven't gone as far as you think. When the relief army gets here from the West. . . .'

Ruth slammed the door in his face. The incident was over and an uneasy feeling pervaded the acrid atmosphere of the basement.

The remaining German troops in Steglitz, SS and Home Guard, were soon routed. The first Russians appeared in the streets. Everyone in the basement was ready to surrender joyfully – to welcome the liberators with a white flag and with open arms.

Then the worst possible thing happened. Fanatics of the Nazi resistance, the 'Werewolves', chose the block above as a base from which to harass the Russians. A patrol of young Russian soldiers advancing up from a bivouac being established at the corner of the street was fired upon. Two dead. Surely they would never stand for this.

Most of the occupants of the basement huddled terrified. A few emerged and tried themselves to take pot-shots with old weapons at the Werewolves. They probably got one, but the Werewolves seemed to be everywhere – 'The irresponsible idiots – why did they have to choose Steglitz? Why our block?'

To have lived through everything. To have reached the moment of liberation. And now this.

Rifle butts hammered on the basement door.

Russians.

Some of the anti-Nazis spoke Russian. One, Andrik, was born in Moscow. Stolzburg was suspected to be a soldier and was taken with Ruth and Andrik, who were reckoned to be the ringleaders.

'Something cold touches the back of my neck. "You shooting", is yelled from all sides. I run. Andrik runs beside me. Stolzburg is with us too: three Russians ahead of us, three Russians behind us. The muzzles of their automatic rifles stare like dead eyes. We are dragged off at a gallop. Our feet run of their own accord, run, stumble, run again. A fence looms before us. We are over it with a bound. I see shrubs, hedges, wooden crosses, the cemetery. A dead man lies directly across our path. German? Russian? What do we care? We just have to jump to keep from stepping on him.'

Ruth knew she would be shot. Behind the shrubbery they slowed down. No, not there. Onwards. The water tower. 'At the iron gate we

Heroic sculpture in Berlin's Treptow Park – Sergeant of the Guards,
Nikolai Masalov, rescues a small German girl on the Potsdam Bridge

The Olympic Stadium, scene of a bloody battle – for once Helmuth Altner found himself on the winning side

The mass grave at Ruhleben, now preserved in a quiet corner of the municipal cemetery

Ruth Andreas-Friedrich was dragged across a cemetery to this water tower where she assumed she would be shot. Shells had blown human remains from the graves into the trees

Berlin's East-West axis, looking from the Victory Column west towards Charlottenburg, Ruhleben and Spandau. For two days the Red Army held this road while the Germans occupied the tunnels underneath

The former headquarters of the Reich Labour Service, now used as Federal Government offices in West Berlin

There was massive loss of life as Nazi remnants entered Spandau over the Charlotte Bridge. Spandau Town Hall is in the distance

All that remains of the old humpback Potsdam Bridge (brickwork in the foreground) where the Red Army broke into the Tiergarten area

No. 2 Schulenburgring where
General Weidling surrendered
Berlin

Stadtmitte underground station was
the last command post of
Krukenberg's Nordland Division
while buildings burned all around

The ruins of Hitler's 'New Chancellery' looking from Voss Strasse
towards the Reichstag

The large house in the foreground was the signalman's house at Salzkorn where ardent Nazis treated Helmuth Altner and other refugees from Berlin as heroes

Bullet holes from 1945 can still be seen on many of Berlin's older buildings – 'Even now!'

DIE TOTEN
MAHNEN
UNS

Memorial to the Socialists who suffered under the Nazis – 'The Dead are
Warning Us'

halt, then grope down a few steps. So it will be in a cellar – with no sky and no stars. . . .'

The astonished prisoners were brought into a room with a Russian colonel seated in a plush green armchair smoking a cigarette.

A rapid conversation in Russian:

'You were shooting?'

'No.'

'You are partisans. We shall shoot you.'

'We aren't partisans.'

'Why do you speak Russian?'

'I was born in Moscow.'

'Why are you living here?'

'My parents are German.'

'Do you listen to our radio?'

'Every morning at eleven o'clock.'

'When was the last time you listened?'

'Last Tuesday, when they broadcast the German news. Then the electricity was cut off.'

'What did we say?'

'That fighting was going on in Lankwitz. . . . We hate the Nazis. For twelve years we have been waiting for you. We were always on your side.'

'Show me where we are on this map. Show me Alexanderplatz.'

'There . . . there. . . . We aren't partisans. We want to help you.'

'Do you know the Soviet National Anthem?'

'I do.'

'Sing it to us. If you know it, you should be able to sing it.'

'*Soyuz Nerushimi Respublik Svobodnikh* . . . [Unbreakable Union of Freeborn Republics . . .].'

Two verses were the proof that was needed.

Now they were comrades. Now they would fight together, Russians and Germans, and the whole anti-Nazi cell in the basement was saved.

Source
R. Andreas-Friedrich, *Berlin Underground*

The Fall of the Wendl Family: Late April to Early June

'. . . You and I can't judge these things, darling. We aren't diplomats or generals, are we? And suppose Russia had suddenly attacked us? We simply had to act first, didn't we?'

The Red Army was now in Potsdam and was expected in Kladow, a few miles down the road towards Berlin, in a couple of hours. The prospect had been made appalling by Goebbels' horror propaganda on the rape and murder which went with defeat.

The meadows and lake at Kladow, and the woods all around, made a beautiful scene on an April morning. The birds sang and no guns fired. The Red Army was on its way.

Resistance in Kladow was light. What was left of the Berlin defence was concentrated in the centre of the city. During the hour or so of fighting the Wendl family hid in their cellar at 12 Quastenhornweg – Elsie and Heiner and their two small children, Wolfgang and Klaus. Almost the last shot in Kladow was a shell which landed next to their house, nearly deafened them, shattered most of the windows and damaged the house next door.

'Heiner, please do as I ask: go into hiding until the Russians pass on.'

'What? Are you mad? Leave you here in this mess? Alone with the Russians.'

'There's that narrow gap in the roof above the stairs; you could just squeeze into it and sit up once you're inside.'

'But what about you? What would they do to you?'

'You can't help me, and you'll only risk your own life. If you promise to love me whatever they do to me, I'll try to be calm and not make things worse for us all than they are.' Heiner just stared. 'I'll go to a doctor as soon as I can afterwards,' Elsie added.

Heiner broke down in tears. Then he hid in the roof.

Elsie went back to the cellar and started to tell the children a fairy story, trying to stay calm. She had got to the point where the beautiful princess was struck blind.

A bang on the door.

'Hands up! Where is the man?'

'There isn't a man.'

'We'll find him.'

They did not find him. When they found the children, they laughed and gave them sweets. Wolfgang declared that he liked Russians; then he remembered and asked, 'What happened to the blind princess?'

The next afternoon, things changed for the worse. A knock on the door and Heiner hid again. A German with a red armband – no one knew he had been a Communist before but he was certainly one now – arrived with a platoon of Russian soldiers. He announced that a Russian doctor and his staff would arrive to take over the house in half an hour. The family was to leave at once. When Elsie pleaded,

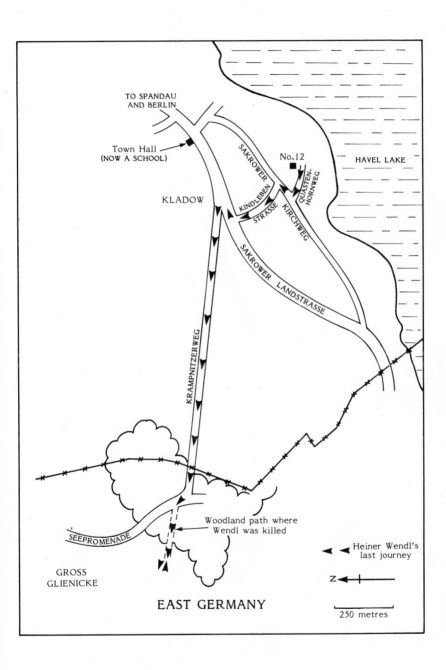

TO SPANDAU
AND BERLIN

Town Hall
(NOW A SCHOOL)

KLADOW

SAKROWER

KINDLEBEN
STRASSE

KIRCHWEG

No. 12

QUASTEN-
HORNWEG

HAVEL LAKE

SAKROWER LANDSTRASSE

KRAMPNITZERWEG

SEEPROMENADE

Woodland path where
Wendl was killed

Heiner Wendl's
last journey

GROSS
GLIENICKE

Z

EAST GERMANY

250 metres

the German shrugged and said he could do nothing about it. Eventually he agreed that Elsie could ask the Russian doctor when he came if the family could stay in the cellar and cook and clean for him and his staff. Alternatively the cellar door could be barricaded and the family could use the side door and never bother the doctor at all.

When the doctor arrived, he allowed them to stay on, provided they kept out of the way. Even when Heiner gave himself up – the alternative was starvation and cramp – the doctor, although rather taken aback, allowed him to join the family in the cellar.

'That first night we couldn't sleep, and I did not even undress. The noise was awful, and there was loud music as well. Were they dancing? Certainly they were drinking as I could hear the shouting become louder and wilder. I became more and more nervous. The Russian doctor had promised that no one should molest me, but I knew the reputation of the Russian soldiers when drunk. How long would I be left in peace even with Heiner's protection?'

One Russian soldier clambered down to the cellar. The soldier was armed and drunk. He gripped Elsie's arm and touched her body. Heiner managed to get out and call the Russian doctor, a desperate plea. The doctor took pity and punished the soldier for disobedience – he had to live out of doors, never allowed in the house, sleeping in the mud in the rain.

The order came in a few days to all Germans to take their radios to the town hall. It was safer for Elsie than Heiner, because Heiner risked being rounded up and taken away to work in Russia. She set off and saw how lucky she and her family had been. In the handing-in queue, she met a friend who had been raped and whose husband had been shot. 'All she could say was, "If only I hadn't screamed; if only I hadn't screamed. . . ."' She dragged herself along, looking utterly dejected, with her little boy holding her hand.' Elsie and her family had had scraps, and the children had even had sweets, from the Russians. Now she met the truly starving, neighbours who had recently been well-to-do. She tried to get bread but there was none, and she tried to get vegetables and there were none. Back to scraps.

'One of the most frightening things in those days was the fact that we were not allowed to lock our doors. All the women had to sleep completely unprotected and the Russians had access to anyone they liked. If they found no woman in the place they would often wreck the furniture in their rage.'

How much longer could the doctor's protection last?

The news came that Hitler had shot himself. Berlin capitulated. 'Berlin is yours.' The Red Army could enjoy its spoils.

It turned out that Kladow was to be in the British zone so, towards the end of May, the doctor and all the others slipped quietly across the new frontier towards Potsdam. The Wendls re-emerged from their cellar into a dirty and damaged home. The situation settled and much of the fear lifted.

The hunger continued. In fact, with so much of the food-producing areas around Berlin now inaccessible in the Russian occupation zone, the hunger became worse. All the Wendls had left were foul potato peelings. The children were emaciated. Elsie and Heiner were ill and starving. The family gorged the potato peelings. Heiner banged his fist on the table and jumped up.

'I'm going to get something to eat. I can't stand this any longer.'

'Don't be mad. . . .'

'I'm going to the Russian zone.' In the Russian zone were the big market gardens. 'If I don't go, we'll all soon be starved to death anyway.'

He cycled up Kindlebenstrasse, and along Krampnitzerweg and passed the checkpoint which marked the edge of the British sector. He cycled on to the outskirts of the village of Glienicke, where he exchanged Elsie's best blouse for some fruit and vegetables. Leaving Glienicke, on a section of road passing through some woods, two Russian soldiers had seen him with the bicycle and demanded it. Heiner refused. He had forgotten who had won the war and who had lost. He was shot in the forehead, and his brains spilled over the path.

Source
E. Wendl, *Hausfrau at War*

A Diary of the End: 28 April to 2 May

An old man slept in his overcoat for the third night running in a dank cellar. Many old people had died of pneumonia in such conditions in Berlin in the past few months. Max Bock, lying there, somehow managed to scratch his impressions into his diary. As a gunner in the First World War, he wondered why the piercingly noisy artillery in the street outside that went on all night was wasting its ammunition. As a decent person, he was sad to see young soldiers dying for evil or for nothing at all – 'So they try to find poor innocent victims to prolong their lost cause. It is a thousand pities for those who have to lay down their young lives for that murderous clique.'

'Another day and more suffering for all concerned.' But Saturday 28 April brought a respite. Bock even wondered if the Russians had

been beaten back. He noticed that the other people in his central
Berlin block in Meinekestrasse looked disappointed. Ordinary Berliners just wanted to get it over with.

By evening, the battle had begun again. Heavy shells were thick in
the air, and Bock settled down to another night in the cellar. As the
small hours passed, he knew the final battle was surely under way.
Now there were not just shells fired from some distance but machine-
gun and rifle fire as well.

'I go up to the flat to see if all is well, have a wash and a cold drink
of coffee, it is impossible to go out on to the balcony because of
passing bullets. In the street, lorries and other vehicles are parked
under the trees. The infantry have laid telephone wires along the
pavement, and troops, rifles at the ready, are advancing in the
direction of the Ranke Platz.'

The major target for Russian bombardment on Saturday 29 April
was Berlin's famous zoo. It had already been badly smashed, and
now Bock could hear all hell breaking loose again. He was sick to
think of the destruction of the zoo. The problem was that the
authorities had put the 'big bunker' there, a massive anti-aircraft
tower built of reinforced concrete.

'Round after round of ammunition is fired in that direction,
probably leaving little intact of the zoo and its gardens. One thinks
with horror of the suffering of the poor helpless animals, possibly
running loose so that one might find oneself face to face with a lion or
a jaguar in the street. And poor Lissy, the big elephant who used to
stand at the entrance, might well be dead. The last of her family. The
others died in an air attack in November '43. Was it really not
possible to find another spot for the big bunker, not so close to such a
famous cultural institution? Typical of the Nazis. . . .

'The streets are full of advancing troops and, now and again, a
trickle of wounded soldiers returning. At lunchtime I saw them bury
a soldier in the grass verge outside my house. A simple mound and a
few shrubs is all that remains – an unknown soldier who has given his
life for a lost cause. Later I noticed another dead soldier lying in the
entrance hall, apparently he had bled to death from a stomach
wound. So we are now on the battlefield – a battlefield among streets
and buildings. The devastation in the street is constantly increasing
– rubble lying around, buildings in ruins everywhere.'

In the evening, a building was blown up in the street behind
Bock's apartment, Fasanenstrasse. By the next day, Monday the
30th, the front line was in Ranke Platz, only 200 metres away, then
Lietzenburger Strasse, then Meinekestrasse itself.

'Bombardment of our district by the Russian artillery had meanwhile assumed such intensity that one fears the worst. It is now

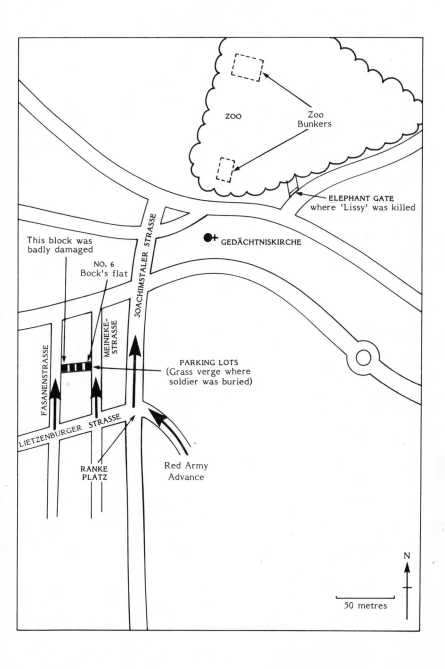

impossible to leave the cellar, so fast and close together are the explosions. The shells are not very heavy – having been in the artillery in the First World War, I have an idea that they are about 10 to 15 centimetres in calibre. Some shells brush past the house so closely, just a few centimetres away, that bricks are lifted and dislodged and some crash down. The tumult is hellish. The entire building seems to shake and threatens to collapse from a tremendous explosion nearby, followed by a hailstorm of falling stones and masonry. It must have hit our building. I hope it is not on fire. No, apart from splinter damage, the house is unhurt as we later establish, but the house backing on to us has been hit and there is a huge hole in the wall.'

The bombardment stopped in the late morning because the Russian front line was nearly there. By noon, they had occupied the buildings in Meinekestrasse down as far as the cinema.

The last Germans withdrew towards Kurfürstendamm between four and five in the afternoon. Bock heard them discussing whether the last stand would be made at the Chancellery. Some had apparently been told that the Americans had declared war on the Russians, so they just had to cling on, and it would be a matter of time.

Meanwhile, the middle and south end of Meinekestrasse were in no man's land. At 7.35 in the evening, two youngsters ventured into the street, shouted 'The Russians are here' and were caught. At 7.50, through a peep-hole in the cellar entrance, Bock saw his first Russians, '. . . keeping close to the buildings, walking in the direction of the Kurfürstendamm. Some wearing steel helmets, most just with their caps on, rifles or bayonets on their shoulders. . . .' The battle moved on towards the centre of the city. Some Russians made a quick search of all the cellars and left peacefully. Buildings burned, but Bock noticed how the people around him now seemed indifferent to danger. The war was over for them, and they wanted to sleep.

Tuesday – May Day – Bock's neighbours made a terrible mistake that put the whole community in jeopardy. Some women trying to make their way to the flats upstairs had been horrified to find a machine-gun at the entrance to the cellar. There had been rumours that when the Russians found weapons, they blew up the buildings and killed all the inhabitants. In a panic, two young men with an older neighbour dragged the machine-gun out into the street. A burst of fire. Some confused shouting in German and Russian. More firing. There was a pool of blood in the street now. Three women were widows; the whole community feared an instant mass execution. The machine-gun turned out to have been left by the Russians.

Bock could hear more intense fighting around the zoo and in the government quarter beyond. Huge columns of smoke poured high into the sky. Berlin had now burned relentlessly for five days.

For the first time for weeks, on the night of 1 May, there was no need to sleep in the cellar. Bock went up to his flat to bed. In the morning he thought he heard the sound of a loudspeaker in Russian and German saying something about the Führer. He hurried downstairs.

'People had picked up bits of the announcement, and the wildest rumours were going around. The Führer is said to have shot himself together with his wife Eva Braun. Goebbels and Ribbentrop had been taken prisoners by the Russians, and the final resistance under the leadership of Hans Fritzsche, the Nazi radio commentator, has collapsed in Berlin. But by lunchtime there is still firing from the Zoo Bunker. Towards the afternoon it is rumoured that the Russians had penetrated the Bunker, and indeed, shortly afterwards firing ceases.

'One of the women went to fetch some water and comes back with a young Red Army soldier who, she says, has been very polite and helpful, conducting her through the streets which was not easy, and also helping her to carry the water. He comes into the flats, gives a brief military salute, shakes each of us by the hand and says, "*Woina kaput, woina kaput*" – "The war is over."'

Source
M. Bock, unpublished diary

The Story of a Berliner Boy and His Uncle: April

'I'm not going back to that shelter where my mother is,' said fifteen-year-old Helmut Lüdicke. 'The underground station is too overcrowded, you can't move and it stinks of the women and children.'

Helmut came to his uncle's flat at 10 Tauentzienstrasse near the zoo, right in the centre of Berlin. His mother stayed behind in the underground station in Nollendorfplatz. After a little hesitation, his uncle, Willy Lüdicke, who was the caretaker and had built a sound air-raid shelter beneath no. 9 next door, let him stay. He liked Helmut; he was good to have around. He finished preparing a potato stew in his flat, where he still cooked between raids, and took it down with Helmut to join the inmates of the shelter next door.

'Imagine what I saw when I went to the shelter. . . . Among the people were Nazis who were celebrating Hitler's birthday. A picture of Hitler was decorated with flowers, and the people were drinking toasts to him as their liberator. I was flabbergasted that there were still such fanatics left. Nothing could help those people. They believed everything that this adventurer told him; they did not realize he had become the grand maniac of the world.'

So deeply embedded was the germ of Nazism that, even at this last stage of collapse, a certain Frau Zimmerman, a refugee from a part of Germany already occupied by the Red Army, who had been admitted to Lüdicke's shelter, told another woman in the shelter that she would report Lüdicke to the SS. His crime? Throwing a picture of Hitler from the attic into the street, where it had broken, while he was putting out a fire after a raid.

By 21 April, food was more important than paintings of Hitler. Helmut was plucky: 'A horse was killed by a bomb in Nürnberger-strasse, and a soldier quickly skinned it. Later I discovered my nephew was missing from the shelter, although I had strictly forbidden him to leave. In about an hour's time he returned with 5 or 6 pounds of horsemeat. At first I felt like giving him a good beating, but I had to close my eyes to his disobedience; all he wanted was to increase our food supply. We made 2 pounds of the horse into mincemeat; with pepper and salt it was simply delicious. The rest I fried a little for preservation.'

The end got nearer, and the situation in and around Tauentzien-strasse got worse. The SS came into the shelters in search of deserters and hanged two elderly Home Guard from the lamp-posts in Augs-burger Strasse, where they died slowly while street urchins twisted their legs for fun. A woman in the shelter took poison and died screaming, and her husband only had the bottle snatched from him at the last moment by Lüdicke diving at him – it was finally agreed that he would be allowed to commit suicide, but out in the street where it was less disturbing for everybody in the shelter.

Nazi propaganda about what the Red Army would be like had been terrifying. An old man of seventy tried to slash his wrists. Lüdicke had to wrestle a gun away from a woman to stop her shooting her children and herself.

As the battle finally closed in on the centre of Berlin, Helmut heard that his mother's underground station in Nollendorfplatz was in Russian hands, and Tauentzienstrasse was hit from both sides. The shelter survived; its occupants were bruised but still whole.

On 28 April, with the Red Army at the end of the street, the people were at their worst.

'I became aware that there was tension in the shelter and I went about quietly enquiring if anything was wrong. I learned that

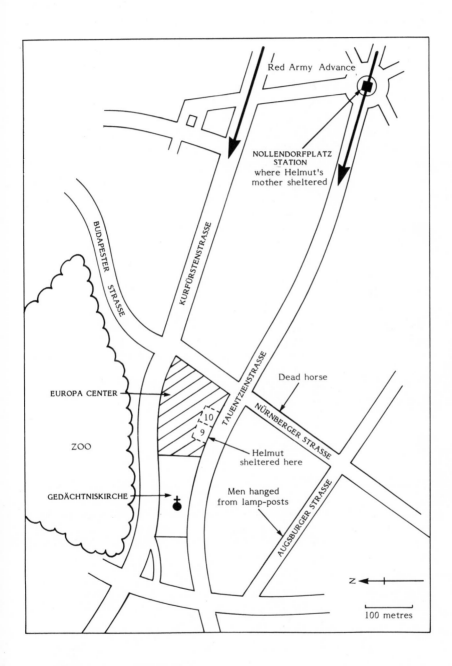

someone had stolen a suitcase and some other personal belongings from two women.

> 'People always say that
> Times get worse.
> Times never get worse
> – it's the people who do.'

Around noon on 30 April fire broke out again next door to the shelter. Willy and Helmut had to build a barrier of sandbags and cement in heat and smoke to stop the fire spreading. They also recovered a badly wounded soldier who would otherwise have been burnt alive. He was a Russian. They carried the soldier to safety. They tended him and pulled out the shrapnel from his back and legs while, fortunately for him, he stayed unconscious. Helmut was holding him while his uncle bandaged him. He mumbled. Willy offered him some schnapps. He refused distrustfully at first. So Willy and Helmut themselves gulped from the bottle. Then the soldier allowed it to be poured down his throat.

That evening the door of the shelter was flung open and several Russians burst in, led by a major. Helmut and Willy led the major straight to the wounded man, who talked at length to him.

'This man says you have been very kind to him. We are grateful to you. He told me about the schnapps. You did a good job.'

The major pinned a medal on Willy Lüdicke. For certain now, Willy and Helmut would be safe.

Source
A. Tully, *Berlin: Story of a Battle, April–May 1945*

The Hotel Adlon, Number 1, Unter den Linden: March to May

Roosevelt, Molotov and Mary Pickford had all stayed at the Hotel Adlon. It was Berlin's Number One hotel. Towards the end of the war it was also the only one left. Bombed-out residents came to the Adlon from the Bristol, the Esplanade, the Habel and the Kaiserhof. From the bombed Hotel Eden one night came a group of atom scientists, in Berlin to report on their progress in the preparation of a new bomb. Guests as important as these had to be protected.

They built vast and luxurious air-raid shelters under the hotel and grounds. They built a protective wall up to the height of the first floor balconies – the wife of the proprietor Louis Adlon hated it: 'It lent the building, of which the graceful architecture had been so essential a part of Unter den Linden and Berlin, a strangely remote and repellent aspect, as though, from being an hotel world-famous for its warmth and hospitality, it had become a fortress where no one might enter.'

The Foreign Ministry was 'at home' at the Adlon to diplomats every Wednesday. Before the war, they had been in the beautiful grounds of the hotel, including the famous Goethe Garden. By 1945, almost all these receptions were underground. Before the war, they had been splendid affairs, with the French, Americans, British and Russians attending. Now you were more likely to meet the Croats, the Slovaks and the Irish. The food and drink, however, remained the best in Berlin, some of it even 'off ration'.

The raids came more and more often, the sirens wailed outside, and the soft, melancholy gong sounded in the hotel. Everyone made for the cellars – 'They sat together in the big shelter, indiscriminately mingled according to the order in which they had arrived, the fighter-pilot beside the Spanish count, the beautiful blonde actress beside the Swedish banker, the Foreign Office official, the company director, the film producer, the surgeon from the Charité Hospital. And, as though by an unspoken compact, the horrors of the time were left outside. The talk was of art and literature and music, and travel in foreign lands.'

Louis Adlon and his wife thought it must have been like the *Titanic*. The edifice was still standing but the people inside could only prepare themselves for death. There was no hope left.

The Adlons watched as the Foreign Ministry finally left Berlin at the beginning of April. A whole column of cars and trucks met outside the hotel in the Pariser Platz and drove west through the one unbarricaded archway of the Brandenburg Gate, the Kaiser's Archway in the centre. Only the Chancellery remained in Germany's capital.

Once the Oder battle was fought and Berlin was encircled, the hotel stopped charging. Money and ration coupons no longer mattered.

The air raids ended; the shelling began. 'Yet the well-tried apparatus of the Hotel continued to function with a smoothness such as only a long-established and deeply-rooted tradition can instil into each member of the staff. Hot meals were regularly served at mid-day and in the evening. Hot water flowed from the taps as it had always done. There were baths, clean beds and, almost to the very end, full hotel service.'

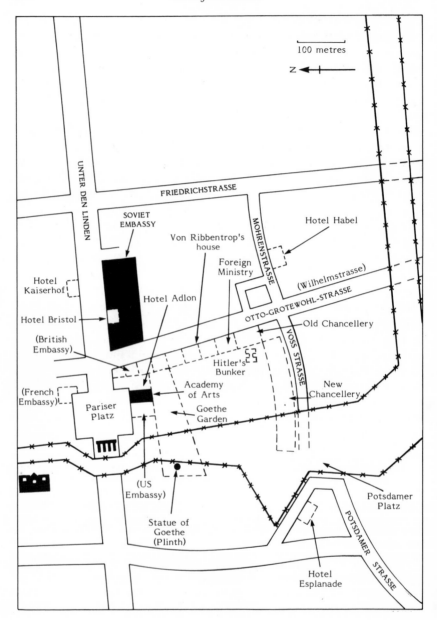

The very end came swiftly.

In the last few days, the hotel doubled as a field dressing station. The barber's shop in the basement was the operating theatre, the air-raid shelter was the recovery ward, and the Goethe Garden was the mortuary. The Academy of Art next door caught fire but guests and staff combined and stopped it spreading.

At eight in the morning of 3 May, the first Russians entered the Adlon. In the evening, some trucks drew up and removed the whole contents of the cellars, one of Europe's finest collections of wine. Later in the night, the hotel caught fire. 'It seemed as though the end of that famous wine-cellar betokened the end of the Hotel, for it was in the cellar that fire broke out. There could have been no better kindling than the piles of empty crates and packing-straw that were left behind. The flames, fanned by the draught from open windows, roared upwards from floor to floor at a tremendous rate.'

No one could deal with the sudden violent outbreak. The panic cry of 'Fire!' drove everyone out into the street, the wounded limping or crawling through the narrow steel door in the protective wall. Some managed to drag themselves to the middle of the Pariser Platz, but others could not do so and remained prostrate on the pavement where the burning debris fell on them.

'Fate decreed that no colour should be lacking from that gruesome scene. At the height of the conflagration there was a sudden blaring of klaxons and shouting of orders. Trucks drove up, cameras were unloaded, and a Russian news-reel contingent filmed the dying Hotel. Searchlights and lenses were turned upon the blazing roof, the glowing façade, the wounded lying near the entrance, the corpses amid the debris.'

Shortly afterwards, Louis Adlon was taken away. He died a few days later. An annex, the Couriers' Wing, later became for a few years a small, inferior hotel in the Communist part of Berlin.

Source
H. Adlon, *Hotel Adlon*

WAR IN THE STREETS

Introduction

By 25 April, Berlin was completely encircled. By 26 April, the nine armies, all part of the million-strong Red Army force now in the heart of Germany, had redeployed and reorganized, so a concerted assault began. This was to be simply a relentless inward drive by each of the armies involved.

The battle was really a foregone conclusion. They estimated that a city the size of Berlin would need 200,000 well-trained troops to stand any chance of putting up an effective fight against the hardened Red Army. Such troops simply did not exist. The vast majority of the 90,000 or so defenders were Hitler Youth or Volkssturm, Nazi Home Guard, badly equipped, trained and organized. The only defending units of any real significance were the remnants of Weidling's 56th Panzer Corps which had retreated into Berlin on Hitler's direct orders after taking the brunt of the assault on the Seelow Heights. The effective Berlin garrison of competent soldiers was probably little more than 25,000.

Time was also on the Red Army's side: May Day was a good

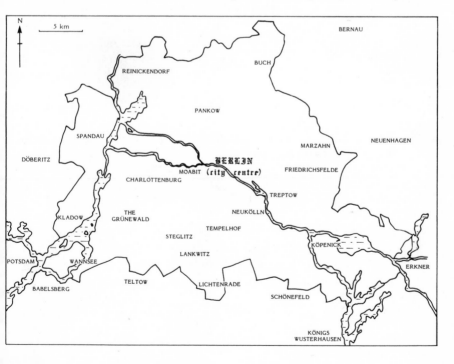

symbolic objective for final victory but if it took a week longer, it would hardly matter now.

In some ways the battle for the city of Berlin was a gigantic mopping-up operation by the Red Army. Especially in the suburbs, the defenders were thin on the ground, and pockets of resistance could be either annihilated by artillery or bypassed and left isolated until their supplies ran out (which invariably brought about a panic of discarding uniforms and more or less successful mingling with the civilian population). Theoretical successive defence rings – for example, using the S-Bahn railway 'circle' – were never adequately manned to be effective.

There were some Germans though who were determined that the battle for Berlin should not be a simple or quick one. In places defence was fanatical. In an effort to prevent desertion and stiffen morale, individual SS officers operated instant courts martial and hanged or shot anybody of military age who could not account for their movements. Every street had lamp-posts which bore witness to this Nazi self-butchery. By contrast, Soviet commanders tried to avoid unnecessary casualties both among their own troops and among the civilian population – for example, by just refusing to fire on boys of the Hitler Youth until they found themselves starting to lose men and tanks to them.

In the centre of the city, resistance stiffened as German-trained troops became thicker on the ground. Fighting was sharp and vicious. Early Red Army attempts to penetrate into the city in armoured columns had been abandoned as two-man vehicles had been knocked out by infantry anti-tank weapons. By the time the city centre was under attack, mixed infantry combat teams with automatic weapons, grenades and flame-throwers, supported by snipers, mortars and individual tanks, had been given the task of clearing the area block by block, sometimes fighting set-piece battles for single buildings, streets and squares.

One of the main problems for the Red Army fighting in the centre of the city was the lack of open spaces in which to deploy their vast superiority of artillery. Tall buildings also obstructed their field of fire. So they had to rely heavily on mortars and the rocket-firing *katyushi* with their much higher trajectories. Sometimes they dismantled the *katyushi* and re-assembled them in the attics of buildings where they could be fired straight across squares or up streets; then they could destroy a whole building in a few minutes. For example, they fired at the Reichstag from the Ministry of the Interior, causing extensive damage even at a considerable distance. The Reichstag was fiercely defended and was finally cleared only after the surrender of the city.

The troops resisting at the very end were an odd mixture of young and old, SS, Navy and Wehrmacht, and at least half were not even German – they were British, Danes, Finns, French, Italians, Latvians, Norwegians, Spanish, Swedes, Ukrainians and a host of others. Most of these foreigners were members of SS volunteer units, like the Nordland Division which was one of the last to stop fighting. The motives of these foreigners defending the German capital to the last varied from a form of suicide to the imagined fulfilment of their role as the élite of the New Order keeping at bay the Bolshevik hordes from the East until the Western Allies inevitably joined the fight on Germany's side. Goebbels' propaganda, until the last days, kept up this belief in an Allied split. Goebbels also held out the hope that Berlin would be relieved by the remains of Wenck's Twelfth Army and Büsse's Ninth Army. It was effective propaganda, and it kept men fighting long after they should otherwise have surrendered. So did the horror propaganda of what would happen if they lost. The SS especially fought simply for their own survival in an attempt to avoid capture and execution.

Surrender was out of the question while Hitler was still alive. Hitler was still in charge of the increasingly debauched, hopeless and claustrophobic bunker, until he finally committed suicide at about half past three in the afternoon of 30 April. Goebbels, who took charge after him, tried to negotiate a truce but failed, and he committed suicide the following morning. This cleared the way for the Military Commandant of Berlin, General Weidling, to arrange the final unconditional surrender. The few remaining members of Hitler's entourage had their chance to escape during the early hours of 2 May. Apart from Bormann who, contrary to widespread rumour, never reached Latin America or anywhere else outside Berlin, most escapees actually made it to the West. In the confusion and rubble, not every exit could be covered.

Up to these very last suicides and break-outs, the Nazi machinery still functioned. Hitler himself was preoccupied more with the problems of succession and with hysterical demands for total loyalty than with the pressing needs of Berlin's defence. A good deal of last-minute scheming was organized by his private secretary, Bormann, who had special access to him. He could control Hitler's supply of information and, while Berlin burned, he busily arranged for Goering to be put out of the succession and then exposed Himmler's dealings with the Western Allies. He even helped to organize the last execution ordered by Hitler, that of SS General Fegelein, on various charges associated with Himmler and an actress who was thought to be a British spy.

By the time Weidling was able to surrender the city, the brief mad bunker world had ended. Only a single technician was left there, and he sat and drank champagne with the Russians when they arrived. There were still, however, pockets of resistance in the Chancellery area and also in the Reichstag cellars, and a few small groups tried to organize a movement north up Friedrichstrasse over the Weiden-damm Bridge. Other resistance centres were the flak towers in the zoo and in Humboldtshain Park. At the same time, quite a large body of troops tried to escape west from the suburbs of Ruhleben and Westend, and a few even made it to the Elbe.

Back in the city, a handful of snipers were dealt with ruthlessly. The battle of Berlin ground to a halt on 2 May.

Escape to Berlin – and Fighting Back: 20 April

Run. The Russians are 200 metres behind. Machine-gun bullets whistling. Friends struck down. Reach the 'collecting point' over-looking Lietzen and look back. The village is in flames, and most of it is in enemy hands.

Enemy planes swoop and rake Helmuth Altner and his friends. Altner is a proud seventeen-year-old. He does not let go of his equipment. More experienced comrades throw everything dispos-able away to run faster.

Through the village of Falkenhagen. Villagers stare horrified. The once-invincible Wehrmacht is in rout. The main road is crowded with refugees. Push past them. Skirt Arensdorf, shelled and in flames.

Hasenfelde church clock strikes mid-day, greeting 20 April 1945, the day of the great Red Army breakthrough on the Oder Front.

Now Altner and his friends take it in turns to carry packs. One is always resting from the weight. They are becoming exhausted. A farm. An order to stop. A whole pig is boiled.

The Red Army is on the horizon. The half-boiled pig is aban-doned.

A metalled road. Agony on the feet. Spare ammunition crashes into the knees. Pack straps cut cruelly into the shoulders. Altner and Stroschn drop behind.

Forty-eight kilometres. They can't go on. Stop at some isolated houses. Surrounded by angry Hitler Youth. Who are you? Deserters? What do you want? Just food and rest. From the Oder Front. The Russians are coming. They won't get here today.

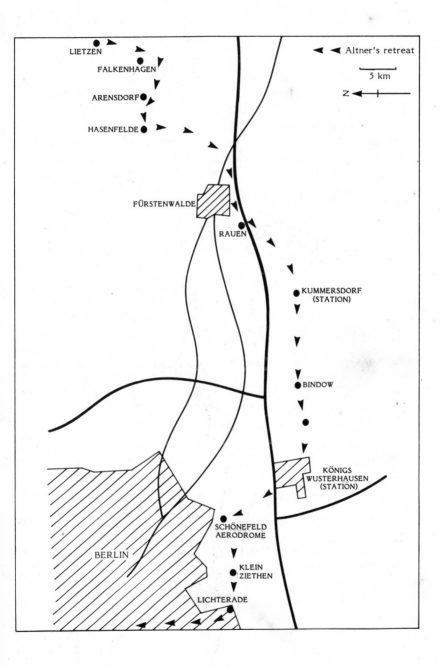

Bread to eat. Malt to drink. Tubs of cold water for bleeding feet.
Straw for beds.

Sleep.

Loud explosions and crashing glass greeted Altner and Stroschn in
the morning. Time to move on – and quickly. Altner's vague memory
of the route was that they should be making for Rauen, a village
somewhere south of the Fürstenwalde *Autobahn.*

'Military Police were trying to control a mass of traffic converging
on the *Autobahn*, while Hitlerjugend [Hitler Youth] and Volkssturm
[Home Guard] worked frantically at improving the defences. Soldiers were marching along both sides of the road heading west as
fully-laden motor vehicles raced down the centre.'

At a blown-up bridge there was a sergeant directing the traffic. A
short distance away, his brand new bicycle was propped up against
the wall. Altner and Stroschn could not resist the temptation. They
pedalled it away furiously, with Altner at the controls and Stroschn
on the carrier behind. They only stopped breathlessly to pick up a
grubby salami from the road – for breakfast. With some trouble, they
managed to find Rauen, and they hoped against hope that they
might find the rest of the Company there.

At the crossroads they decided to separate to find some water.
Stroschn had the luck to find the whole Company, but Altner ran
into trouble. Two young subalterns confiscated his bike and ordered
him at gun-point to run off and report to the barracks in Fürstenwalde. Humiliated and angry, Altner stormed away and for a time
was alone. Must he really go to Fürstenwalde? He started in that
direction and then crept back. Where was Stroschn? Would he be
shot by the subalterns? Indeed, where were they now? After a few
minutes of heart-stopping panic, he found Stroschn and the Company and was safe – at least from other Germans, if not from the
Russians.

It was like being home again. It was good to be striding through
woods, led by Lieutenant Fricke, a comfortable, reassuring figure,
and to be with all the others. The news was bad, but it did look as
though they could get back to Berlin if they moved quickly to
Kummersdorf and got on a train due to leave that night. The
resourceful Fricke even found an isolated farm for hot milk and
a good supper. Then they piled onto the goods train and fell
asleep.

'Suddenly the wagon doors were wrenched open with a shout:
"Everybody out." The Russians had blocked the line up ahead and
now the only way forward was on foot.

'They piled out of the train despondently and marched off in single file each man automatically placing one foot after the other blindly following the man in front. . . .'

They stumbled on, past sleepy villages, some making desultory Home Guard preparations for defence – so obviously hopeless – against the Red Army. Bindow – Senzig – only seven kilometres to Königs Wusterhausen, the last chance for a train home, a big station on the main line to Berlin.

The station was deserted when they got there. The last train for Berlin had left hours ago. Altner and his friends collapsed exhausted, many now in tears. It looked like the end. Fricke called a break, Sleep.

Every way seemed to be blocked. They heard the Russians were now shelling the centre of Berlin and were trying to block off all the southern approaches to the city to keep reinforcements away.

But they revived after some sleep. The women in Königs Wusterhausen fed Altner and his friends with rations they could hardly spare and encouraged them. They decided to have one last go – on foot – the last forty-four kilometres.

By detours and back roads and last-minute dodges, Fricke managed to lead his weary band of youngsters as far as Schönefeld aerodrome before they came under direct attack. They escaped to a farm next to the village of Klein Ziethen. It was evening again and they desperately needed more rest. The farmer was reluctant. He feared Russian reprisals, but he had no choice and had to surrender one of his old barns. It was the end of their third day on the run. 180 kilometres so far, twenty-five kilometres to go. Again they were disturbed at 11 p.m. The Russians were in the next village and approaching.

'They marched on silently through the night each man engrossed in his own thoughts. The moon hung over the sleeping villages like a pale disc in the sky. The anti-tank barriers were closed, the cobbles dug up in places and anti-tank mines strewn in the ditches to catch the unwary. Sometimes a civilian sentry would accost them at the barricades as they passed.'

The suburb of Lichtenrade meant Berlin and, for now, safety. They staggered painfully, these sixteen- and seventeen-year-olds, like old men.

They had made it. They knew now they would reach their barracks at Ruhleben in the north-west corner of the city. Success.

'Now they could see Home Guard, mainly dressed in Waffen-SS camouflage uniforms, guarding the barricades, and Hitler Youth strutting around with bazookas. SS were patrolling the streets in cars checking individual identities and occasionally picking someone up. Two SA men were standing smoking beside a lamp-post from which hung a tightly-bound man in civilian clothes, his dead eyes staring out from his blue face. A label pinned to his chest pronounced that he had been executed for cowardice and desertion.'

Altner felt sick. Was it all worth fighting for?

There was a brief respite from fighting when they got back to Ruhleben Barracks, not much food but plenty of schnapps and alluring girls from an SS 'Death Battalion' who had decided to die rather than surrender but who also, evidently from their behaviour, had decided to have a good time first. For this purpose they found a quiet corner of the barracks.

Then it was back to battle. Spandau was the last part of the ring round Berlin which was still German. If Spandau were lost, Berlin would be surrounded. Altner and Stroschn were sent out as part of a new Company made up from the motley collection of Wehrmacht, SS and Hitler Youth now occupying Ruhleben Barracks, and found themselves eventually in a trench next to the big hospital in Spandau, the Johannesstift. The Red Army was known to be just on the far side of the hospital, and there were 500 badly wounded soldiers in it. There was only distant firing, and nothing happened in Altner's trench all day. Night fell and it grew colder, so cold that neither Altner nor Stroschn could sleep for more than a few minutes.

The next morning, 25 April, Altner and Stroschn learned that the hospital would be handed over to the Russians without a fight. To almost everyone's relief, the SS had been overruled and another chapter of horrors averted.

The new order was to march to the northern outskirts of Spandau along Niederneuendorfer Allee and then to cut across a meadow to some trenches next to a deserted slave-labour camp. Beyond the camp were some woods, and to the north some industrial buildings. As Altner and his comrades ran across the meadows, they were raked by shellfire and machine-gun fire. Most of them made it to the trenches, only to find that they were barely waist-deep.

One section was detailed to cross a small track facing a small clearing to the rear of the labour camp. Altner followed them, as his job was to liaise between this advance trench and the main trench in the meadow. All but two of the advance section were killed outright when a tank loomed in front of them and blew them and the trench to pieces. The sergeant, who had the only bazooka in the Company, had his head blown neatly off his shoulders before he had the chance to use it. Now the tank turned to the main trench, to which Altner had managed to return:

'There was the roar of an engine and the rattling of tracks from the right flank where a massive tank emerged from the trees. The Staff Sergeant called for a bazooka but there was none available. The gun

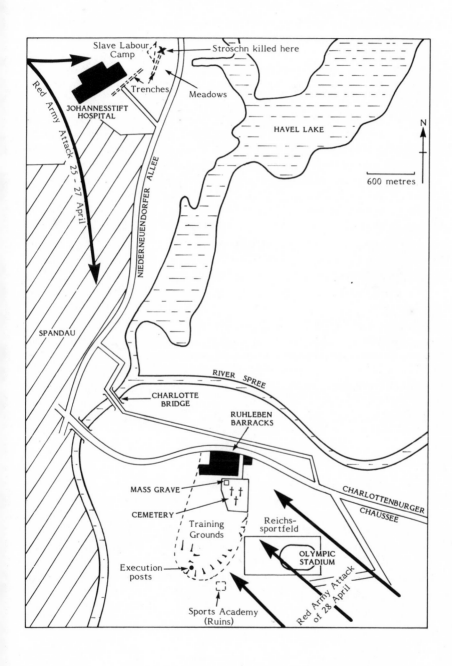

Slave Labour Camp

Stroschn killed here

Trenches

Meadows

JOHANNESSTIFT HOSPITAL

Red Army Attack 25 - 27 April

NIEDER-NEUENDORFER ALLEE

HAVEL LAKE

N

600 metres

SPANDAU

RIVER SPREE

CHARLOTTE BRIDGE

RUHLEBEN BARRACKS

CHARLOTTENBURGER CHAUSSEE

MASS GRAVE

CEMETERY

Training Grounds

Reichs-sportfeld

OLYMPIC STADIUM

Execution posts

Red Army Attack of 28 April

Sports Academy (Ruins)

dipped and fired along the length of the trench. Only Altner had any
cover, being round a slight bend next to the labour camp. The gun
kept on firing methodically destroying the trench and killing its
occupants. Someone tried to run but was immediately gunned down
by the tank's machine-gun. . . . The survivors started crawling back
through the dead and dying while enemy fire continued unabated
over their heads.'

Altner's pal Stroschn died. Altner himself survived and cried
hysterically that night in a cellar back in the centre of Spandau.

There were some desultory attempts to defend odd buildings in
Spandau now, but nobody really wanted to fight there any more.
The town was evacuated on 26 April. Before finally withdrawing
over Charlotte Bridge, Altner heard a Red Army broadcast in
German on a wireless in a house in which he was sheltering. Berlin
was surrounded. Dozens of familiar places were occupied.

Ruhleben Barracks themselves were soon barricaded against the
attack which was expected from Spandau, now in the hands of
the Red Army. In the event, the Russians stormed the rear of the
barracks from the direction of the Olympic Stadium, across the
Reichssportfeld (a series of playing fields west of the stadium itself)
and down through the ranges and assault courses behind the barracks.
It was in the practice ranges that Altner for the first and only time found
himself winning a battle against the Red Army.

From one of the practice trenches, Altner and various Hitler
Youth and other more or less trained men and women fired into the
woods which skirted the complex of stadiums making up the 1936
Olympic complex. Clear on the horizon, as dawn broke, were the
barracks' three execution posts for deserters and traitors. Altner
remembered how, in the past, he had had to witness executions
there, but those posts would not be needed any more.

A Russian tank appeared with a white flag and broadcast this
message: 'Comrades, give yourselves up. There is no point in
continuing to fight. The Russians have you covered and the Barracks
are completely surrounded. Run over and report to the Russian
troops on the Reichssportfeld. You will be well treated, and as soon
as hostilities have ended you will be allowed to go home. Soldiers,
there is no point in it any more. Do you want to die in the last hours of
a war already lost?'

Some broke loose and disappeared in the direction of the Reichssportfeld. They were mostly machine-gunned by their former comrades from behind.

Then Altner – who had not been tempted to defect – found himself
in a counter-attack, his first. It was exhilarating. He was actually
advancing, winning. This is what he had always expected to do. It

was so very sad that his friend Stroschn was not by his side now. He thought of him.

The order came to advance across the practice grounds. Enemy fire was heavy but the obstacles of the assault courses and mock villages made it difficult for the Red Army to aim their fire and to resist the assault on their positions in the woods, even though they had the higher ground. Several hundred motley German troops advanced in surprisingly good order into trenches which had been built for training and now provided cover very much in earnest.

The Russians retreated from the woods and the suburbs around. They had plainly miscalculated. They had thought the Ruhleben Barracks was on the verge of surrender. They were shocked and badly mauled by a fierce counter-attack using every weapon available – many of the Hitler Youth came onto the battlefield unarmed and relied on taking weapons from the dead.

Terrible crossfire on the Reichssportfeld from Russian positions in the ruins of the nearby Sports Academy took a big toll. In all, there were 2,000 German casualties – and probably a good many more Russians killed and injured. It was a dramatic and unexpected German fight-back. Helmuth Altner was pleased to have taken part.

Source
H. Altner (ed. T. Le Tissier), *Totentanz Berlin*

A Doctor is 'De-Nazified' and Meets Hitler: 23–30 April

Professor Ernst-Gunther Schenck had been an ardent Nazi and an enthusiastic anti-Semite as a student and a young doctor. He had abandoned a promising civilian medical career to join Leibstandarte Adolf Hitler, the élite Panzer regiment of the Waffen SS, in which he had eventually been promoted colonel. He was woodenly loyal to Hitler even as Germany collapsed, and it was out of this loyalty that he travelled from the safety of Bavaria to an emergency operating table in a cellar under the New Chancellery in Voss Strasse in the centre of besieged Berlin. Hitler was in his own bunker under the Old Chancellery in Wilhelmstrasse, connected by a labyrinth of underground passages to Schenck's operating room. It was 23 April 1945.

The first thing Schenck had to do in Berlin was to get supplies. He had to go out at night searching long-forgotten medical centres and hastily abandoned hospitals. The Red Army was already shelling the suburb of Steglitz when Schenck arrived there to salvage what he could from the remains of the Augusta-Viktoria Hospital:

'. . . in the basement where I was prowling about with a flashlight in search of supplies, I suddenly came upon some dozen very elderly, moaning women. When this hospital had had to be evacuated, two days before, they had been left behind. Apparently there was just no transport. When I entered the basement ward at midnight, they thought I was the first Russian. They began screaming like Valkyries. I made the familiar bedside rounds, gave each patient a few placebo pills. Then I, too, had to abandon them to their fate – hungry, distraught, forlorn. It was ghastly. I simply had to leave them alone in the midnight dark.'

He managed to pile some supplies into his truck – bandages, morphine, splints and other basic medical commodities – and made it out into Schloss Strasse. On the way back he saw properly for the first time the distress of Berlin. Although it was night, he saw how few houses were still standing, how fires raged out of control, how there was no hope for the refugees, no hope for Berliners and no point in continuing the fight. When he got back to the New Chancellery, he was shocked by the Nazis there. To be exact, he was shocked by two sorts of Nazi, the strutting sort and the decayed sort.

The strutting sort he quickly dismissed as madmen sending children into a hopeless battle – they might as well have thrown their sons and daughters into a furnace. They talked of a 'military situation' but rarely, if ever, left the bunker. It was the decayed sort of Nazi in the bunker who really persuaded Schenck that Nazism was hollow. Amid all the misery, blood and death, he met high Nazi Party functionaries, 'clad in gaudy uniforms and decorations not earned on any wartime front'.

'These functionaries, most of them portly and middle-aged, for-mer stormtroopers I suspect, had nothing to do except bemoan their fate and lost privileges. Nor could I induce them to volunteer to do anything, even make their own beds. None would help in my casualty station; that was beneath their rank and dignity. One told me, haughtily, "I simply cannot stand the sight of blood." Not one of these worthies would venture out into the city with me in the evenings, to forage for medical supplies. After two or three nights, exhausted as I was, I could not even sleep because of their noisy strutting about and their sodden drinking bouts. When they began dragging stray whores in, I got General Mohnke to shift my bunk assignment. . . .'

Now Schenck worked night and day at the only contribution he could make. He performed 370 operations in the last week of the war. Some of them were on screaming children as young as ten years old,

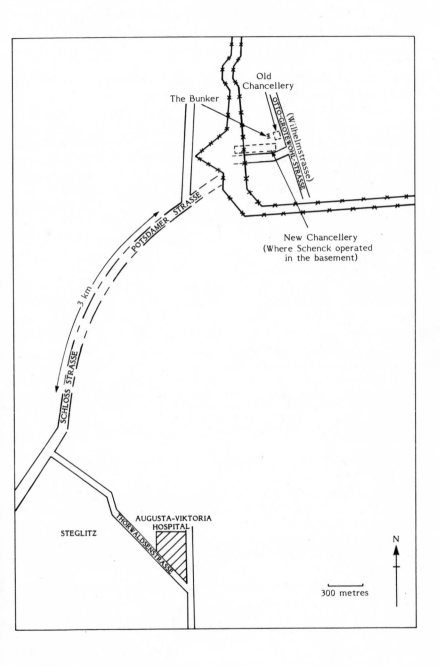

with Hitler Youth uniforms caked in their own and their former playmates' blood and with their limbs broken and bodies torn. Some of them were men of retirement age now dying bewildered. Some were the soldiers of the French, Danish, Latvian and Spanish SS units caught up in Germany's Armageddon. Schenck found himself half-awake, half-asleep, performing operation after operation, amputation after amputation, applying bandages to the living taken from the dead.

The last troops flown in to defend Berlin were two Navy battalions, totally untrained in infantry warfare. They were told to help defend the Reichstag. They nearly all died – some on Schenck's operating table, but most in the Reichstag. He could recognize them by the remains of their brass-buttoned uniforms.

By 29 April, the Red Army's artillery could pinpoint with fearful accuracy Target 106, the New Chancellery. The operating cellar shook violently as the lights flickered every few seconds. The slaughter of the innocents intensified.

Schenck went on operating and started to use up the last few drugs. He was assisted by Sister Erna, '. . . a kind of German Florence Nightingale, standing in a clutter of amputated arms and legs and entrails which she later stuffed, like slop, into ashcans. The orderlies could bury the fallings from the operating table only during the spells when artillery let up.'

Late in the evening, Schenck and Sister Erna were summoned to see the Führer himself. Excitedly, they filed through a maze of dark underground passages leading to the special bunker under the Old Chancellery still carefully guarded, the inner sanctum. Immediately they entered, they saw the man just a few yards away.

'I was a mere colonel. He was the Führer. My whole body seemed to freeze. A chill went up and down my upper spine. . . .'

Hitler responded with a handshake, 'A cold-fish flapping gesture . . . really only a jerky reflex, although it was meant to be amiable enough.'

The small company stood for a few minutes of rambling conversation in which Hitler mumbled his thanks for the help of his medical staff at this late stage of the struggle.

'He wore his golden Party badge and his World War I Iron Cross on his left breast pocket. But the human being buried in these sloppy, food-stained clothes had completely withdrawn into himself. . . . I could see Hitler's hunched spine, the curved shoulders that seemed to twitch and tremble. Somehow his head seemed withdrawn into his shoulders, turtlelike. He struck me as an agonised Atlas with a mountain on his back. . . . His eyes, although he was looking directly at me, did not seem to be focussing. They were like wet pale-blue porcelain, glazed, actually more grey than blue. They were filmy, like the skin of a soft white grape. The whites were bloodshot. I could detect no expression on his vapid, immobile face. Drooping black sacks under his eyes betrayed loss of sleep. . . . Deep folded lines ran down his rather large pulpy nose to the corners of his mouth. . . . At fifty-six, the Führer was a palsied, physical wreck, his face puckered now like a mask, all yellow and grey.'

Sister Erna broke down: 'My Führer, keep up your faith in final victory. Lead, and we shall follow.'

'One must not, like a coward, seek to avoid one's own destiny,' was Hitler's reply.

The whole interview lasted only a few minutes, and Schenck saw that Hitler was very near the end.

On his way back to his cellar, Schenck was surprised by the sound of clinking glasses and merry-making. He was invited in and was soon joining in a party with General Krebs, General Burgdorf and others who had little left to do but eat and drink. They were joined after a while by Eva Braun (by now Eva Hitler) and a couple of her companions:

'She was not drunk, but well on the way, tossing her glass back regularly. She was seated at the head of the long oak table in the gangway and was the real life of the party – like a Rhineland Carnival Queen. I was at the other end.

'The Führer's bride talked away, in a chirpy, rather pleasant Bavarian accent, to this audience of some fifteen or sixteen men and women. It was all small talk, gossip, rather pointless anecdotes. . . . But she was not the sweet simple woman she seemed to be. She was deeply neurotic. And she did not strike me as particularly intelligent. She was banal.'

In those few days, Schenck had seen the top echelon of Nazi Germany at first hand. He had met inferior people, unheroic, only really concerned by the destruction they had brought about because it touched themselves. He considered afterwards that he had been 'denazified' by all this. Perhaps he was – obviously too late.

Source
J. P. O'Donnell, *The Berlin Bunker*

The Last Flight from Berlin: 24–28 April

Goering had suggested that he should now be Führer, since Hitler was cut off in Berlin.

Hitler reacted: 'None of this is anything new to me. I have always known that Hermann Goering was lazy. He let the Luftwaffe fall apart. The man was a monumental crook, and his bad example let corruption flourish at lower levels. He has been a drug addict for years. I have known these things all along.'

Goering was dismissed by telegram, and a new chief of the Luftwaffe was needed. In the world of make-believe which shrouded the bunker, new life in the Luftwaffe might be just what was needed to save the day. They sent for Colonel-General Robert Ritter von Greim.

Von Greim received the order to go to Hitler on 24 April at a Luftwaffe base near Munich. His mistress, test-pilot Hanna Reitsch, flew with him to Rechlin, some hundred kilometres from Berlin. There they intended to take a helicopter to the Chancellery. Hanna Reitsch, slight, blonde, blue-eyed Nazi heroine, knew a great deal about helicopters – in fact, she had performed for Hitler the feat of flying a helicopter indoors, the only time it had ever been done. Just before arriving at Rechlin, the last helicopter had, however, been destroyed in an air raid.

They decided to try to force their way to Gatow, an airport on the western outskirts of Berlin, by Focke-Wolf 190 with an escort of twenty fighters. They made it, but ten of the fighters were lost. There was still the problem of getting from Gatow to the centre of Berlin, past suburbs where the Red Army was already entrenched. They decided to commandeer a tiny training plane, a Fieseler Storch.

Von Greim took the controls, and Reitsch crouched behind him. They flew low to avoid attracting attention, startling the Russians in the Grünewald park. It was only when they flew below the level of the trees up the wooded valley south of the Olympic Stadium that the Russians had a chance to take aim. Russian infantry fired and some tank crews with machine-guns joined in. Bullets flew and hit the fuselage, the glass, the propeller, but amazingly failed to blow up or ground the plane. It zigzagged on, until suddenly von Greim lurched forward as blood poured from a bullet-ridden foot. Reitsch grabbed the controls, leaning over von Greim, and five minutes later landed the remains of their plane just west of the Brandenburg Gate.

The journey from Munich had taken two full days. They had answered the summons of the Führer presumably to evacuate him

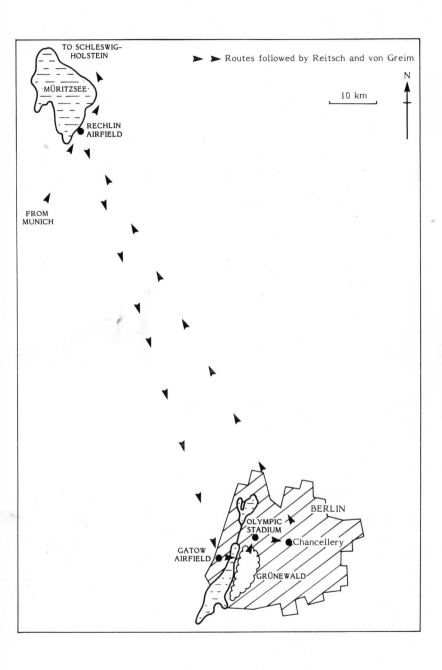

TO SCHLESWIG-
HOLSTEIN

MÜRITZSEE

RECHLIN
AIRFIELD

FROM
MUNICH

➤ ➤ Routes followed by Reitsch and von Greim

N

10 km

BERLIN

OLYMPIC
STADIUM

Chancellery

GATOW
AIRFIELD

GRÜNEWALD

and his Court to safety. But within a few minutes of entering the bunker from the exploded city above, they realized that the rumours of a madhouse were true. Instead of entering the seat of a crisp, clear-headed government at bay, they were entering an asylum run by the inmates.

Von Greim was brought on a stretcher to Hitler for he could no longer walk. He believed in Hitler. He found it difficult to believe what he now heard.

'I make you Field Marshal and turn over to you the command of the Luftwaffe of the German Reich. I am now working out plans for the relief of Berlin, and in these plans you will take a very important part. Wenck's Army is opposed by the Third Russian Army, but if you can open the way for him through the circle around Berlin, he can break through and lift the siege.'

'My Führer, how am I going to open up the way?'

'By every bomber at our command. You will rest for a while, and then at the appointed time you will need to take over.'

Von Greim was carried away for surgery on his foot. Reitsch was detained for a diatribe against Himmler, who was seeking peace with the Western Allies. She then joined Magda Goebbels and helped her entertain her children. She taught them to yodel and talked about her adventures as a flying ace. She knew the children were doomed. Their mother, outwardly calm, would murder them all with chocolate laced with cyanide. The plans were already laid. They were so innocent and young. Their father was preparing even now a diary entry on 'the meaning of sacrifice'. Reitsch saw this madness being sullenly prepared. She saw the little brass phials of cyanide. Magda Goebbels was no longer even interested in the possibility, however remote, of escape by plane which Reitsch offered to do everything she could to make possible.

After two days in the bunker, the same daring young pilot who had flown the Focke-Wolf 190 from Rechlin to Gatow, flew a little Arado-96 up to the Brandenburg Gate. He brought in some supplies and took off a few minutes later with Reitsch and von Greim. Shells and bullets were flying everywhere. The Russians were surprised by a dramatic take-off to the east, just missing the top of the Brandenburg Gate. Reitsch and von Greim were squeezed in behind the cockpit and got away from Berlin. A few bullets whizzed up from Unter den Linden but the three were soon safe in the clouds.

The new Field Marshal and head of the Luftwaffe flew briefly to Plön in Schleswig-Holstein, to confer with Grand Admiral Dönitz, head of the Navy. There was nothing to be done and nothing to command. As she had promised Hitler, Reitsch denounced Himmler, but there was little point. All hope was lost, and what did his feeble attempts at a separate peace with the West matter anyway? The head of the Luftwaffe and his mistress retired for the last few days of the war to a Luftwaffe sanatorium in the Austrian resort of Kitzbühel, away from poison and bombs and far from the dreadful insanity of the Berlin bunker. But von Greim's world had collapsed, and he killed himself before he could be arrested after the final surrender. Reitsch made her way home but most of her family was dead.

Source
J. P. O'Donnell, *The Berlin Bunker*

The Battles of Moabit: 26 and 27 April

The Third Reich had made it clear that it would fight to the last man, the last woman and the last child. Young Germans and young Russians would be forced to die in battle, even when the outcome was obvious and known.

There was no doubt whatever that the Red Army would get across the Westhafen Canal into Moabit, the working-class inner suburb of Berlin. It was inevitable because they had more men and more guns. How many more heroes would be turned to corpses crossing this stretch of water? Quite a few, reckoned Captain Stepan Neustroyev, leading a battalion mainly of members of the Young Communist League, as he watched the first attempt at a crossing fall back in pain and confusion.

The Westhafen Canal was cold, deep and as wide as an *autobahn*. The bridge north of Beusselstrasse Station was the obvious place to cross but it was badly damaged and had to be used gingerly. Unless you crossed it quickly, though, the chances of survival were slim. From buildings on the south bank, the Germans raked the bridge with machine-gun fire. From further afield, they bombarded it with light shells. If this bridge could be taken, one of the last rings of defence of the centre of Berlin would be penetrated. An operation was planned for the night of 26 April.

In the darkest part of the night, a small group of engineers slid down the canal banks, under the damaged bridge, to remove the mines which the Germans planned to use if the Red Army started to cross again. They worked softly and quickly and nearly escaped but, just as they were in the last stages, German machine-guns opened

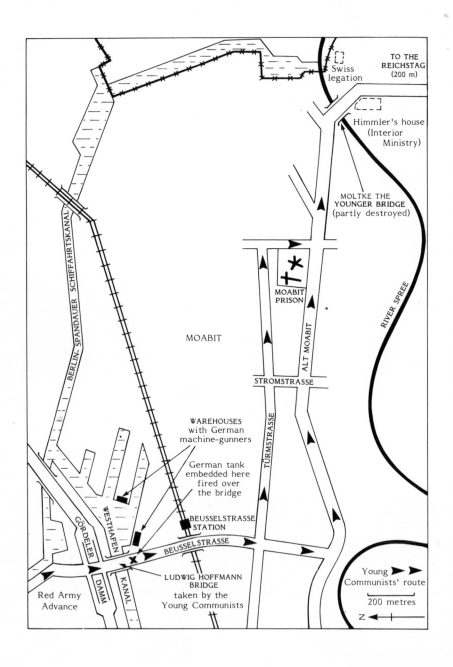

TO THE
REICHSTAG
(200 m)

Swiss
legation

Himmler's house
(Interior
Ministry)

MOLTKE THE
YOUNGER BRIDGE
(partly destroyed)

MOABIT
PRISON

ALT MOABIT

RIVER SPREE

BERLIN-SPANDAUER SCHIFFAHRTSKANAL

MOABIT

STROMSTRASSE

WAREHOUSES
with German
machine-gunners

TÜRMSTRASSE

German tank
embedded here
fired over
the bridge

BEUSSELSTRASSE
STATION

GÖRDELER

WESTHAFEN

DAMM

KANAL

BEUSSELSTRASSE

LUDWIG HOFFMANN
BRIDGE
taken by the
Young Communists

Red Army
Advance

Young
Communists' route

200 metres

z

up. One stubborn engineer, Private Stankevich, was decorated for bravely carrying on under fire; unfortunately the decoration was posthumous.

Still, the charges had been removed and the damaged bridge was open. Early the next morning, Captain Neustroyev watched a rather desultory artillery barrage which did not even appear to damage one of the most dangerous German-occupied warehouses on the opposite bank. Then he watched the first assault force picking its way across the bridge, to be driven back by a tank half-embedded in the road beyond the bridge and by machine-guns in an undestroyed warehouse. The assault force, made up partly of recently liberated Russian slave-labourers, became the victim of one of the small groups of Germans frantically defending the last few square kilometres of Nazi Berlin.

Another rather low-key artillery barrage. The whole thing needed thinking out again.

Captain Neustroyev agreed that his battalion of Young Communists should lead the next assault but this time there would have to be better back-up. He arranged with his colleague, Captain Gorodov, to use his 'chemical defence weapons' to get up a dense smoke-screen. In this more organized way, most of the Young Communists did manage to get across the canal alive – the Germans could only fire wildly through the smoke – to take on the defenders man to man, an unequal fight between well-fed superior numbers buoyed by victory and the remains of the Wehrmacht clearly on the point of surrender.

While Neustroyev's Young Communists defended the bridgehead, a second battalion fought its way through to Beusselstrasse Station some 200 metres beyond the bridge, but the bridge itself was still under fire. Indeed, some of Neustroyev's men had to return to try to sort out an unpleasant muddle caused by four horses in a gun team killed by machine-gun fire as the smoke lifted; they collapsed on the bridge itself and had to be manhandled into the canal. Meanwhile the resulting traffic jam became a series of sitting targets for the Germans who were still in the warehouse.

It took several more hours to overcome German resistance on the Moabit side of the Westhafen Canal, floor-to-floor and room-to-room fighting. Then it got much easier. In Moabit proper, there was neither SS nor Wehrmacht, only Hitler Youth and Home Guard right up to the Spree, the next main defence line. Even Moabit Prison was virtually undefended.

Neustroyev's battalion swept through Moabit in a few hours. They were soon converging on the banks to the Spree from which they could see the Reichstag a few hundred metres further on. They were so quick that there was initially a good deal of confusion. When the colonel in charge was told on the wireless that Neustroyev had reached the Spree, he insisted that it was impossible, that they must have lost their bearings and returned to the canal. He ordered them to check at once.

They checked. It was the Spree. The centre of Berlin was burning beyond. Across the river, bristling with machine-guns, stood Himmler's Ministry of the Interior.

To reach the Spree so quickly, Neustroyev's battalion had really just crossed Moabit rather than conquering it. They had not stayed. It was left to others to mop up behind them. Captain Boyev's company, which had taken Beusselstrasse Station, now moved on to deal with the inhabitants of Moabit, who consequently lost their watches and, in many cases, their virtue. Some phoned their friends in the city centre to say they had been conquered.

There was, in fact, some disagreement among their officers as to whether Russian soldiers should be free to rape the women of Moabit or not. For one thing, this was a working-class and potentially Communist area. For another, Stalin had apparently forbidden rape in his Order of the Day. There were some cases where soldiers were, literally, ordered off their victims by their officers, who then themselves raped the women who thought they had been rescued. More commonly, officers simply turned a blind eye. One woman complained to an officer, and he explained that worse things had been done to his sisters by the Germans in Russia and added that, on the whole, his men were fairly clean.

Some of the incidents were far uglier. One pretty German girl, Lotte Behn, had her SS uniform cut open and was raped. But being in the SS, it was felt that she deserved something more. She was hacked to pieces, and the group of soldiers, larking around, made her friends watch as they played a game of football in the street using her head as the ball.

More serious business, meanwhile, was under way on the banks of the Spree. The Germans had mined the Moltke the Younger Bridge, the last bridge standing in the area, but they had not had enough explosive to do a proper job. They had only damaged the bridge severely enough to make the preparations for crossing long, slow and painful. The mistake at the Westhafen Canal was not repeated. There was heavy covering fire aimed at the Ministry of the Interior and other buildings such as the Swiss Legation which the Germans were using as a defence line between the Spree and the Reichstag. Then slowly, and with some casualties, Neustroyev's leading men clambered over twisted girders, eventually clearing a path over the ruined bridge. A small bridgehead was established east of the Spree.

The Red Army now had a toehold on the administrative centre of Nazi Germany.

Source
S. A. Neustroyev, *Storming the Reichstag (Shturm Raikhstaga)*

Organizing the Defence of Berlin and Running Away: 24–29 April

Goebbels was realistic enough to know that a good many of the troops whom Hitler intended using for a heroic defence of Berlin were unreal. They were paper flags on optimistic maps.

People like Major Arnulf Pritzsch who had fought in the East, been injured, returned to Berlin and then been drafted back into Army administration, knew all the real details. There were between 75,000 and 95,000 men and boys who could reasonably be expected to shoot at the Russians. They would have to stand up to 225,000 troops, more experienced and better equipped.

From his office in Unter den Linden and, when that was bombed out, from his office at 1 Jebenstrasse, Pritzsch had helped to plan the defence of Berlin. Press gangs had gone into youth clubs, schools and even hospitals. Civilians had been forced into ill-fitting uniforms to die for Hitler in a hopeless battle. Defensive rings, which looked good on maps, had been set up around the city, each a kilometre or two nearer the city centre.

When it came, the battle was not heroic. It could not be, with the poor German remnants. It was at times a bitter fight, with a great many casualties, mostly German.

As one defence post fell after another, Pritzsch, 'a trim, slender man with a longish face and an air of fatalism', organized and reorganized the deployment of fewer and fewer troops. Each time, his face grew longer and his attitude more fatalistic. Then his information dried up.

Pritzsch and his colleagues sat and waited. They could hear the war in the distance clearly enough, and it was getting nearer, but no news came, so they could make no new dispositions. 25 April. 26 April. Nothing.

Pritzsch decided to go and see for himself. 'He wangled a Krad motor-bike with a driver and, plumping himself in the side-car, ordered the driver to head for the Grünewald. They made their way unmolested along the Hohenzollerndamm to Roseneck, to the begin-

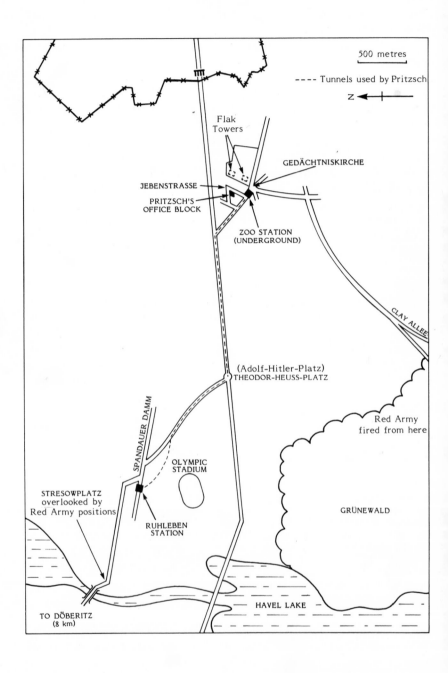

500 metres

- - - - Tunnels used by Pritzsch

z ←——+——

Flak Towers

GEDÄCHTNISKIRCHE

JEBENSTRASSE

PRITZSCH'S
OFFICE BLOCK

ZOO STATION
(UNDERGROUND)

CLAY ALLEE

(Adolf-Hitler-Platz)
THEODOR-HEUSS-PLATZ

Red Army
fired from here

SPANDAUER DAMM

OLYMPIC
STADIUM

STRESOWPLATZ
overlooked by
Red Army positions

GRÜNEWALD

RUHLEBEN
STATION

HAVEL LAKE

TO DÖBERITZ
(8 km)

ning of the Kronprinzenallee, where they ran into heavy artillery fire from the Grünewald. There was no aimed fire at first, but when they lingered it became clear that they were under observation and that the Russian guns were zeroing in on them.'

Quite shaken, Pritzsch and his driver got back alive to Jebenstrasse. Pritzsch reported that the Russians were in the Grünewald and moving towards the centre. He also reported that there was not a great deal to stop them reaching Jebenstrasse.

Surprisingly though, it was from the other side, from the east, that the actual threat to Jebenstrasse appeared – on 29 April:

'Within twenty-four hours, the Russians had become next-door neighbours. They moved on the Gedächtniskirche and kept going to the Zoological Garden. Here they milled about in seeming confusion, under heavy attack from the huge Zoo Bunker in a corner of the Zoological Garden by the Landwehr Canal. Watching the scene from a top-floor room in the seven-storey administration building, Pritzsch found it a weird sight. Russian T-34 tanks had nosed into the Zoological Garden, among the various animal houses, but the numerous Soviet troops appeared to be annoyed at finding themselves there. With fire from the Zoo Bunker filling the air, they didn't dare to cross the square and move on the Zoo Station or Jebenstrasse.'

Pritzsch went up to the roof and fired his machine pistol into the zoo, taking pot-shots. For a time, this caused confusion amongst the Russians, who could not make out where the bullets were coming from. There were several casualties.

Then the Russians worked it out. 1 Jebenstrasse was plastered with shells and rifle-grenades. Pritzsch dived inside and rushed down into the cellars.

It was time to get out – while it was still possible to get to the Zoo Station and down into the underground tunnels. The decision was confirmed by a 'special order' from the Führer's bunker. 'Hitler has been killed fighting at his command post, and orders all military forces to make their way west. . . .' They could hardly wait.

About 300 from the Army administration made their way into the tunnels. They were nearly at Adolf-Hitler-Platz when the chief of staff, without thinking, lit a cigarette. The struck match attracted a burst of machine-gun fire. Fortunately, however, for the 300, it was not followed up; the Russians were taking no risks now. The group made it by tunnel right up to the suburb of Ruhleben and marched on through the night towards Spandau and the West.

In the wide Spandauer Damm, they made an error of judgement. They came across some Tiger Tanks manned by Austrians who were also trying to make it to the West. Tanks were obviously safer to hide behind, but they attracted massive fire – in the Stresowplatz, many of the 300, along with civilians who had sheltered with them, were mown down by machine-gun fire from all sides.

A few escaped. Pritzsch was among them. He got as far as the west side of the training grounds at Döberitz just outside Berlin, where he and a few companions were soon surrounded in a house where they had taken refuge. They fired a few shots and quickly ran out of ammunition. Then they surrendered.

Source
A. Tully, *Berlin: Story of a Battle, April–May 1945*

Toughness and Tenderness on the Potsdam Bridge: 26–29 April

'The Tiergarten is an island defended by picked SS troops and battalions forming the bodyguard of the Hitlerite government. It is dominated by tall, solid buildings, from which all the approaches to the water barriers were kept under full observation and covered by armed fire' – from General Vasili Ivanovich Chuikov's report.

Despite the fact that the SS were still out for the kill and despite all the horrors of a long war which could harden the soul, many ordinary soldiers in the Red Army were never really toughened. They kept that civilian human decency which separated the way they behaved from the way the Germans behaved. The Red Army taught the German population a hard lesson, particularly through widespread rape, but it was rape and not rapacity.

Of course, there were as many bad Russians as anyone else, but the Red Army gave its soldiers a different environment and different expectations from other armies; the main difference was the high-profile role in the Red Army of enthusiastic Communists. Every battalion had a hand-picked political deputy who was usually one of the very best soldiers and also totally committed to Stalinist Communism. The political officers were believers. They were enthused with the ideals of Lenin and Stalin, and they fought for the destruction of Fascism and the liberation of all people from Hitler, including the German people.

The political officers' main job in the field was to keep up morale. This they could easily have done by simply adding to the hatred and natural desire for revenge felt by the ordinary Russian soldier.

Instead of negative loathing, however, they talked only about their own positive cause; they instilled a spirit of comradeship and purpose among the men who took Berlin. The best political officers talked to soldiers face to face and gave them faith in their cause and in the inevitability of final victory over Fascism. Coming from men and women who were also good soldiers, the arguments were very convincing.

General Vasili Chuikov, who was in charge of the attempt to force an entry into the Tiergarten, stopped the attack for a full twenty-four hours, to allow time for his political staff, in whom he had great confidence, to get among his soldiers:

'Where is the guarantee that when the signal "attack" is given the regiments and battalions will rise as one to make the final storm?

'There was, is, and will be such a guarantee. The officers, the Communists, the Young Communists, and their personal example, and every man's full consciousness of his responsibility towards his comrades, his conscience and his country – there is the constant and inexhaustible source of the army's fighting morale.'

Political discussion also made ordinary soldiers think of life beyond the regimentation of an army at war. They saw German children innocently caught up in the horrors, and they fed the starving even if they themselves went hungry. Indeed, Chuikov had to issue a special order to his officers to ensure that their men were keeping enough back for themselves.

Chuikov himself was guilty of a bad misjudgement about some older children, twelve- to fifteen-year-old Hitler Youth, when on 26 April they openly marched towards Red Army positions in the Kolonnenstrasse. How could he order a massacre of the innocents? Would such an order even be obeyed?

'Refrain from firing: find some way of disarming them,' ordered Chuikov over the radio-telephone.

The children charged, with their hand-held anti-tank weapons, 'blowing men and horses to ribbons'. Tearfully, Chuikov ordered that the children be slaughtered. The order was carried out without hesitation.

By 29 April, after the rest-period for political activity and for softening-up by artillery, the time had come to cross the hump-backed Potsdam Bridge, to enter the Tiergarten. There was still substantial German resistance there, and it needed to be stamped out.

It was the hour before zero hour when Sergeant of the Guards Nikolai Masalov heard a child's voice on the far side of the canal near the Potsdam Bridge, the main chosen point of entry into the Tiergarten: '*Mutti, Mutti . . .*' 'Mummy, Mummy . . .'.

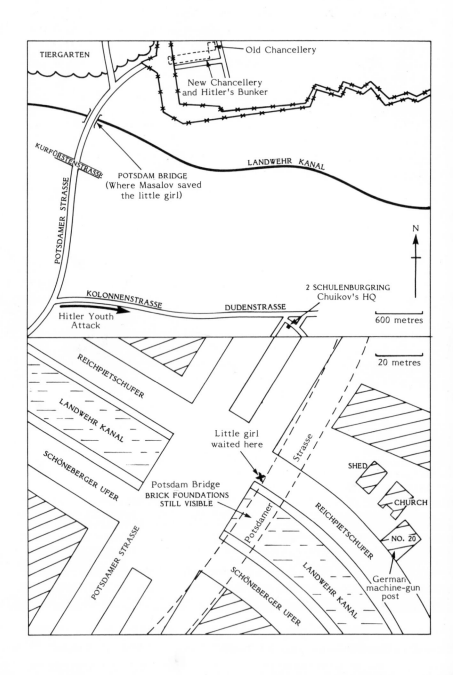

Chuikov was preparing to attack across the bridge when he saw Masalov – who was also the standard-bearer – crawling forward alone over the bridge. Masalov, who had fought his way ruthlessly from Stalingrad to Berlin, had been unable to stand the child's cries any longer.

'It was calling its mother, pitifully, persistently, seeming to ask Masalov to hurry. The Guardsman stood right up. A tall, strong Soviet soldier, proud wearer of several orders – neither bullets nor flying splinters could stop him.

'Machine-guns were chattering. This was our gunners opening counter-fire, without waiting for anyone to tell them to do so. Masalov leapt the parapet of the canal. . . .

'Five minutes past; ten minutes. The machine-guns fell silent. The child too was quiet now. Had Masalov risked so much in vain?

'Several Guardsmen, in silent accord, began to get ready to make a rush for the ground under the bridge.

'Then all heard the Sergeant's voice, calling, "I've got the child. There's a machine-gun on the right, on the balcony of the building with pillars. Shut it up."

'Just at that moment the Commander of Artillery, General Pozharski, gave the order "Ready. . . . Fire."

'Thousands of guns and mortars opened up in the preliminary bombardment, and their bursting salvoes covered Masalov's retreat from the mouth of death, a small German girl of three years in his arms.'

Back to war.

The Guards' first attempts to force their way across the Potsdam Bridge failed. German outflanking fire from left and right was too intense. It came from places the artillery could not reach without exposing itself dangerously. Mortars had some success, but German machine-gun fire took a fearful toll of any unit which tried to cross the canal. A Panzerfaust – long-range fire from tanks dug in to the ground – would put out any Red Army tank which dared cross the bridge ahead of the infantry.

'One might have thought that this would be the end of our efforts to get tanks through to the Tiergarten. But no, the infantry came up with the answer. They proposed that a storm-group tank (designed to carry a raiding party), with its protective covering of sandbags, should be doused with crude oil and solar oil, have smoke canisters lashed to its sides and be sent off as if on fire.

'The experiment worked. The leading tank "burst into flames" as it approached the bridge. For a moment, the SS men did not know what to make of this – a burning tank continuing to move and to fire its guns. The crews of our other tanks took advantage of this hesitation. The tanks got over the bridge and into the courtyard of the corner building, and once there worked together with the storm-group with tommy-guns to clear the block of the enemy.'

By land, by water, by underground tunnel, the German strongholds in the Tiergarten fell one by one. It was to be several days' painful work. It was still unfinished when Berlin surrendered.

Source
V. Chuikov, *The End of the Third Reich*

Iron Crosses: 28 April

Hilde Lemke, captain in the anti-aircraft command, was on her way to the front at Schmargendorf Station. She passed a group of SS stoking a huge bonfire.

'What's this? I smell food burning.'

'Fräulein Captain, your nose is working fine. This is food. We're burning it so that the Russians won't get it. It's a big job – there was a four-year supply for the battalion in that building.'

Within a few days, in the same street, a horse collapsed. People were so hungry that they swarmed over it before it was dead and, while the animal screamed horrifically as chunks were cut from it, they squabbled, using their pieces of meat as weapons.

It was war to the end.

The Soviet Third Guards Tank Army was in Grünewald, and the next serious line of defence was along the railway cutting from Schmargendorf Station to Hallensee Bridge. Hilde Lemke was at the headquarters of the Reich Labour Service out west of the canal and at risk of imminent attack. She had originally commanded a company of girls on anti-aircraft duty. When this was deemed too dangerous for women, she was sent out to help where she could.

The boys of the Hitler Youth were fighting bravely along the whole front, and Lemke was asked to go to the Chancellery to get some Iron Crosses to encourage the brave.

On her way up the Charlottenburger Chaussee, she noticed other forms of encouragement to the less brave – the SS warning exactly what would happen to any soldiers who deserted, Nazis to the last: 'Dirty Cowards And Defeatists – We've Got Them All On Our Lists.'

When she reached the Chancellery, she saw SS General Fegelein being pushed into the building to be shot for treason. There were

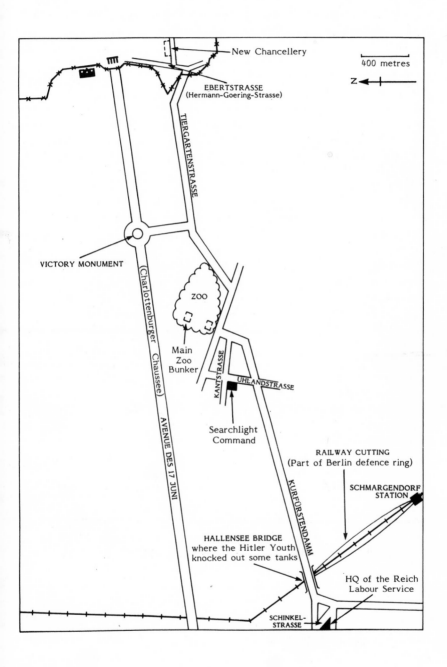

New Chancellery

400 metres

EBERTSTRASSE
(Hermann-Goering-Strasse)

TIERGARTENSTRASSE

VICTORY MONUMENT

(Charlottenburger Chaussee)

ZOO

Main
Zoo
Bunker

KANTSTRASSE

UHLANDSTRASSE

Searchlight
Command

AVENUE DES 17 JUNI

RAILWAY CUTTING
(Part of Berlin defence ring)

SCHMARGENDORF
STATION

KURFÜRSTENDAMM

HALLENSEE BRIDGE
where the Hitler Youth
knocked out some tanks

HQ of the Reich
Labour Service

SCHINKEL-
STRASSE

Russian shells plastering the street outside, and they were still shooting each other.

Lemke had a glass of champagne with the major, who gave her 130 Iron Crosses for dishing out to the Hitler Youth. The Chancellery was the last piece of luxury in Berlin. The major, who was impeccably dressed, told her a ridiculous story about the impending relief of Berlin that was apparently believed in the Chancellery. Lemke, who was wearing only the tattered and dusty remains of her uniform, listened to a story of this Army Command in the north and that Army Command in the south. When the major had finished, she left, disillusioned, for the Searchlight Command on the corner of Uhlandstrasse and Kantstrasse, where she exchanged something to eat from old friends for some Iron Crosses.

When she got back to the scene of the fighting, she found that the fiercest part of the front line had shifted from Schmargendorf Station to the Hallensee Bridge. Here the battle for Berlin was in full swing. The Hitler Youth had already knocked out five T-34 tanks, and Lemke was asked to observe for one of the last German tanks which had drawn up on the eastern side of the bridge. The tank was hidden behind a broken stone wall, and she directed its fire so skilfully that it knocked out three T-34s and causes havoc among the attacking infantry. For the moment, the Red Army was effectively blocked at one of the main access points to the western part of central Berlin. Lemke knew it could not last long, but the scene exhilarated her for the time being.

She admitted afterwards that she found herself exhilarated by the violence itself, the thunder-and-lightning end of the Reich, as much as by the bravery of the youngsters whose Iron Crosses she carried. The adrenalin was still flowing when she was insulted with, 'This is no place for a woman,' from a Wehrmacht major.

Lemke hastily distributed the Iron Crosses and then went back in one of the last trucks in German hands to the Zoo Bunker, the mammoth concrete complex which now housed 29,000 people (instead of its official capacity of 15,000) in the greatest imaginable squalor. But it was safe from the shells and machine-gun fire which, by this evening of 28 April, could be encountered everywhere in the centre of Berlin.

Lemke slept, exhausted, in one of the very few places in Berlin which still had electric power, a water supply and a partially equipped hospital.

Source
A. Tully, *Berlin: Story of a Battle, April–May 1945*

Attacking the Reichstag: 30 April

'Captain Guselnikov had been severely wounded, and Senior Sergeant Syanov, the Party organiser of the company, had been appointed in his place. The men with minor wounds remained on duty. Senior Lieutenant Kuzma Gusev's orderly, the lively little Vasili, was dead.'

Syanov was sad about his friend Vasili. Why should he die? From Stalingrad to Berlin, he had stayed cheerful and determined. Now, in front of 'Himmler's House', the Nazi Interior Ministry situated between the Spree and the Reichstag, he was dead. In a few hours he would have seen the end of the war.

Syanov was normally calm, friendly and open. Now he pondered the life and death of Vasili. The few hours that were left of the war would be the time when Vasili's death would be avenged.

Syanov had been involved in the crossing of the Spree in the night. The Germans had mined the Moltke Bridge leading to the centre of Berlin from the suburb of Moabit, but they had insufficient explosive to do a proper job. They had only damaged it. The Red Army poured across, among them new recruits from the prisoners in Moabit gaol, each hastily given a meal and the brown uniform of a Red Army infantryman. Prisoners and slave-labourers were keen to destroy the last remains of their oppressors' city.

Syanov had also been involved in the taking of 'Himmler's House', fighting for each room and corridor. The SS had defended it every inch of the way. Vasili had been killed, and so had hundreds of others – for one building – and now, ahead of him and his comrades, stood the domed and pillared Reichstag.

'Alright, Sergeant, go back to your company and when you get the signal go into attack. Don't wait for anything or anybody – but draw the 2nd and 3rd Companies along with you as you advance. You're first for the Reichstag.'

'Right, comrade Captain,' Syanov replied to Neustroyev.

'You're to have a great honour, Sergeant Syanov,' joined in Captain Prelov, the regimental political officer.

'Let's hope I live to enjoy it, comrade Captain. But I'll do my best,' Syanov grinned. 'I'm a Party member you know.'

The Reichstag came alive as Red Army troops started to emerge into Königsplatz, the big square in front of it. Königsplatz had been one of Berlin's finest open spaces. Between there and the Spree were the expansive buildings of ministries and embassies, now all ruins. On the east side, the Reichstag, now shattered by artillery, was a nest for machine-guns, anti-tank guns and anti-aircraft guns which were

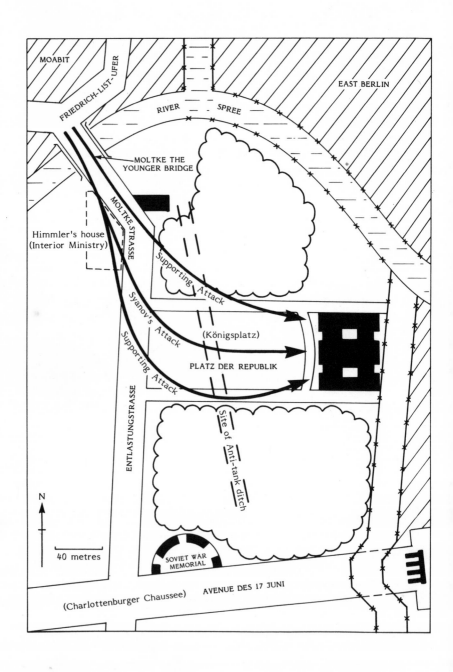

MOABIT

FRIEDRICH-LIST-UFER

EAST BERLIN

RIVER   SPREE

MOLTKE THE
YOUNGER BRIDGE

MOLTKE STRASSE

Himmler's house
(Interior Ministry)

Supporting Attack

Syanov's Attack

Supporting Attack

(Königsplatz)

PLATZ DER REPUBLIK

ENTLASTUNGSTRASSE

Site of Anti-tank ditch

N

40 metres

SOVIET WAR
MEMORIAL

(Charlottenburger Chaussee)   AVENUE DES 17 JUNI

re-directed down onto the infantry starting to advance across the square.

Syanov led his attack under the hail of all this fire from the Reichstag itself and under artillery fire from the Tiergarten to the south. He was supported by his own artillery, but it seemed to Syanov that not enough had been brought up in time. When he saw that there was a deep anti-tank ditch to cross, which stretched the width of the square, he wondered if the whole attack might have to be called off.

He watched amazed as his men hardly hesitated, plunged in and waded. Shells exploded all around them. Machine-guns played on the water and on the anti-tank defences either side. Syanov followed them across and then resumed the lead.

By now, more artillery had been dragged up to the second and third floors of the remains of 'Himmler's House' and was playing on the Reichstag defences. It was time for the final rush.

'Now it seemed as if hundreds of soldiers were on their feet, running towards the Reichstag. In the van, a red flag was unfurled and the banner fluttered in the concussion of hundreds of explosions . . . twice shell splinters sliced into Syanov's arms and chest, but he went on.'

They stormed up the broad steps and past the giant pillars to the blind zone where they were safe up against the wall. They were safe, but where could they go next? The entrances were not just bolted but bricked up.

'Stand back,' ordered Syanov.

The men cleared away from the immediate area, still clinging to the wall.

'Two mortars were depressed to aim point-blank at the bricked-up entrance and then fired simultaneously. There was a thudding crash and a shower of bricks and mortar and a four-foot hole suddenly appeared in the barricade.'

'Let's go.'

Syanov was first in the Reichstag. With his heart in his mouth, he jumped through the one-man-sized gap blown in the wall, half-expecting to be killed as he did so. He lived. The German defenders had been confused by the point-blank explosion and had withdrawn to the side-chambers and upstairs. More infantry soon poured in, gradually widening the rough entrance.

Everywhere in the pitch-dark, smoke-filled Reichstag was soon confused and deadly. Knives and bayonets and rifle-butts were the weapons of those pitched medieval-style battles in the two side-chambers on the ground floor and on the main staircase.

Then a grenade exploded, which blew to pieces Russians and

Germans quite indiscriminately. There was a moment's stunned silence. More Russians poured in and charged up the staircase. Wild firing. Screams. More explosions. Fire. Flames spread quickly over the plush furniture and wood panels and in some of the rooms actually stopped the fighting while men gasped for breath or desperately tried to stop their scorched uniforms burning.

Syanov reached the first floor. He saw a German with a Red Cross armband. He did not fire. The German pulled the pin from a grenade and dropped it into the lobby, killing a number of Russians. Syanov just stared in horror. The German escaped.

The fighting carried on. The Germans, inevitably and by sheer weight of numbers, were thrown out of the Reichstag, only hanging on for a few extra hours in the cellars.

Back on the roof of the Reichstag, there remained only one last act. Mikhail Yegorov and Meliton Kantaria clambered to the statue of Germania. By the left front hoof of her horse they found a gash in the metal suitable for a flagpole, probably caused by a shell exploding nearby. There they placed the Red banner over the Reichstag.

Source
S. A. Neustroyev, *Storming the Reichstag (Shturm Raikhstaga)*

Hitler Dispatches His Final Testament: 29 April to 1 May

'It is not true that I or anyone else in Germany wanted war back in 1939. It was desired and provoked solely by those international politicians who either come from Jewish stock or who are agents of Jewish interests. After all my many offers of disarmament, posterity simply cannot pin any blame for this war on me. . . .'

Hitler dictated his political testament during the day before his suicide. It was probably originally drafted by Goebbels. Apart from diatribes and nonsensical assertions, it dealt with the succession. Goering, who had tried to make a separate peace agreement and had said he was 'taking over' for the purpose, was dismissed from the Party, and Grand-Admiral Dönitz was made Reich President and Supreme Commander of the Armed Forces. Signed and witnessed by Bormann, the testament had no particular legal force, since a new leader of the Nazi Party really required an election, but as a document dictated and signed by Hitler himself it was deemed to have immense importance. It had to reach the new German leaders, and bearers had to be found to carry it.

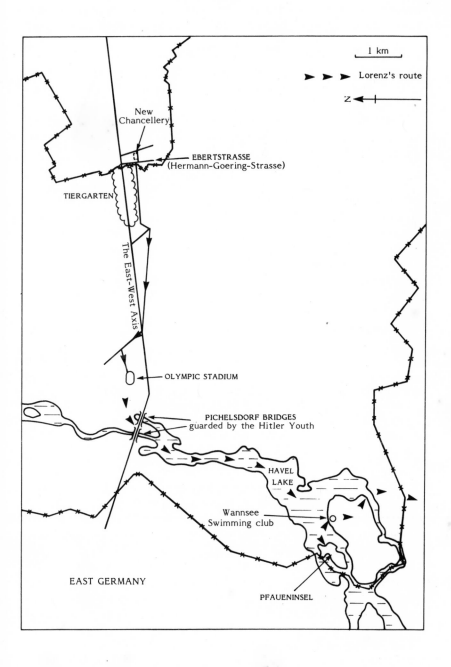

1 km

► ► ► Lorenz's route

N ◄———

New
Chancellery

EBERTSTRASSE
(Hermann-Goering-Strasse)

TIERGARTEN

The East-West Axis

OLYMPIC STADIUM

PICHELSDORF BRIDGES
guarded by the Hitler Youth

HAVEL
LAKE

Wannsee
Swimming club

EAST GERMANY

PFAUENINSEL

One of Goebbels' chosen men at his Ministry of Propaganda was Heinz Lorenz. He had stayed behind in Berlin to be with his boss and perhaps, as a journalist, to live and tell the story of the last days of the Reich. In the bunker he operated the radio set, the only contact with the outside world, so he knew what was happening. He knew the reality of the military situation in Berlin. He knew that the time was now if he were to get out at all.

The need to get Hitler's testament to Dönitz in Schleswig-Holstein was the opportunity needed. He smartly volunteered and found himself one of the chosen three bearers, along with an SS colonel, Wilhelm Zander, and Hitler's Army adjutant, Major Willi Johann-meier. They shook hands with the Führer and were off. Each clutched a copy of the testament, their passports out of the bunker.

They rushed out through the Chancellery garages into Hermann-Goering-Strasse and into the Tiergarten. Only then did they realize that they had come out not only with no papers but with no food or drink either. None of them had any intention of going back, whatever the reason, so they pressed on, sometimes within yards of Red Army positions, until they reached an isolated Hitler Youth battalion holding the bridges at Pichelsdorf.

It was now late afternoon on 29 April and they rested till dark. Lorenz slept right through till 10 p.m. through sheer nervous exhaustion, curled up in a corner of the Hitler Youth headquarters; compared with the various types of military all around him, he looked every inch a journalist in his crumpled suit.

When it was properly dark, they climbed into a small pleasure boat and rowed it down the Havel Lake to an outpost of German resistance, Pfaueninsel, a small island off Wannsee with a few luxury houses and a lot of paraphernalia for water sports, altogether better equipped for holidays than for war. This turned out to be fortunate for Lorenz and the others, as they jumped into canoes and paddled off shore to avoid a long bombardment. The three canoeists met together on an anchored yacht and radioed Dönitz to send a sea-plane to pick them up. The only response for a full day was more enemy shells and bombs.

While the three were on the yacht, Hitler and his new wife retreated to their room in the bunker. Together, they bit their cyanide capsules, and Hitler blew out his brains as well. His testament was presumed to be with his successor. It was not. It was still on Pfaueninsel, just outside Berlin.

On the evening of 30 April the sea-plane arrived. Lorenz was the first to spot it and canoed out to it; he tried to shout to the pilot that he had to go and get two others who were back on shore. But a few minutes later shells started falling around them, and a munitions ship exploded a little further down the lake, lighting the whole scene for enemy artillery. Lorenz, hardly a canoeist at the best of times, fell in the water. The others came to the rescue. The pilot took fright and flew off.

All three bearers, soaked, despondent and frightened, made their way back to the island and waited another day. If they stayed much longer, either capture or death was certain.

On the night of 1 May they rowed to the deserted Wannsee Swimming Club and headed west. They crossed the Elbe the day after Dönitz had surrendered. Lorenz was caught and reluctantly handed Hitler's testament over to the Allies. The others disappeared.

Source
H. Trevor-Roper, *The Last Days of Hitler*

Bluster and the Loss of the Reichstag: 28 April to 1 May

Fierce, fat and bald – and well behind the lines – the SS Obersturmführer talked about final victory. He cursed cowards and traitors. And he ruled his little cellar, a hundred metres behind the Reichstag, with an iron fist. He had detailed maps of the whole area, and he was in command. It had taken him until this stage in the war to be in command of a pitched battle, and he was relishing it.

Babick was incapable of military planning. He resorted to bluster about loyalty and victory. Luftwaffe NCO Gerhard Zilch of the Third Heavy Flak Battery had the misfortune to be with him on 29 April:

'He had divided his men into groups of five to ten. One group was again commanded by SS Untersturmführer Undermann . . : posted south of the Moltke Bridge in the Ministry of the Interior. . . . Then an SS ensign, aged about nineteen, came to Babick with a report that Undermann and his men had come across some alcohol and that they had got roaring drunk. As a precaution, he had brought Undermann along; he was waiting outside. Babick roared out the order: "Have him shot on the spot". The ensign clicked his heels and ran out. Seconds later we heard a burst of fire from a submachine-gun. The boy reappeared and reported: "Orders carried out". Babick put him in charge of Undermann's unit.' Undermann's unit was virtually all wiped out or taken prisoner by now anyway.

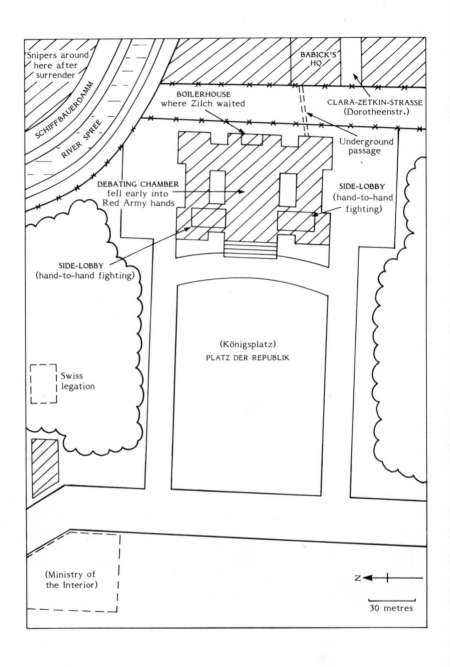

Snipers around here after surrender

SCHIFFBAUERDAMM

RIVER SPREE

BABICK'S HQ

BOILERHOUSE
where Zilch waited

CLARA-ZETKIN-STRASSE
(Dorotheenstr.)

Underground
passage

DEBATING CHAMBER
fell early into
Red Army hands

SIDE-LOBBY
(hand-to-hand
fighting)

SIDE-LOBBY
(hand-to-hand fighting)

(Königsplatz)
PLATZ DER REPUBLIK

Swiss
legation

(Ministry of
the Interior)

z

30 metres

By 30 April Luftwaffe NCO Gerhard Zilch of the Third Heavy Flak Battery found himself being reduced to a messenger between SS Obersturmführer Babick and his artillery commanders, who now had no guns and were holding out desperately with pistols and rifles in the lobbies surrounding the Reichstag Debating Chamber. Zilch was mad with impotence as Babick wasted young men's lives in battle plans belonging to a make-believe world of reinforcements that never came and victories that never happened. How could such an idiot be in charge of the last battle of the Reich?

Babick had under his command the gunners, some Hitler Youth, some SS and a few of the last reinforcements to be parachuted in from the West, a detachment of marines under a lieutenant-commander. When Zilch arrived at Babick's candle-lit cellar, via a network of underground tunnels from the Reichstag, the lieutenant-commander was slumped on a dirty sofa with nothing to do, unable to get a sensible decision out of the blustering Babick.

Zilch reported on the latest situation in the Reichstag. The first Red Army assault had been held up by flame-throwers, but in the end the numbers had been overwhelming. There had been some successful hand-to-hand fighting in the ground-floor lobbies and in some of the upstairs offices, but it was obvious that there would soon be hardly any resistance except in the cellars. The Red Army had the power to wipe everyone out. Babick had nothing to say.

Later Zilch reported that the Red Flag flew over the Reichstag and that such resistance as there was mainly continued down in the cellars. He then hurried back along underground passages to the Reichstag without receiving further orders. Babick bolted a few minutes later, since the situation in the Reichstag was obviously hopeless. His moment of glory was over.

The Red Army was less careless of lives than the SS Obersturm-führer and they decided to leave the last German resisters in the cellars and outhouses of the Reichstag until they inevitably gave themselves up in due course.

Zilch and a few comrades waited twenty-four hours in the washroom of the boilerhouse, where they changed into civilian suits before anything else happened.

On 2 May Berlin surrendered and the Russians felt it was safe at last to send a group of three armed emissaries looking for the Reichstag commandant. All they found were Zilch and his friends, who surrendered gladly. Their captors took their watches and herded them into the Reichstag Debating Chamber. It did not look good. Zilch thought he was going to be shot.

There was still sporadic shooting outside, and Zilch did not like the look of it when he and a group of other captives were taken to the

Reichstag steps and told to march – unaccompanied – to the Swiss Embassy building, across the open space of Königsplatz, for interrogation. 'The Russians pointed to the Swiss Embassy and said: "You, over there." The square was full of smashed German guns and dead German soldiers. Our Russian guards stayed behind. After a hundred yards we saw why: bullets started whistling round our ears. We covered the rest of the way on all fours. SS snipers in the ruined Schiffbauerdamm were shooting at anybody they saw moving. . . .'

The man who interrogated Zilch was a good deal more interested in the busty German prostitute sitting on his knee than in Zilch's ramblings. When it was over, to Zilch's great relief, the sniping had stopped. He was marched safely off to prison.

Source
E. Kuby, *The Russians and Berlin 1945*

Hitler – The End and After:
30 April to 9 May

Hitler had stated in 1938: 'Upon my death, my remains shall be transported to Munich. They shall be properly displayed on a catafalque before the Hall of the Field Marshals. After the state funeral, which is to be a solemn yet simple one, my body is to be removed to the Temple of National Socialism on the Königsplatz. There I shall rest – under the eternal flame.'

The practical and immediate reasons for Hitler's decision to commit suicide may seem obvious, but they are not enough properly to explain why he chose to take his own life. Even in the most extreme circumstances, suicide is unnatural and unusual. It defies the basic drive for survival which everyone has. Towards the end of 1945, Hitler's position as leader of Nazi Germany was untenable, but there were various ways in which he could reasonably have tried to escape death, even with the limited power which was still at his disposal.

Suicide gratified Hitler's aggressive personality. He wanted to punish those around him. 'Nothing is spared me, no allegiances are kept, no honour lived up to . . . no betrayals I have not experienced. . . . Nothing remains. Every wrong has already been done me.' Let Germans now suffer. Let his friends, most of them traitors, suffer. Let them be punished. This was Hitler's psychosis. This was the explanation.

Hitler and his new bride, Eva, sat on the blue and white sofa in

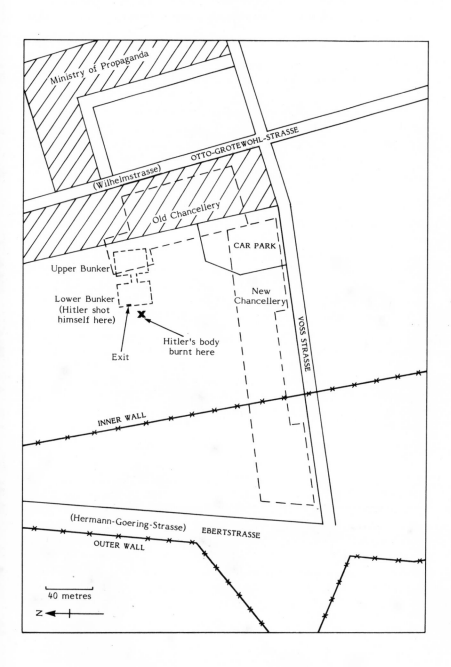

their private apartment in the bunker. It was 3.30 p.m. on 30 April. Hitler took a capsule of potassium cyanide in his hand. Simultaneously he put a pistol to his temple. He put the capsule in his mouth, bit it hard and blew some of his brains out at the same time. Eva Hitler bit her poison capsule as she heard the shot.

The bodies were carried out of the bunker about fifteen minutes later into the Chancellery Garden, where a trench had been prepared. They were put into the trench and soaked in over 400 litres of petrol. They burned well but not by any means to ashes – the bones and teeth were hardly affected at all. The burial party, including Martin Bormann and a handful of other bunker inmates, all stood to attention and gave Nazi salutes for the first few moments of the cremation, then they retreated to the bunker for cover from the constant Red Army shellfire and also to get away from the awful smell, 'like sweet burning bacon'. A few hours later the trench was filled in, making a shallow grave.

By the time the Red Army entered the bunker, on 2 May, the only person remaining was a machine-room operator. When pressed to do so, he managed to find Goebbels' grave but he did not know where Hitler was buried. The bodies of Hitler and his wife lay undisturbed until 4 May, when Private Ivan Churekov noticed some pieces of material, poked around and revealed the charred and now stinking remains. At that time, however, another body found in the Chancellery was thought to be Hitler's, so no one took much notice. It was on 9 May that a dental assistant identified Hitler's teeth as those from Churekov's find and not the Chancellery body. A post-mortem a few days later clearly showed a good deal of cyanide in the system and possibly (though this has never been confirmed) a missing left testicle, thus firmly identifying Churekov's find as the genuine one.

The post-mortem was carried out in a hospital at Buch near Berlin. Then the body was probably cremated properly and the ashes were thrown into the surrounding forest.

The Russians were absolutely determined not to create the possibility of a shrine. No one knows for sure where Hitler's remains were scattered and, of course, there is no grave and no memorial.

Source
J. P. O'Donnell, *The Berlin Bunker*

Joseph and Magda Goebbels – Infanticide and Death: January to May

Dr Goebbels and the rest were so very ordinary. One of the frightening things about the Nazi leadership was its striking ordinariness. Their strength was that they were really just like the people they led down the path to the gas chambers of Auschwitz and to the ruins of Berlin. They knew how the people thought. They could empathize and manipulate – none better than Joseph Goebbels.

As Nazi Propaganda Minister, Goebbels had broadcast on 24 June 1941, right at the start of Operation Barbarossa in which Hitler had attacked the Soviet Union: 'God's high court of history is now passing judgment on the Soviet state . . . the day of reckoning has come.' More astutely he commented in his diary, 'If we win, we shall then have right on our side.'

Now, in 1945, Goebbels was Gauleiter of Berlin. He was busy inspecting the city's defences against the final Soviet revenge on Nazi Germany. Then he would go to his office in the Ordenspalais in Wilhelmplatz and prepare atrocity propaganda against the Red Army – rape of nuns, detailed descriptions of appalling tortures, slavery in Siberia and so on; and to the black threatening cloud he always added the ray of hope, the vague but wonderful miracle that would save Nazi Germany in the final battle, a separate peace with the West.

Magda Goebbels and their five young children lived out of Berlin in the winter of 1944–5, away from the bombing raids, in a villa near Lanke (which had cost 3 million marks, 'a contribution from the German film industry'). By January, it was only forty kilometres from the Eastern Front and so, when at first the big offensive was expected in early March, the Goebbels family moved back to Berlin, to the Gauleiter Minister's official residence at 20 Hermann-Goering-Strasse. When it was badly bomb-damaged the very next night in an American raid, they all moved out to yet another official mansion, Schwanenwerder by Lake Havel.

There were several attempts to persuade Magda at least to allow her children to leave Berlin. From Schwanenwerder there were plans to float them down the Havel in a barge till they reached the Americans on the Elbe. Goebbels himself dithered about what to do with his children. Sometimes he wanted them to go and sometimes to stay.

Magda had no doubts. She worshipped the Führer. As SS Colonel Erich Kempka had observed, 'Whenever she was in the presence of the Führer, I could hear her ovaries rattling.' Life without him was

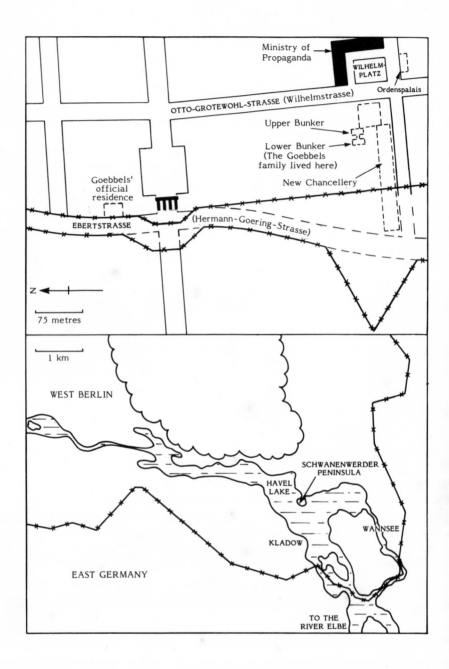

unimaginable. Life for her children without Hitler would be life without meaning. She was completely wound up in her husband's simple propaganda of gods, demons and heroes. When Goebbels shied away from murdering his children, she stiffened him. They would stay behind in Berlin and die with her Führer and her husband. She had firmly decided to kill them.

Like many psychopaths, Magda Goebbels retained her outward composure, the hostess and the mother. Now she graciously received a gift of out-of-season lilies-of-the-valley from Hitler, then she played rough-and-tumble with four-year-old Heidi.

Meanwhile, her husband had to stiffen the Führer's own resolve to die in Berlin. On 29 March Hitler had nearly been persuaded to move to Berchtesgarten and was always under pressure to get out of the Berlin trap. Goebbels made it his business always to be around to make sure that Hitler stayed. Goebbels had written so much of the story that he himself now believed the Hitler myth. He was determined to write the last chapter too. His obsession in planning the defence of Berlin, his eventual move into the bunker, his drafting of Hitler's testament and the planning of his own suicide – all were aimed to give the appearance of a *Götterdämmerung*, a death to shake the world. It had to be in Berlin, the imperial capital. It had to be a great drama. Then, he averred, it would be the greatest thing since Calvary.

. Hitler invited Goebbels to move his whole family into the bunker on 22 April. This was as planned, and they accepted. Goebbels himself made sure that all his personal mementoes – old photographs and school reports – as well as incriminating Propaganda Ministry files which could spoil the myth, were burned. He gave his last radio broadcast saying that Hitler would die fighting in Berlin, and virtually closed his Ministry, which had been active right up until the past few days. In his last talk with his top officials, he complained about the German people who had not deserved the noble ideals of Nazism – 'What can you do with a people whose men are no longer ready to fight when their wives are being raped?' Finally he sent his mother and sister on the refugee trail west. Hitler's suicide and testament went more or less as Goebbels had scripted. Goebbels himself became Chancellor and even made a crude attempt to parley with the Russians through Chief of Staff Krebs, but he would not agree to unconditional surrender. It was his last act of government.

Magda Goebbels in the bunker was more popular with the men than with other women; everyone agreed she was very maternal, and she had a reassuring high-cheekboned smile which put guests and children at ease. She retained the calm poise that goes with money and power.

She now murdered all her children. 'My darlings are simply too good for this bad world.'

She drugged some chocolate and told her children that an aeroplane was coming to lift them away in the night. They had to take the chocolate to prevent travel sickness. Only the oldest child, twelve-year-old Helga, did not believe her and did not finish the chocolate. About an hour later, she woke when Magda went back into the room and struggled while her mother forced cyanide into her mouth. The other five children never woke.

The childless couple now made their way up to the New Chancellery courtyard, past the jerricans of petrol brought up for their cremation, and bit on their own cyanide capsules.

Magda had become a mass murderess. Joseph could not stand the sight of blood but was surely responsible for many more deaths than she had been. 'He was clever, charming, cultivated. . . . He was self-satisfied and snobbish, and at the same time immature and unprincipled, labile. He was vain, ambitious and harried with complexes. . . . One shouldn't be fooled by his dreadful end. A bad joke can't be made into a tragedy by the mere fact that a vast amount of blood is shed in it.'

Sources
L. P. Lochner (ed.), *The Goebbels Diaries*
H. O. Meissner, *Magda Goebbels: A biography*

The End of the French SS Volunteers: 30 April to 2 May

Grenadier Pierre Soulier noticed how quickly and eloquently the Ukrainian Red Army prisoner spoke. The treatment of prisoners who failed to speak in the hands of the SS was well known. The Ukrainian was very puzzled though; he was sure these were not Germans. Yet they wore SS insignia and were fighting to the last in Berlin in 1945.

They were members of the French SS Volunteer Division 'Charlemagne', now only ninety strong and incorporated into the Nordland Division (11th Volunteer SS Panzer Grenadiers) which contained 1,500 or so other volunteers from all over Europe. The new commanding officer of the Nordland Division, appointed for the defence of Berlin, was SS Brigadeführer Dr Gustav Krukenberg, and the Division's biggest success in the current battle was in knocking out some sixty-four Red Army tanks and causing the Red Army to think again about some of its tactics in taking the city centre of Berlin.

Pierre Soulier, eighteen years old, had already knocked out four tanks with his hand-held Panzerfaust. The Ukrainian prisoner said that Soviet tank commanders quaked at the thought of advancing any further. He flattered his captors. Ninety French fanatics caused upsetting pinpricks but they were no real threat. One of Soulier's comrades, Eugène Vaulot, won one of the last Knight's Crosses of the war for destroying tanks in Neukölln. But there were so many more. At the gates of Berlin stood an army of at least a million. The 'division' of 1,500 French, Danes, Croats, Slovaks, Norwegians, Spaniards and a few others was pitted against not just the Red Army but other East European Communist forces, including nearly 200,000 Poles.

It was 1 May. Hitler was dead. Krukenberg had no idea what was now expected of him and his men, who clung on to a more and more precarious part of the centre of Berlin. The morning brought no new orders, so he set out for the Bendlerstrasse Army Headquarters where General Weidling, Commandant of Berlin, was staying. Even covering that short distance was now dangerous. Before Krukenberg could go, Soulier and a small élite troop checked out the sewers and underground tunnels which he was obliged to use. Then the Brigadeführer went to the meeting.

He never found Weidling, but he did learn that peace negotiations had failed. Another attempt might be made later in the day; meanwhile he decided that all he would do was defend his position as effectively as possible.

Holed up in a few cellars and running out of ammunition, there was not much the remains of the Nordland Division could do. One Soviet tank came too close to Krukenberg's command post at Stadtmitte Station and was put out of action; its crew scuttled away into the ruins.

The ninety Charlemagne men also took over the defence of an SS administrative building two hundred metres away, at 8 Prinz-Albrecht-Strasse, just next to the headquarters of the Gestapo. This was practically on the front line by the afternoon of 1 May, as the Frenchmen found out to their cost when two or three Red Army sappers crept across the crumbling roofs of Prinz-Albrecht-Strasse, keeping in touch with another small group who were making their way through the sewers. Simultaneously both groups let off incendiary devices and withdrew. Within minutes the whole area was in flames. Everything was tinder-dry. Red and orange tongues of flames seared through the floorboards of the occupied buildings below and burned away the ceilings above.

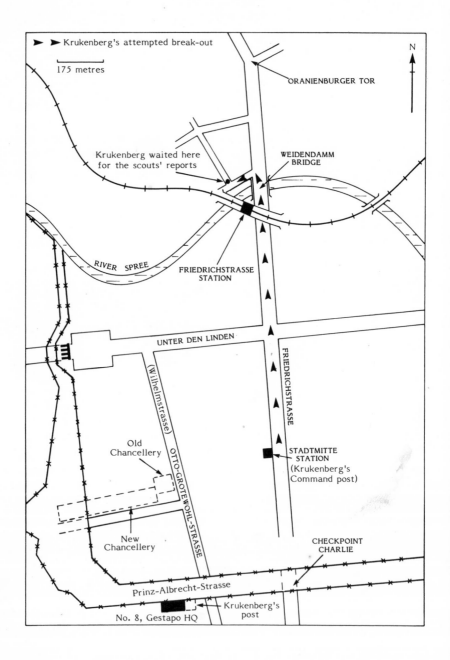

The Nordlanders poured out into the street and received a hail of shellfire. Soulier helped a former Paris fireman, a fellow Grenadier, fight the flames. There was never a chance. Nearly all the Nordland equipment and supplies were gone in half an hour. There were no human casualties in the fire but the shelling took its toll. Soulier and the fireman were last out of one of the office blocks, followed by thick black billowing smoke. Then small explosions rocked the buildings as boilers and ammunition blew up.

In the ruins of 8 Prinz-Albrecht-Strasse, at 9.30 on the night of 1 May, Krukenberg issued his last order to the French. They should join the rest of Nordland and meet at Friedrichstrasse Station at midnight, strike north-west and try to escape from Berlin.

Krukenberg, along with Soulier and a few others who were to form an advance guard, moved back to Stadtmitte underground station at once to avoid being cut off by the steady building-by-building Red Army advance. At 11 p.m. the advance guard made their way to the Weidendamm Bridge, turned left along the bank of the Spree and then turned up a side street to receive reports from scouts who were looking at what lay ahead in the suburbs.

The 1,500 Nordland men now gathered at Friedrichstrasse Station and started to attract Russian attention. They decided to move at 11.30, before Krukenberg had had a chance to report back.

The main column advanced slowly. All the men were worn out, and they were dangerously exposed. There were just four vehicles, including the last Tiger II tank in service in Berlin. It led the way and broke through the barrier on the north side of the bridge. Red Army artillery and tanks opened fire from north, east and west at the Oranienburg Gate. Every street the column scattered down seemed to have a Russian tank at the end firing back. The French had almost nothing with which to return fire.

The whole break-out was soon an obvious fiasco. There was nowhere to turn. Ninety per cent were lost that night. Krukenberg himself slipped into a workshop and found some carpenters' overalls for disguise. He was still taken prisoner the next afternoon. Soulier had no future in France. How could a volunteer in the SS go home? He stood right in the way of a tank whose machine-gun was mowing down his comrades as they tried to scramble out of the way over the ruins, and purposefully raised his Panzerfaust. He knocked out his fifth tank just as it crushed him.

Sources
C. Georgen, *Berlin 1945: Sur les traces de la division 'Charlemagne'*
D. Littlejohn, *Foreign Legions of the Third Reich*

Bormann's Escape and Suicide: 1–2 May

Hitler's pilot, Hans Baur, had planned an escape to Japan, to Greenland, to Manchuria, in fact to anywhere in the world Hitler wanted to go. He need only get to Rechlin Air Base, which was still open and accessible by tank from Berlin. Hitler had refused.

Hitler said: 'Dönitz will be my natural successor. I have given Bormann several messages for Dönitz. See to it that you get Bormann out of Berlin and to Dönitz by means of your planes at Rechlin.'

Baur was fiercely loyal to Hitler and, although he did not care at all for Hitler's former secretary, Martin Bormann, he did his best to carry out instructions. Of the less reliable Bormann it was said, 'He could cut a throat with a thin whisper.'

At 11.40 p.m. on 1 May, Baur, Bormann and a small group of other top Nazis slipped out of Hitler's bunker, through the Chancellery and out by a shellhole in the wall. Although there were a few Red Army snipers, they were probably not observed, and they made it to the relative safety of the Wilhelmstrasse underground station.

Most of the Red Army meanwhile was concluding its celebrations of its most victorious May Day ever. Groups of infantry and tank crew roasted an ox by the Brandenburg Gate, drinking the remains of a nearby hotel's cellar. Others sang and danced where they stopped for the night before finally drawing the Battle of Berlin to a close.

Probably some message about a group leaving the Chancellery Bunker reached the artillery, as there was some half-hearted shelling of the streets around. Nothing came of it.

Once in the tunnels, they were safe – but it was eerie. A few of them had pocket torches but they soon lost their way and decided to struggle to the surface at Stadtmitte Station. They moved east to avoid having to go straight up the main Friedrichstrasse but the cold night was hot from burning buildings – a theatre and the cathedral were on fire.

Baur, Bormann and the others made their way gingerly up Friedrichstrasse, drawing no fire. It was only when they had crossed the dangerous Unter den Linden and almost reached the Weidendamm Bridge that battle broke out and they were nearly caught in the middle of it. The remains of the SS Nordland Division, all foreign volunteers, were making a final attempt to break out by forcing their way north in half a dozen tanks. The Nordland tanks blasted the anti-tank defences north of the Weidendamm Bridge, tried to move further north, and battle ensued. Shells exploded all around the

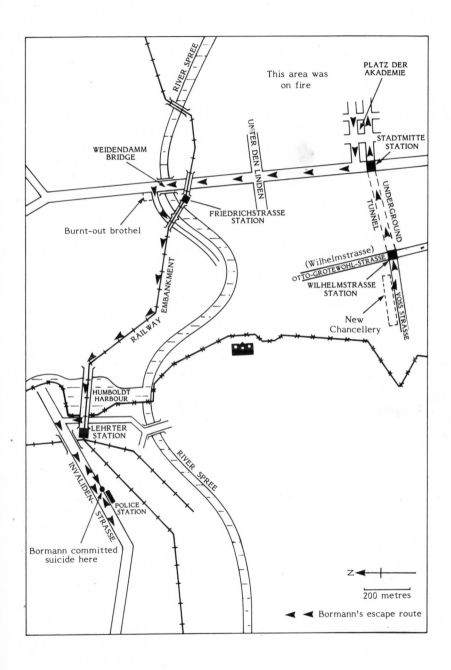

escape route. Baur and Bormann lost sight of each other as they were hurled to the ground and nearly blinded by blast upon blast.

After twenty minutes, Baur caught sight of Bormann again. He was sitting alone, dazed, at the entrance to a cellar of a bombed-out brothel on the corner of Friedrichstrasse and Schiffbauerdamm. A dead Russian was sprawled in front of him.

The brothel-keeper and her daughter took in Baur and Bormann, until the brief battle was over and the remains of the SS Nordland Division retreated back down Friedrichstrasse. There followed hasty discussions about the best route to follow now, with the Red Army newly alert and suspicious. They talked about how much they needed a *Kellerkind*, a local urchin, to guide them through the sewers and railway tunnels, but there was no hope of finding one now. All the *Kellerkinder* had picked their way through or under the ruins to safer places than this. The Saxon Bormann and the Bavarian Baur decided to take the only way they knew for sure, the railway embankment to Lehrter Station. They met up with three other survivors of the break-out and inched along the side of the railway line for about 1.5 kilometres, passing only a few hundred metres from the embattled Reichstag. By now it was about 3 a.m.

They jumped down from the bridge at Lehrter Station only to be immediately surrounded by a Red Army platoon. One of their companions, Artur Axmann, recalled that, '. . . to our amazement and joy they simply kept announcing in a boisterous chorus, "*Hitler kaputt, Krieg aus.*" Then they engaged us in a very pleasant chat in broken German. . . . They graciously offered us *papirosi*, cigarettes with paper mouthpieces. Apparently they thought we were simple Home Guard returning from a long, hard evening at the front.'

Martin Bormann and another break-out companion, Dr Stumpfegger, slipped away from the merry-making. They ran up In-validenstrasse. They encountered more Red Army tanks and retreated as far as the railway bridge half way back to the station. They looked both ways along the railway line for an escape route and saw only the Red Army. They knew that in the end their true identities as aides to Hitler would be discovered. There was no hope of escape.

They took cyanide.

Source
J. P. O'Donnell, *The Berlin Bunker*

The Surrender of Berlin: 1 and 2 May

The nerve-centre of German resistance in Berlin after the death of Hitler and his entourage was Army Headquarters in Bendlerstrasse. The acres of office buildings still stood there damaged but by no means in ruins.

Inside the shelter in the old courtyard was General of Artillery Karl Weidling with his staff. Weidling could not claim to control all German fighting in Berlin but, considering that the Red Army was now in the Reichstag, Unter den Linden and much of the Tiergarten, there was a surprising amount of Army discipline. Weidling's writ ran in most areas of resistance, and on May Day he sat receiving reports from the fighting still going on in the city. At 8.30 p.m. on May Day evening, he decided to call a conference of sector commanders to discuss surrender.

About a dozen sector commanders made their way from the remains of German-held Berlin to Bendlerstrasse that night. They stood around Weidling's room looking just as they felt – soldiers in a lost battle, exhausted, covered in mud and dust from hazardous journeys across the city to reach the conference.

Weidling wasted no time: '. . . his face grave and obviously strained, his eyeglass tightly screwed in, Berlin's last Nazi Commandant took up his position behind the desk and in brisk and firm tones announced his decision to surrender with a heavy heart.'

A radio message was sent to the Soviet 79th Guards Division operating to the west of the Potsdam Bridge, only a couple of hundred metres from the Bendlerstrasse conference room. The radio operator of Weidling's 56th German Panzer Corps knew Russian and had the Red Army frequency ready for the message:

'Hello, hello. This is the 56th German Panzer Corps. We ask you to cease fire at 05.00 hours, Berlin time. We are sending envoys to parley with you, to the Potsdam Bridge. Mark for purposes of recognition – a white flag. We await your reply.'

The reply came at last after the message had been broadcast five times: 'Your message received. Message received. Your request passed to our superior officers.'

The message went straight to General Chuikov. It was the one he had been waiting for. An earlier fruitless discussion with a member of Hitler's immediate staff and another with a supposed appointee of Goering could not have delivered the goods. It was the Army General's message he wanted.

At 5 a.m., as agreed, members of Weidling's and Chuikov's staff met on the bridge and discussed the details of a surrender meeting

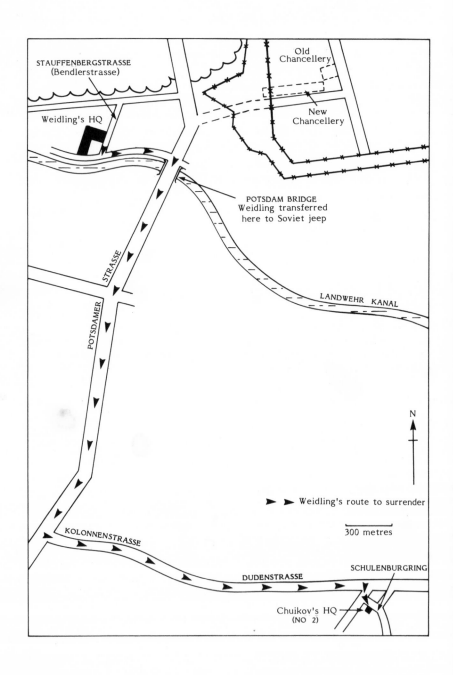

STAUFFENBERGSTRASSE
(Bendlerstrasse)

Weidling's HQ

Old
Chancellery

New
Chancellery

POTSDAM BRIDGE
Weidling transferred
here to Soviet jeep

POTSDAMER STRASSE

LANDWEHR KANAL

N

Weidling's route to surrender

300 metres

KOLONNENSTRASSE

SCHULENBURGRING

DUDENSTRASSE

Chuikov's HQ
(NO 2)

between the generals. The courtesies were agreed. Weidling and his senior officers would be allowed to keep their side-arms and would be treated honourably. It was understood that they were not trying to negotiate, simply to arrange unconditional surrender in the most organized way possible.

Half an hour later Weidling, his adjutant and four other officers walked to the Potsdam Bridge. A Red Army jeep was waiting on the far side to take them to Chuikov's temporary headquarters, 2 Schulenburgring, and straight to Chuikov himself, who stood at his desk and asked as Weidling entered the room:

'Are you the Commandant of the Berlin Garrison?'

Weidling nodded gravely when the question was repeated in German: 'Yes, I am Commander of the 56th Panzer Corps.'

The conversation, through interpreters, was carried on with both generals seated. Weidling explained the extent of his authority and assured Chuikov that no buildings or bridges were mined. He recited what he knew about Hitler's suicide and the end of the Goebbels family.

'So the war is over.'

'In my opinion any further sacrifices would be an act of folly and a crime.'

Weidling, commenting that this was the second war he had lost, sat down at Chuikov's desk and wrote out the following order:

On 30th April 1945, the Führer, to whom we had all sworn allegiance, forsook us by committing suicide. Faithful to the Führer, you, soldiers of Germany, were prepared to continue the Battle for Berlin, although your ammunition was running out and the general situation made further resistance senseless. I now order all resistance to cease forthwith.

Weidling,
Artillery General,
Commandant, Berlin Defence Region.

Various Soviet officers started suggesting changes but Chuikov stopped them – 'It's his order.' Then it was typed and Chuikov made arrangements for it to be distributed to Weidling's staff waiting back at Bendlerstrasse.

An hour later Weidling recorded the surrender order, and Red Army vehicles broadcast it all over Berlin. It was successful. Virtually all fighting stopped at once.

They fetched Weidling's coat from the Chancellery and gave him a glass of Russian tea. 'It's hard for him,' someone said. Weidling was in tears.

On 2 May Berlin became free from the Nazis.

Source
E. Kuby, *The Russians and Berlin 1945*

Break-out and Capture: 2–3 May

It was obvious by 2 May that the few hundred troops holed up in Ruhleben Barracks in the north-west corner of Berlin could contribute nothing towards saving the city. They had been told about the horrors of what would follow conquest by the Red Army. Death would be a better option. Soviet soldiers were portrayed as devils whose greatest pleasure was to rape, destroy and cause pain. This was a powerful message for young soldiers like Helmuth Altner, aged seventeen, who had been in the Wehrmacht for only a month; he had been brought up to believe that Nazi propaganda was all true, word for word, down to the last hyperbole. He was not a bit surprised to see the sergeant-major prepare his family for a hazardous walk to the Elbe and the Americans, rather than risk surrender to the Red Army.

One Nazi lie which most of the soldiers in Ruhleben believed was that General Wenck's Twelfth Army was on the point of relieving Berlin. It was said to have reached the Döberitz training grounds. If only the Ruhleben troops could break out through Spandau, they could link up with Wenck.

Soldiers and civilians set out together for Spandau. They had not realized just how dangerous it would be. They took the Red Army by surprise and managed to force their way through, but the cost was appalling.

Altner was well behind the spearhead of the break-out. He and his friends had to climb over the bodies of the leading assault groups, the bodies of soldiers and civilians alike. He had never witnessed, on the Oder Front or in the centre of Berlin – he had served in both places in the last few weeks, a more dreadful scene than the one he witnessed on the Charlotte Bridge over the River Havel, which led into Spandau town.

'Altner could see more and more people streaming on to the bridge behind him regardless of the bullets reaching out to get them. Women with babies in their arms holding other children by the hand, Hitlerjugend, girls, old men and women, many collapsing to the ground and dragging others down with them while tanks continued to roll over the centre of the bridge ignoring all who got in their way and grinding them to a bloody pulp. The Havel below was red with blood as it bore away the bits and pieces of the bodies that fell into it from this press.'

Altner made it through Spandau and (he never quite knew how) to Gartenstadt Staaken. Almost every house seemed to be occupied and defended by the Red Army.

A group of soldiers and civilians decided on a 'death drive'. They clambered onto a lorry till it could bear no more – Altner himself was on the front left wing with his fingers curled into the engine ventilation slots. The lorry accelerated. The firing started. A civilian girl, probably about the same age as Altner, hanging on to the opposite set of ventilation slots, was shot and fell off the speeding lorry into the road and screamed.

They roared on, street after murderous street. Altner was in the small minority who survived that journey through Gartenstadt Staaken.

The Döberitz training area was just beyond. It was deserted. The propaganda and the lies were exposed. True there were no Russians, but equally there was no sign at all that a German army, Wenck's or anybody else's, had been there in recent days. There was nothing for it but to keep trudging west in the hope of meeting either some German armed forces or else, as now seemed slightly more probable, the Americans or British.

Altner joined untidy knots of refugees forcing themselves onwards. They were shelled occasionally, and during one of these attacks Altner was injured in the foot. A sizeable metal fragment bolted the sole of his boot to the ball of his foot. He limped painfully but carried on walking. What else was there to do? The injury was not serious, only painful, and the sharp agony gradually reduced to a dull, continuous ache as the dust and clotted blood formed a more or less solid glob.

Groups of refugees who had followed slightly different break-out routes sometimes bumped into each other. One of these groups had an ambulance with them which, almost unbelievably to Altner, was filled with belongings and not with people. He and some others held down the driver while the goods were chucked out and people got inside. But there was no room for Altner, and he was left behind as night fell.

He decided to follow the tracks of tanks which had led the break-out in the first place. If anything had got through, they must have. He passed villages which had indeed been taken back from the

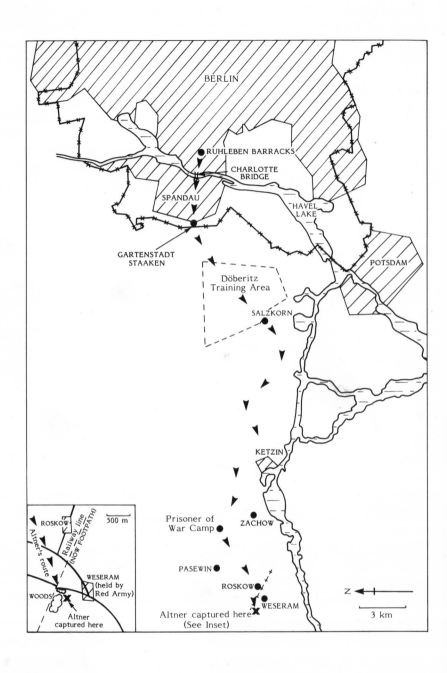

BERLIN

RUHLEBEN BARRACKS

CHARLOTTE
BRIDGE

SPANDAU

HAVEL
LAKE

POTSDAM

GARTENSTADT
STAAKEN

Döberitz
Training Area

SALZKORN

KETZIN

Prisoner of
War Camp

ZACHOW

ROSKOW

500 m

Railway line
(NOW FOOTPATH)

Altner's route

PASEWIN

WESERAM
(held by
Red Army)

ROSKOW

WOODS

WESERAM

Altner
captured here

Altner captured here
(See Inset)

N

3 km

Russians. Some were delighted – he was treated like a hero in the signalman's house at Salzkorn, but not all were glad to see Germans in uniform again. The village of Ketzin, for example, had avoided the war till now, and its people were clearly unhappy to find their houses on fire and themselves in the front line. Some of the local Home Guard had been taken prisoner and locked in a barn by the Russians; Altner and others went to free them; the prisoners told them to go away and leave them alone.

Dawn was now on the horizon. It was essential to find somewhere to hide. Altner and his assortment of companions made for a distant wood. It looked deep and safe. When they got there, however, they discovered it was only 100 metres or so across and was already full of refugees whose tracks could clearly have been seen leading up to the wood by anyone pursuing them. To make matters worse, it turned out to be a rather thin wood offering few good hiding-places, and it was altogether cold, damp and unsafe.

There were in total about 150 people in this wood – really little more than a copse. About one-third were soldiers with weapons (with an average of ten rounds each), and there were two girl-soldiers who spoke in Russian to a captured 'Ivan' who carried their packs. A couple of scouts made contact with a local farmer, who told them that German lines were beyond the village of Pasewin, the last in the hands of the Red Army. They could skirt the small villages of Zachow and Roskow on the way by going through the fields, but marshes and lakes meant they would probably have to fight their way through Pasewin.

When the time came to attack, the small troop advanced bravely across the fields. They were totally outnumbered and outgunned and they were decimated by superior fire power and finally dispersed by a single shellfiring tank.

Altner ran off and found himself outside a deserted prisoner-of-war camp. As he rested, its wooden structure was suddenly blown to pieces by Russian shellfire. He ran on in a panic across the middle of a marsh. The water poured into his boots, and every step was heavier than the last. Finally he joined up with some other survivors. They found a bogged-down truck, pulled it out of the marsh and got it started, shoved the injured into the back and sent them all off with a driver displaying a white flag, to surrender to the Russians.

Those who were left behind joined up with a Home Guard officer. 'He said that he required unquestioning obedience on pain of death. The others laughed but decided to humour him. Only eight decided to go with him; a Flak Auxiliary lad, a wounded Air Force clerk, two policemen, a civilian, two soldiers and Altner.' They were too tired for caution. They headed west in broad daylight, sometimes crouching in ditches or behind hedges but sometimes, through necessity, walking in the open.

'They crossed the railway and stopped in a clump of bushes for a break. When a Soviet armoured car passed close along the road they buried their faces in the earth until it was gone. Then they came to a thick hedge separating the fields and pushed their way through. They were so tired they could scarcely move but they forced themselves on. . . . Suddenly they heard voices calling behind them and, looking back, they saw the Russians. They started running in panic towards the haven of the woods but firing broke out and bullets started flying all around them. They carried on running, but the Russians were gaining rapidly. Altner who was out of breath, stopped and threw his pistol away. It was over, the Russians were all round them.'

The Russians led them back to the road. Altner stumbled on his injured foot. A Russian picked him up, steadied him and gave him a cigarette.

Altner burst into tears.

Source
H. Altner (ed. T. Le Tissier), *Totentanz Berlin*

AFTERMATH

Introduction

Within days of the surrender, military trains ran to Berlin, and within a month public transport started up. Within two months, water supply, sewerage and electricity were all restored. Some observers had said that Berlin could never be a city again because so much had been destroyed. The truth was that a good deal of the infrastructure and many of the suburbs had survived without serious damage. At the very end, Nazi defences had been so weak that it was only in the city centre that they could put up a really effective fight.

The centre was badly damaged. Many beautiful buildings were lost. One of the finest cities in Europe had become a photographer's model of destruction and devastation. Still, nearly 2 million people lived on in Berlin, in suburbs and in the cellars, basements and bomb-ruined, shell-ruined apartments nearer the centre.

From 2 May for two months, the Red Army was in sole control of the city. The control was simple and ruthless. Berliners found they were the *Untermensch* – the inferior race – now. They suffered appallingly but they were fed and for the most part allowed to carry on living where they were. As Soviet-controlled newspapers now reminded them, their suffering never compared with what they had brought a few years earlier to Kiev, Warsaw, Minsk and many other towns and villages, let alone compared with the calamities they had brought to the millions of their slave-labourers and their families, and let alone compared with what they had done in Auschwitz, Treblinka, Sobibor and the rest.

The new Soviet rulers made serious efforts to sort out the handful of anti-Nazis from the rest. Sometimes they made mistakes in the scramble by all and sundry who claimed that they had really hated Hitler all along. In the end, though, they usually got the truth. It was easier for people like Max Bock who was among the few Jews who had managed to survive in Berlin. He was now free to point out the ardent Nazis who had made his life hell before he went into hiding, and who had hailed the SS and the excesses of the regime at every turn. The Nazi enthusiasts soon found themselves the labourers rebuilding the Soviet state. They were no longer allowed to run free in Berlin.

Within a fortnight some less disciplined regiments had been removed from Berlin, and by the end of June the whole first wave of Red Army troops had been replaced by regiments that had not been briefed with the somewhat chilling 'Berlin is Yours' order of the day. They were ready to get on with the American, British and French troops who would make Berlin a four-power city following the Yalta Conference decisions and the details subsequently agreed by Eisenhower and Zhukov at their meeting on 5 June.

Berliners welcomed the entry of the Western Allies into their three-quarters of the city in early July as a virtual liberation. They thought that life would be much better for them now. In some ways they were right. The Western forces were undoubtedly more disciplined and inclined to be better disposed towards the native population than the Red Army had been at least in the early days of occupation. It may have been an end to political and personal oppression, but it was no liberation from starvation, poverty, disease and death in the island in the Soviet zone of Germany which made up the Western-held sectors of Berlin.

The British and other Western officers who were supposed to liaise with the local population soon found out that the privations of the ordinary Berliners were hard indeed. Almost every family had lost someone in the war and, to add to the misery of this personal loss, there was the experience of recent suffering in the early days of occupation, the total disruption of most people's lives and now an increasing risk of out-and-out starvation.

Berliners living in the Soviet sector had access to some of the products of market gardens and farm produce from the outer Berlin area. In the Western sectors, some Soviet zone supplies were made available, but not enough. A lot of people went hungry. Some found a way out through prostitution and black-marketeering. Some of the rest starved.

The whole problem of civilian supplies intensified through the autumn and icy winter of 1945–6. The four-power political administration of Berlin was very difficult to operate, and the aims of the Soviet and Western sides were quite different. The Western powers wanted the city quickly rebuilt and to stop being a financial liability. The Soviets wanted a reliable Communist administration to emerge as soon as possible, to stop their part of Germany being a political liability.

The intelligence services of the Western powers stopped the development of Communism in their zones in the very early stages, but in the Soviet zone they could only watch. At the same time the Western administrations encouraged rebuilding and the redevelopment of industry, much of which, undestroyed, had been shipped lock, stock and barrel out of Germany to the Soviet Union during the period of exclusive occupation. Eventually different priorities meant that inevitable differences in the standards of living emerged between what quickly became rather clearly demarcated Communist East Berlin and capitalist West Berlin.

Both sides were agreed on the need to de-Nazify. Leading Nazis were quickly executed or imprisoned. But the bacillus was deep in the population. In the development of the new Communist state, the Soviets were on the whole more thorough in their re-education and purge. The Western powers were inclined to use some of the old institutions, and some of the former administrators were allowed to carry on; in the West, they were not quite so inclined to turn everything upside down and start again.

The bacillus was truly dangerous. One Christian who had gone through the Hitler Youth training found that anti-semitism was deep-rooted in his psyche. He at least thought about these things. Most people did not. They just felt and were hardly aware that within themselves Hitler had planted a germ which only constant vigilance could keep in check.

The Potsdam Conference set the agenda for post-War Europe. It left Berlin in an anomalous position unless there was to be real East–West co-operation, which never happened.

By 1948 East and West were polarized. A row over currency and the development of an embryonic West German Government without reference to the Soviets led to the blockade of West Berlin. Stalin thought the Western Allies would leave, starved out, but an airlift of heroic proportions brought up to 10,000 tonnes a day into West Berlin.

It took nearly a year but the tension eventually relaxed. Then the East and West German states developed more or less successfully for the next three decades, the Democratic Republic in the East and the Federal Republic in the West.

Riots in 1953 and the Wall from 1961 onwards have symbolized the tension in a city where the world's two most powerful rival systems have developed in each other's backyards, a disappointing outcome of a great victory.

Nazis Don't Get Away With It: 20 May

Berliners quickly realized that surrender would bring retribution. Max Bock, who as a Jew had hidden throughout the war, now joined the Anti-Fascist Action Group whose job it was to eradicate everything to do with Nazis and Nazism. Bock was particularly determined to pursue an unpleasant woman who had not even been commandeered into the workforce yet but '. . . complains loudly to the shops if the bread is not delivered on time'. Under the Nazis, this same woman would follow Bock and his wife when they went out, then she would come right up to them and spit on them. She encouraged her children to do the same. There was nothing the Bocks could do to escape or fight back, because they were wearing the Star of David. Bock was now to make sure the tables were turned on her and many others like her.

There was urgent need of the Anti-Fascist Action Group in the suburb of Lankwitz where friends had hidden Max Bock after his wife had been seized by the Nazis and murdered. These friends themselves had risked deportation and death. Now Bock heard they were threatened with arrest for, of all things, being Nazis.

Bock set off for Lankwitz. It was only a few miles but it was a long journey on Whit Sunday, 20 May 1945. The suburbs of Friedenau and Steglitz were relatively undamaged but the whole area around the Teltow Canal was wrecked. The bridge at the end of Halske-strasse had been destroyed, although Bock managed to clamber over planks at crazy angles, tree trunks and jagged pieces of masonry lying in the canal and reached the other side without a long detour and, rather to his surprise, without getting wet. In Lankwitz he heard the worst:

'For safety, the last few nights my friend has not slept at home and is still out when I arrive, a repetition of my own years on the run. I listen to all that has happened and realise the despicable truth. For years my friend has been the manager of the flats, a job which is often open to accusations and to dispute, and the holder of which has not always hit the right note. But that has not been the case here. The owner of the flats, in recognition of a job well done, has given my friend the use of the courtyard for the purpose of keeping chickens and rabbits, and for years some of the tenants have been envious of the privilege. And now they have found an opportune moment, with the changeover to a new regime, to level accusations. These are based on fact to some extent which my friend has never denied, namely that in 1933 he was a Party Member for a few months because of Union pressure, and threat of boycott from his trade association. Already in November of the same year he was thrown out. He hated the whole system, never took part in the activities and soon risked differences with the local Party leadership and later had to fight against many obstacles as the Nazis decided to boycott him.

'And his accusers? There is Herr M, the ring-leader, who used to annoy people constantly by forcing them to respond to his endless Hitler salute, and who now claims to have Jewish blood in his veins, a well-kept secret as even before the War he used to strut about in

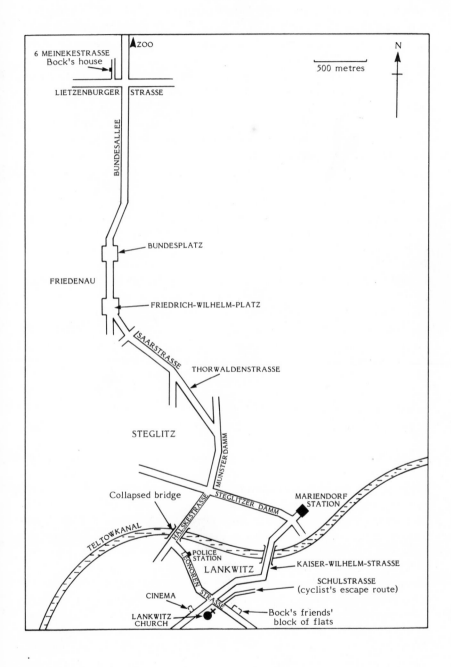

Nazi uniform. His wife was not to be trusted either, and my friends used to hide me if she happened to call if I was there. One has to be wary of people like these who today claim to be the opposite of what they were and who will use any means available to achieve their aim. In this case, their aim is to have the courtyard for their own use.'

Bock and his friend went to the police to make a statement about his friend keeping Bock in hiding, proof of an anti-Nazi. The first thing they discovered was that Herr M had not only been accusing all kinds of people of being Nazis, he had also been wearing an official red armband illegally. He had no authority. His name and address had been supplied to the Russians, who would deal with him properly.

Bock signed the statement and was assured his friends would now be safe. They were lucky. They were all left wondering just how many old scores were now being settled in Berlin and how many innocent people were suffering at the hands of the likes of Herr M.

As they walked back along the streets of Lankwitz, there was little to alleviate their feeling of depression. A dead horse was being hacked to pieces for meat in one street – someone even went off with the head and ears under her arm – Bock wondered who could possibly fancy eating those, however hungry they were. A cyclist was very nearly shot a few minutes later for not giving up his bicycle to the Russian sentry posted at the junction by Lankwitz church – the cyclist disappeared up Schulstrasse at top speed, with bullets flying round him.

Some cinemas had reopened. Why not try a film to get away from it all? *Lenin 1918* was showing locally. The film was about the relationship between Lenin and Stalin during the critical year following the October Revolution. 'Apart from the fact that a film like that must necessarily contain a great deal of propaganda, one must admire it not only from a political, but also from a technical and artistic point of view and look at it from a different standpoint from one's own. We left the cinema, pleased to have had a new kind of experience.'

The great events portrayed in the film were ultimately worked out in the streets of Nazi Berlin. They were reinforced by the only German newspaper on sale which Bock bought, *Nachrichtenblatt für die Deutsche Bevölkerung – Information for the German Population*: 'Goering and Kesselring have been captured by the English. Goering is reported to have been rather tearful, claiming that he was no longer a follower of Hitler, having not long ago praised his "passionately loved Führer" to the sky. Yes, that is what true Nazis look like when things go wrong.'

Bock was determined to get on with his own role of avenger. As he made his way back through the ruins of Berlin to his home in Meinekestrasse, he thought of his wife and family, all murdered. He clambered through the ruined allotments in old Lankwitz and followed the road to Mariendorf – the canal bridge on the direct route was now blocked by the Russians. Near the Kaiser Platz he met a young Russian officer who, after checking his papers, asked Bock if he knew any Nazis or Tsarist *émigrés*; Bock was somewhat taken aback about the *émigrés* and certainly did not know any, but as for Nazis . . . the woman who spat and whose children spat, the man who insulted, the shopkeeper who refused to serve – their days of freedom were numbered from the moment Bock met that officer.

To his surprise, when he got to Kaiser Platz the first post-war Berlin bus was waiting and took him to the zoo, near his home. Back in his flat, Bock really started to believe that Nazism was finished and that he could play his part in finishing it. The whole ghastly edifice had crashed.

Source
M. Bock, unpublished diary

A British Officer Explores – and Finds Japanese Aphrodisiacs: July to December

Defeated Berliners were not nearly so bitter or resentful as they were described in the British press. Some were sullen. Most were hungry. The Berliners who were best off were those who ran the gangs which controlled the black market. They were all pleased that one way or another the bombing had stopped. Some remained Nazis until they died and passed the ideas on to their children and grandchildren. Most, however, wanted to be the people of Goethe and Beethoven and to forget about being the people of Hitler and Goebbels.

Captain Richard Brett-Smith was in the 11th Hussars, the first British regiment to enter Berlin, the first to see the drab ruins '. . . and the dark crowd of Germans which lines the pavements and clusters in knots on the uneven rubble.'

The 11th Hussars entered Berlin from Potsdam on 6 July and followed the west bank of the Havel up to Spandau. In Pichelsdorfer Strasse, it was four o'clock so they stopped for tea and did some polishing before a drive-past: 'The cars shone brilliantly . . . the little scarlet jerboas, or desert rats, looked especially fine' – the emblem had made it from El Alamein to Berlin. Then they settled down at von Seeckt barracks in Spandau.

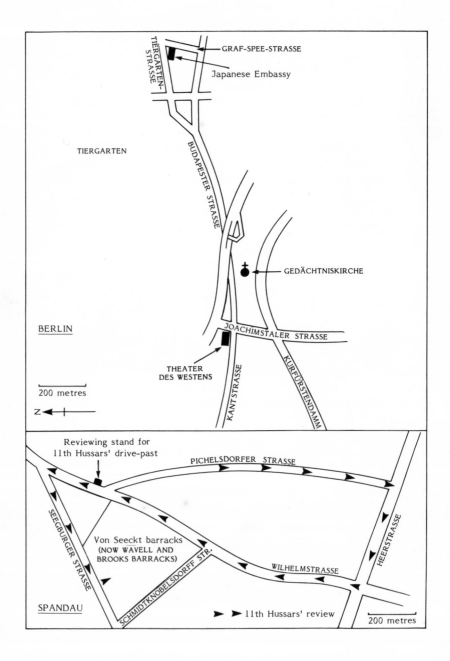

GRAF-SPEE-STRASSE

Japanese Embassy

TIERGARTEN-STRASSE

TIERGARTEN

BUDAPESTER STRASSE

GEDÄCHTNISKIRCHE

BERLIN

JOACHIMSTALER STRASSE

KURFÜRSTENDAMM

THEATER DES WESTENS

KANTSTRASSE

200 metres

N ←——

Reviewing stand for 11th Hussars' drive-past

PICHELSDORFER STRASSE

SEEGBURGER STRASSE

Von Seeckt barracks (NOW WAVELL AND BROOKS BARRACKS)

SCHMIDTKNOBELSDORFF STR.

WILHELMSTRASSE

HEERSTRASSE

SPANDAU

► ►11th Hussars' review

200 metres

As soon as he could, Brett-Smith was out and about, exploring Berlin. It was a forest of ruins. He headed for a central point he knew about, the Gedächtniskirche, the Memorial Church built by the Kaiser – 'in its heyday the most hideous church outside Maida Vale', the poet Stephen Spender had called it. Brett-Smith concluded that it was much improved by having been blown to pieces, leaving only striking remains of the spire sticking up.

In the Kurfürstendamm, the old decadence was still there. Prostitutes, seedy nightclubs and brothels, along with rats, had survived every assault.

The Japanese Embassy – Brett-Smith climbed inside:

'Crates of plated silver carefully packed up and labelled "Tokyo via Königsberg" – the Russians had missed them. The safes had been blasted open by high explosive, but in one unharmed safe someone found a thick wad of Bank of England £5 notes, which we burned conscientiously after they had been pronounced German forgeries. The lavish cocktail bar that General Hiroshi Oshima, the last Japanese Ambassador to Berlin, had had built in his Embassy, which was well-stocked also with recent English and American books on politics, economics and the war, with foreign periodicals such as *Time* and *The Economist*, with skis (in Japanese sizes) and, interestingly enough, with little tins and bottles of hormone and vitamin tablets, mostly intended to assist the overworked Japanese diplomatists' sexual prowess. (A doctor who put them to the test made a disappointing report on them: he was Irish, however, not Japanese.) It was sad to see how the Russians had gone through room after room full of fine furniture and pictures with fire and the sword, or with their modern counterparts, the Bazooka and the bayonet; they had shot holes in Old Masters, ripped the stuffing out of French and Italian chairs and sofas of the 17th, 18th and 19th centuries, and scoured and defaced exquisite carpets, panelling and mirrors. Nevertheless, because they had also moved like a whirlwind and had been bad and indiscriminate pillagers who had destroyed for the sake of destruction and also emptied their guns for the fun of it, they had missed a picture here and a settee there.'

Brett-Smith managed to salvage a few bits and pieces. A piano from the Japanese Embassy rests in an officers' mess of the 11th Hussars to this day.

Back to Kantstrasse and the Theater des Westens where the Berlin Philharmonic were presenting Mendelssohn (forbidden under the Nazis as Jewish music), playing to a rapt audience. Brett-Smith became a regular visitor to the Berlin Philharmonic until Leo Borchard, the brilliant principal conductor, was accidentally shot by a British sentry at a military checkpoint.

Brett-Smith stayed in Berlin through Christmas. When he heard a 'great swelling surge of Adeste Fideles' from a partly wrecked Berlin church, he was sure, after all, that there was some hope for this new breed of dwellers-in-the-ruins, Nazis-turned-troglodytes.

Source
R. Brett-Smith, *Berlin '45: The Grey City*

Churchill at the Potsdam Conference: 15 July to 2 August

Wednesday 18 July
Potsdam

The PM, since he left London, has refused to do any work or read anything. That is probably quite right, but then he can't have it both ways: if he knows nothing about the subject under discussion, he should keep quiet, or ask that the Foreign Secretary be heard. Instead of that, he butts in on every occasion and talks the most irrelevant rubbish, and risks giving away our case at every point.

Truman is most quick and business-like. He was only trying, at this first meeting, to establish a list of the questions we must deal with. Every mention of a topic started Winston off on a wild rampage from which the combined efforts of Truman and Anthony [Eden] with difficulty restrained him. . . .

The meetings take place in the Cecilienhof, a palace that was built, I think, for Little Willie [Crown Prince Wilhelm of Germany] after his marriage. It stands in a lovely park, strewn with Russian sentries, but the house is pretty ugly. . . .

From a letter from Sir Alexander Cadogan,
Head of the Foreign Office, to his wife,
Lady Theodosia.

Winston Churchill lived at 23 Ringstrasse in Babelsberg during the Potsdam Conference, and the rest of the British Delegation occupied the houses around. The military and civilian team of 260 people took over fifty houses – 'each with their Steinway or Bechstein Grand Piano', enthused one British lady domestic administrator. 'Everybody who was anybody was there. It was the last great beano of the War.'

Anthony Eden, British Foreign Secretary, was there, and he was

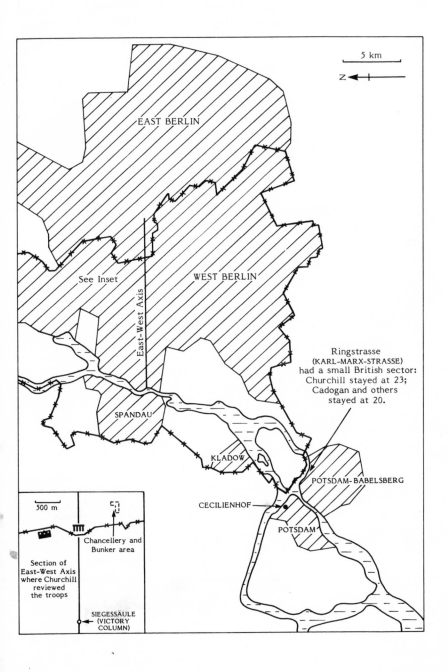

in a bad state. He had just received news that his son was missing, feared killed, in the Far East. He was jittery about his Conservative Party's chances in the General Election. He was maddened by Stalin's ability to get Churchill under his spell – 'I want that man to like me,' Churchill would say.

Eden minuted to the Prime Minister on 17 July:

'The truth is that on any and every point, Russia tries to seize all that she can and she uses these meetings to grab as much as she can get. . . . If we were to talk generously to the Russians this time about access to the wider oceans, I fear that they would only regard it as an indication that we had not been shocked by their demands on Turkey, and would proceed to make more and more demands on Persia and on other countries in the Middle East. . . . I am deeply concerned at the pattern of Russian policy, which becomes clearer as they become more brazen every day.'

Eden did at least make Churchill more bullish on Poland. Churchill put up a good fight to ensure that Poland, for which Britain had gone to war in 1939, was given the promise of independence and free elections. When he set his mind to it, the old man could still be impressive and a formidable opponent in debate.

Cadogan stayed behind after the meeting on Poland for a meeting of officials to clear up the details and then, well satisfied that all that could be done for Poland had been done, set off back to Babelsberg.

'As I was driving back from the meeting this evening, when I was half-way out of the park of the Cecilienhof, I was held up by Russian sentries at a cross-road. From the road on the left emerged a platoon of Russian tommy-gunners in skirmishing order, then a number of guards and units of the NKVD army. Finally appeared Uncle Joe on foot, with his usual thugs surrounding him, followed by another screen of skirmishers. The enormous officer who always sits behind Uncle at meetings was apparently in charge of operations, and was running about, directing tommy-gunners to cover all the alleys in the park giving access to the main road. All this because Uncle wanted five minutes exercise and fresh air, and walked out to pick up his car 500 yards from the Palace.'

One of Britain's main concerns at the conference was to avoid mass starvation in Germany. The British, French and Americans occupied most of the industrial part of Germany but the Soviet Union occupied well over half the food-producing part. Berlin, now a four-power city encircled by the Soviet occupation zone, risked being starved. 'Reviewed coal and food situation in Berlin. It's not so bad as indiscretions by some blockhead British Officers make it seem,' Sir Alexander Cadogan had jotted in his diary in London, but when he went to Berlin he got a shock: he had never seen so much utter devastation and came to the conclusion immediately that it could never be rebuilt.

'I don't know what will happen, this winter, to the population living in the ruins. At present the sewers are mostly bust (with unpleasant results). There is, I believe, a water-supply system, but the suffering and the disease will be awful.

'We stopped at the Reichstag building. . . . We got out of the cars and wandered about which I thought rather a questionable proceeding as there were no elaborate security measures and quite a number of Berliners. They seemed to take a vivid interest (Winston of course was recognised, as he kept a cigar in his mouth the whole time), but there were no obvious signs of hostility. Then to the Chancellery. . . . It was frightfully hot, milling about in such a crowd, stumbling over the dusty debris with which all rooms and passages are littered.'

Then to the bunker: 'We were shown the room in which, according to one story, Hitler died. Next door was another room said to have been Eva Braun's. On one table there was still a vase with a branch in it which had evidently been a spray of blossom. . . .' Churchill clambered back out of the bunker, mopped his brow and commented that Hitler must have '. . . come out here to get some fresh air and heard the guns getting nearer and nearer'.

Back to conference business.

Churchill was determined to avoid the mistake he had made at the Teheran Conference in 1943, which had been to allow Stalin and the American President to get too close together – this was really crucial now because, with Truman, Churchill did not have the warm friendship he had had with Roosevelt. He launched quickly at the next meeting of the Big Three into the question of the German eastern frontier, knowing that this would divide the two budding superpowers. Stalin wanted the Oder–Neisse line which would take into Poland the coal-rich, grain-rich province of Silesia. This in turn would compensate Poland for large chunks of Polish territory now to be taken into the Soviet Union.

'I have been told,' said Churchill, '. . . that the Poles are selling Silesian coal to Sweden. They are doing this when we in Britain have a shortage of coal and are faced with the coldest and harshest winter without fuel. We start from the general principle that the supply of Germany within her 1937 borders with foodstuffs and fuel must be shared proportionately to the size of her population, regardless of the zone in which this food and fuel is located.'

Stalin asked: 'Who is to mine the coal? The Germans are not doing it; it is the Poles who are. . . . The Poles would hang the Germans if they returned.'

Churchill's ploy worked to some extent, as Truman took his side, envisaging an indefinite financial commitment to feeding West Germans, and a row between Truman and Stalin ensued until it was time for a banquet.

'Stalin gave his State dinner,' the President wrote afterwards, 'and it was a wow. Started with caviar and vodka and wound up with water melon and champagne.'

Still, the British Delegation managed to be up at nine the next morning to attend the parade of their troops in the centre of Berlin.

'It was a very good show,' reported Cadogan. 'A stand had been put up on the main avenue in the Tiergarten leading up to the Siegessäule. We all met there and we [the principal guests led by Churchill] were put into little motor lorries that stretched right away nearly to the Brandenburg Gate. A very impressive sight, but we felt rather like French aristocrats being driven in tumbrils through the streets. We eventually got back to the saluting base, and then the whole show marched past, including some of the grenadiers to their regimental march.'

In the car park to Potsdam, Churchill was lectured by Eden and Cadogan about the new-fangled world organization to be called the 'United Nations', the Communist threat to the Greek Government, Stalin's claim to part of the Italian Mediterranean fleet and all the issues which would have to be decided within the next few days and which would affect many millions of Europeans for at least half a century.

A week into the conference, Churchill and Eden announced they would have to leave for a couple of days for the results of the British General Election. No one doubted that they would be back. The round of official meetings would of course continue, now working hard on the vexed question of reparations by Germany to the Allies. It was agreed that Cadogan would act as Foreign Minister in dealings with Molotov and Secretary of State Byrnes, and the date set for the next Big Three meeting was two days later, Friday 27 July.

Churchill's visit had been brief, often ill-informed, and ended with his overwhelming electoral defeat. The new Prime Minister, Clement Attlee, took his place at the conference. But Churchill knew, better than anyone because he had such a profound under-standing of the ebb and flow of world history, that he had shared at Potsdam, the long-anticipated 'Berlin Conference' of the three victorious powers, in the creation of a new Europe, quite different from the ruins of the old.

Source
D. Dilk, ed., *The Diaries of Sir Alexander Cadogan, O.M.*

Attlee at the Potsdam Conference:
15 July to 2 August

Tucked away in a small, dull house that had belonged to an engineer was Clement Attlee, leader of the British Labour Party. He sat at the conference table but played no part in the conference discussions. Churchill had asked him as a constitutional formality because a General Election had been held in Britain and the results were delayed because the service votes from all over the world had taken a long time to assemble and count. Theoretically Attlee could have been the rightful Prime Minister, although everyone agreed it was unlikely, to say the least. Attlee had told Stalin that the result of the election would be close. Stalin had commented to Churchill that Attlee did not seem to him like a man hungry for power.

On 28 July Clement Attlee returned to Potsdam, backed by a massive election win for Labour. He had been kept up-to-date on conference matters by the Head of the Foreign Office, Sir Alexander Cadogan, by telegram and by secret documents sent across to London by Mosquito plane for him to read on his flight out. With the new Foreign Secretary, Ernest Bevin, he went straight to see first President Truman with Secretary of State Byrnes, and then Stalin with Molotov.

Attlee recalled: 'Molotov's smile never seemed to go beyond his lips, but Stalin had a lively sense of humour. It reminded me of the Renaissance despots – no principles, any methods, but no flowery language – always Yes or No, though you could only count on him if it was No. . . . Molotov kept saying, "But you said the Election would be a close thing and now you have a big majority." I said, "Yes, we could not tell what would be the result." But he kept repeating the same phrase. He could not understand why we did not know the result. I am sure he thought that Churchill would have fixed the Election and that the change-over by Democratic process was a great shock to him.'

Even the Americans, Western and democratic, were rather taken aback by Attlee's appearance with Churchill's valet and Churchill's Principal Private Secretary. For the sake of security and comfort, Attlee moved reluctantly from his engineer's house into 23 Ringstrasse, the suburban villa allocated to the British Prime Minister. Attlee was self-effacing and modest – the others at the conference were left wondering how this most uncharismatic of men could have such evident appeal to the British masses.

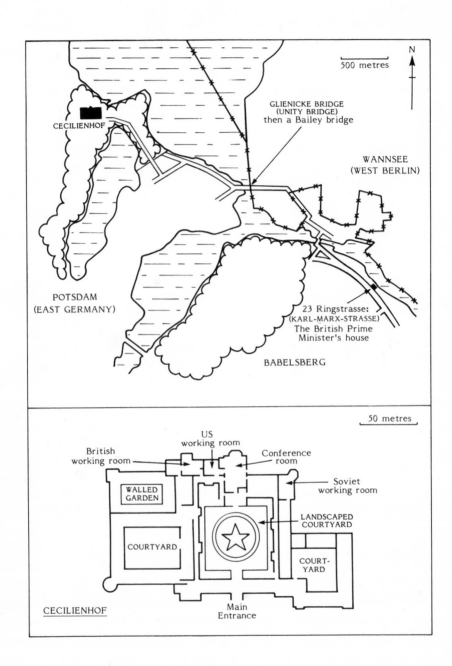

Attlee dined with some junior officials on the evening of 28 July while he was briefed for the full conference session due later that night. It had been quite a day, starting with a Labour victory rally in the City of London, flying to Berlin, meeting the two most powerful men in the world on supposedly equal terms, and now only the prospect of a further tiring session of the conference late at night. Night-time meetings suited neither Attlee nor Truman; Stalin, however, was often at his best at one in the morning. Attlee certainly did not feel like a long wrangle.

In the event, the 28 July conference meeting was short and inconclusive. More important that evening were the details of the first Atom Bomb given to Attlee when Truman visited him in the small room in the conference mansion, Cecilienhof, reserved for the British delegation. Truman told Attlee that a massive explosion could be caused by the Atom Bomb and that it was sure to help bring about the surrender of Japan. He did not anticipate how destructive it would be in Hiroshima and Nagasaki, and he made no mention of the possible fall-out or genetic effects. A secret agreement with Churchill on 21 July meant that Britain had formally forgone any influence over the use of the bomb. Finally Truman said that he had told Stalin on 24 July about the bomb but a polite 'thank you' had been the whole reaction. In fact, Stalin probably knew more details about the bomb than either of the other two leaders, through his American spies Fuchs and Greenglass.

All three leaders were impatient to get home from the conference, not least Attlee to his new Government. The business was to be concluded quickly, and Attlee was just the right man to have around for this purpose. His sharp mind and modest manner were a contrast to the Churchillian style of bluster and speechifying. Although the conference was duller and poorer without Churchill, it had a much better chance of providing quick and effective conclusions. They reached agreements all round by Thursday 2 August: boundaries for Poland, four-power government of Germany, reparation payments, progress towards final peace treaties with Italy, the disarmament and demilitarization of Germany and Austria. Bevin did virtually all the talking for the British delegation. Attlee did a good deal of the organization but said little, just nodded and smoked his pipe – 'You don't keep a dog and bark yourself; and Ernie Bevin was a very good dog.'

On 2 August Attlee was driven to the centre of Berlin, looked at the remains of the Chancellery and the ruins all round, thought briefly about what difference the new bomb would make if conventional bombs could bring about this amount of destruction, and then flew home to greet the first ever Labour majority in the House of Commons.

Sources
D. Dilks, ed., *The Diaries of Sir Alexander Cadogan, O.M.*
K. Harris, *Attlee*

Survivors of the Destruction of Berlin: Christmas Eve

Lieutenant-Colonel Byford Jones was with the Intelligence Corps. He was posted in one of the few buildings that was left standing in the centre of Berlin, the Hotel am Zoo.

One day he had the idea of making contact with some of the grey and ghostly figures, the civilians who still populated Berlin. It was something he thought might be fascinating, seeing how they lived – and how they starved. The starvation was appalling in the British sector. Even the Russians provided civilians with extra rations at Christmas time, but not the British.

Scraps of paper fluttered from every tree and tree-stump left standing in Berlin. Everything could be bought and sold through tree-notices, goods and services, black market and legal. Also, more

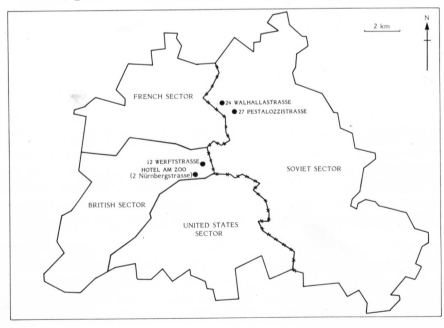

sadly, there were thousands of notices asking for information about relatives or giving information about changes of address as buildings collapsed or family members died. Byford Jones got the hall porter at the Hotel am Zoo to put up a notice, which he had written, on a prominent tree:

'I wrote out in German a message to the effect that a British officer who spoke German would like the privilege of visiting a German family, the members of which had not been supporters of Hitler. I considered it necessary to add that I had no ulterior motive in asking for invitations, and I think I made it clear I was not interested in visiting Black Marketeers or "lonely girls", though I did not mention the facts specifically.'

One hour later the porter went out again and came back with three names:

Rippe, Walhallastrasse 24

Pisarek, Werftstrasse 12a

Drehme, Pestalozzistrasse 27

Byford Jones visited the three addresses and discovered stories of suffering under occupation, and worse suffering under the Nazis.

Frau Rippe had a child who was half black. She had blatantly broken Nazi race laws. From 1933 to 1945 she had been a social outcast. Old friends isolated her and spat at her. Her most chilling comment was her parting one: 'The people who did that to me have not changed . . . they are Germans without soul and without character.'

Whatever they said to Byford Jones, the truth is that the Pisareks were among those who would have spat at Frau Rippe and her son. They had backed the Nazis and had duly sacrificed two soldier-sons in the East; each son left a baby boy. Now they were making the best of Christmas Eve. They lit their traditional Advent candles, and the grandfather dressed as Santa Claus, but it was very cold and there was almost nothing to eat. The two fatherless children received gleefully little home-made gifts from Santa Claus, were enraptured with American chocolate bars from their British visitor and talked chirpily about their recent outing to *Hansel and Gretel* at the State Opera House.

'They are really quite happy,' said Mrs Pisarek. 'After all, what have they been used to? – no fathers, nights in cellars, bombs, fighting, not enough food. You can get used to anything. And I feel I can endure anything, now that the bombs have ceased.'

Frau Drehme and her two elderly companions were pathetic.

'Not much like Christmas,' said the old man. 'Fact is there is only one thing to be glad about, and that is that we do not have to go running down to the damp cellars or the shelters every hour as we did last year. I lost my first wife after many years together because she got pneumonia through being all night in damp cellars up in Schillerstrasse. As she died she begged me to get married again to have someone to look after me. I did, last year. I buried that wife in the winter, pneumonia again, through the damp in the shelters. So many people died of that, old and young, almost as many as died of bombs.' Tears ran down his cheeks, and the two old women spoke quietly to him.

The two old women and the old man insisted on preparing a substitute for the traditional Christmas Eve carp. The fish was made of potato, seasoned and fish-shaped and served in a sauce made from black bread, beer, onions, carrots and gingerbread. Frau Panner, the lodger, was pleased to have a visitor but she knew there was no hope of information from a British officer about the boy she had lost at Stalingrad.

'This week there will be thousands of cards from Moscow coming here from our sons,' said Frau Panner. 'It says so in *Das Volk*. Sixteen bags have already arrived. Perhaps there will be a letter from him. I am sure he is alive; perhaps someone is being kind to him this Christmas, far from his home.'

Source
W. Byford Jones, *Berlin Twilight*

The German Communists: 15 January 1946

The new heroes of the Berliners in the Soviet sector were Karl Liebknecht and Rosa Luxemburg, Communists who had tried to end the First World War and had been murdered back in 1919. It was felt that the Germans needed new heroes to replace the Nazi ones.

'For thirteen years no one had mentioned their names. Most people had forgotten them. Young people had never heard of them. Suddenly Russian newspapers in Berlin began a campaign, and the two Communists became political saints overnight. Russian-inspired appeals by newspapers, posters and speeches were used to advertise a procession and a ceremony on the anniversary of the revolutionaries' deaths.'

Lieutenant-Colonel Byford Jones, British Intelligence Officer, had the job of watching these Communist developments. The British were anti-Communist, and Byford Jones was too – actually he had had Nazi sympathies in the early days and was a rather unpleasant

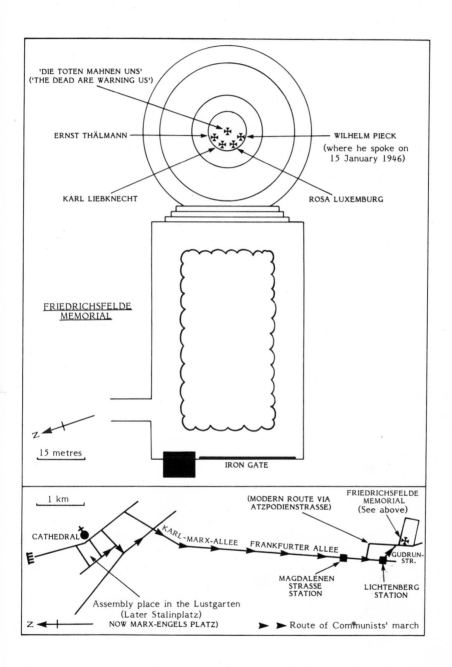

'DIE TOTEN MAHNEN UNS'
('THE DEAD ARE WARNING US')

ERNST THÄLMANN

WILHELM PIECK
(where he spoke on
15 January 1946)

KARL LIEBKNECHT

ROSA LUXEMBURG

FRIEDRICHSFELDE
MEMORIAL

Z

15 metres

IRON GATE

1 km

CATHEDRAL

KARL-MARX-ALLEE

(MODERN ROUTE VIA
ATZPODIENSTRASSE)

FRIEDRICHSFELDE
MEMORIAL
(See above)

FRANKFURTER ALLEE

GUDRUN-
STR.

MAGDALENEN
STRASSE
STATION

LICHTENBERG
STATION

Assembly place in the Lustgarten
(Later Stalinplatz)
NOW MARX-ENGELS PLATZ)

Z

Route of Communists' march

person. Incredibly, for example, after all that had happened, he believed a neo-Nazi story that the Polish Jews were buying up cheaply all the gold and jewels in Berlin. Now he was directing his unwelcome attention to the Communists. They were marching through the Soviet part of Berlin, so, to his chagrin, there was nothing he could do but watch and report.

A vast crowd of some tens of thousands of men, women and children gathered in the former Lustgarten, by now renamed Stalinplatz. Social Democrats and Communists together. Their alliance had been engineered by the Soviet authorities, who knew it had been the split between the two parties of the Left that had destroyed German revolutions in the past. Now that had changed.

The German Communist Party had recruited vigorously, half spontaneously and half because of the better treatment which Communists received if they lived in the Soviet sector. The same would apply to those who allied themselves with the Communists, which goes some way to explaining the sudden burst of comradeship on the part of their old enemies, the Social Democrats. So together they marched. Singing the 'Internationale'. Waving red banners.

The procession wound its way out to the working-class suburb of Friedrichsfelde, which was, conveniently, in the Soviet sector of Berlin. It also had an important symbolic association with German Communism, because a memorial to Liebknecht and Luxemburg had been unveiled there in 1926 which had become a shrine in its day. It had been smashed to pieces by the Nazis but a replica had been built. It was a red block with two mottoes: 'I was, I am, I shall be' and 'The Dead are Warning Us'. The purpose of the march was to unveil this new monument.

They marched through the late morning, through the ruined city. The leader of the procession was Wilhelm Pieck, a Communist survivor of the concentration camps who had escaped to lead a small group of German Communists in Moscow; hardly formidable to look at, he was seventy years old, short, white-haired and blunt.

The people of Berlin looked out from their shattered buildings. Some recalled the distant past when the Communists had marched. Now they saw the start of a Communist new order.

The procession arrived at the monument next to Friedrichsfelde cemetery in the early afternoon. There, on that freezing January day, by the red slab with the simple inscription, the fir trees for a backdrop, Communist Germany began.

'Never again shall Communists and Social Democrats oppose each other,' Wilhelm Peck told the gathering. 'We must prevent reaction such as in 1919. Together we will conclude the closest friendship and enter into the most determined fight for our great cause. Over this grave we extend the hand as a symbol to all our people, in the holy vow that through the mutual struggle we will guarantee the victory of our just aims and our entry into the union of all free and freedom-loving peoples of the world.'

Social Democrats and Communists duly embraced.

Byford Jones knew that the eastern sector of Berlin was now Communist. It would remain for the British, Americans and French to persuade Berliners that they would not give up their island in Communist Germany and that it was safe to oppose Communism there. It was not until after the Airlift of 1948 that most Berliners realized that the split was permanent.

Sources
W. Byford Jones, *Berlin Twilight*
H. Vosske, ed., *Wilhelm Pieck, 1876–1960*

The Hitler Youth Returns: 1944 to 1946

At grenade-throwing practice they told thirteen-year-old Reinhold Kerstan, who could not throw far enough, 'Think of the target as a Jew.' He still failed. 'What's the matter Kerstan? Don't you want to kill a Jew?'

Kerstan's father was a pastor. Every day he read aloud from the family Bible. He really lived his Christianity and therefore rebelled against the anti-Jewish hatred and all the barbarity of the Nazis. But Reinhold had been born in 1931, and he had known Nazism only beyond the family. He had been taught at school to despise the God who cares for the meek and downfallen. He loved Adolf Hitler and wore with pride the brown shirt and black shorts of the Hitler Youth.

Reinhold Kerstan really changed when he was sent away to a training camp in the Sudetenland in Czechoslovakia in 1944. There he was subjected to all the violent routines of the camp bullies. He had a Bible from his father and when he read it on Easter morning, he was stripped and mock-crucified on the bunk beds. His faith in God strengthened and in Hitler weakened as he learned quickly and the Nazis crumbled. Soon Reinhold and his platoon ended up at the mercy of the Americans in Tyrlaching in Bavaria.

All Reinhold now wanted was to get back to his parents, if they had survived, in Berlin.

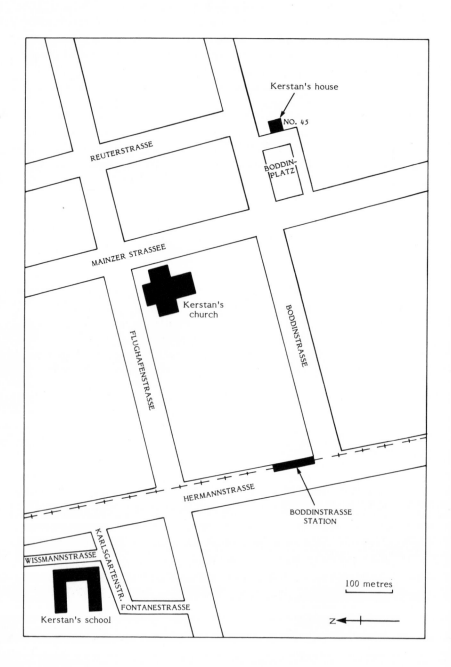

Reinhold and the rest of what was left of his platoon lived in the American Army stables – along with the horses – in what had once been the local dance hall in Tyrlaching. In October the mother of one of the boys in the platoon arrived from Berlin. Some letters had got through and she had been able to chase some names and addresses. One of the names was Reinhold Kerstan. His mother had survived.

Kerstan's journey back to Berlin was illegal. A group of children with families in Berlin were smuggled by two of the mothers to Helmstedt on the edge of the Soviet zone of occupation. Then they had to walk through the woods at night, through thick snow, to cross the zone frontier, because they had no papers – it was touch and go as they were nearly caught by a patrol. Finally they were smuggled onto a train at Magdeburg for Berlin.

They were used to ruined cities by now but they were still shocked by the centre of Berlin. Still, some trains were running and Reinhold made it from the zoo station to Boddinstrasse. To 45 Boddinstrasse – '*Mutti, Mutti*, Reinhold is here.' '*Mein Junge, mein Junge. . . .*'

Reinhold was refused a permit to live in Berlin but nobody suggested sending him anywhere else. No one wanted this remnant of the Master Race. There were no rations and no school for him.

His father soon returned from a prisoner-of-war camp in Italy and set about being pastor again. He and Reinhold started to rebuild his local ruined Apostolic church. It soon became a real community effort: every brick was saved and if necessary repaired; the old roof was propped up, and ancient boilers creaked into action.

It was a bitterly cold winter and there was not enough food or warmth. At one time the Kerstans were reduced to just two pieces of coal, and the temperature dropped well below zero. Wind whistled through the one-room apartment which was separated from the next only by a large wardrobe. There was hardly any privacy, and the unnaturally large room was icy cold.

In the new year Reinhold was given permission to live in Berlin and from now on received his own rations and was allowed to go to school. There he made friends with a boy called Paul.

'He was a slightly built, dark haired boy with a good sense of humour. One Saturday I walked over to his house to give him a few books for a school assignment. He'd been sick and I had volunteered to help him make up lost time. A bearded old man with a small cap and long curls dangling down both sides of his head opened the door.

'I must have stared at him for a moment, because he offered, "You must be Reinhold. Please come in. I'll take you to him."

'As he shut the door to the bedroom, I burst out, "You didn't tell me you had a servant. What a strange man."

' "He's my grandfather." '

'I wanted to crawl under the bed. "I'm sorry," I stammered. "It's just that he . . ."'

' ". . . looks funny. . . ." Paul helped me out.'

' "Right." Paul didn't say anything for a moment then he calmly told me, "He's an Orthodox Jew. Have you never seen one before?"'

'Instead of answering him, I said, "And you are a Jew?"'

' "Yes, I am. My father was not Orthodox but my mother was."'

' "Where are your parents?" But even as I asked, I recalled that he had not mentioned them before and I had a sinking feeling.'

' "In Auschwitz."'

' "You mean. . . ."'

' "Yes."'

'With the pride of a young and dedicated Hitler Youth, I had despised the Yellow Star of David. On many occasions I had joined the gang mocking harmless Jews. But I had been an innocent child then who had known nothing of politics. Certainly, I didn't know any better – or did I?'

Source
R. Kerstan, *Blood and Honour*

Epilogue

The main concern of Nazism was power. The untrammelled exercise of power over others was exciting. Mentally and physically, Nazis were stimulated by acts of domination. Nazi political philosophy was characterized by a rigid and disciplined hierarchy of power; its policies on race and conquest were preoccupied with power through superior armed might.

When they lost the war, Nazis learned to experience in turn the vengeance and lust of conquerors. They experienced what they had imposed just three or four years before. They now had to submit in every way to the whims of others. *Battlefield Berlin* has aimed to provide new insight into how, at the end, this submission came about and how it was enacted. It was not very quick, and sometimes it was painful and unpleasant.

At the same time, the conquerors – the Red Army in the case of Berlin – only really behaved like conquerors in the very early stages. The thrill of power and the excitement of battle had gone. Peace became genuinely appealing to all but the most extreme fanatics. So

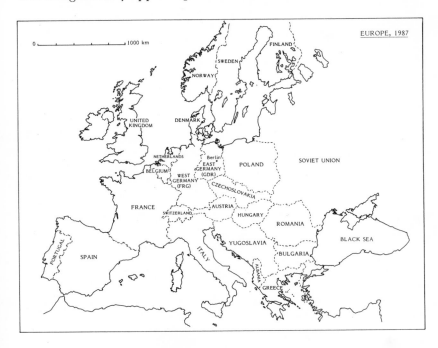

Nazis escaped all but the most short-term consequences of their defeat. It is attributable both to sheer exhaustion and to a superior set of values that the Red Army treated Nazi Germany so leniently; both of these are clear from the personal records in *Battlefield Berlin*.

The defeat of Nazism was never completed. There are still Fascist governments all over the world. There is even a limited revival of 'Neo-Nazism' in Germany; in West Germany in particular Nazis and Nazi ideas were never adequately suppressed. Their conquerors were lenient with the builders of Auschwitz.

The experience of Nazism in defeat and of more peaceful values in the ascendant is uplifting. However haphazardly, however horribly, for however short a time, a great evil was struck down.

Appendix

Berlin 1940–45 – Facts and Figures

25 August 1940	The first time Berlin was bombed by the Royal Air Force.
18 November 1943	Air battle of Berlin begins. RAF Bomber Command starts its offensive. 16 major attacks, each containing 400 to 1,000 bombers. RAF losses: 537 bombers and 4,000 crew. Berlin's losses: 6,166 dead, 18,431 injured, 1½ million homeless and 9 square kilometres destroyed.
2 March 1944	Air battle of Berlin ends. RAF Bomber Command withdrawn for Normandy landings.
20 July 1944	The 'Bomb Plot' to kill Hitler fails.
25 September 1944	Allied strategic bombing of Berlin begins, United States Air Force by day and RAF by night.
18 January 1945	Vistula offensive launched by the Red Army which sweeps across East Prussia and Poland.
1 February 1945	Zhukov's Red Army spearhead reaches the River Oder.
2 February 1945	First bridgeheads built across the River Oder.
mid-February 1945–mid-March 1945	Air raids by the RAF and US Air Force, 30 consecutive days and nights.
14–15 April 1945	Red Army reconnaissance on the Oder Front begins. Germans anticipate massive attack.

The Battle of the Oder

Opposing forces:

Red Army 2½ million troops, 41,600 artillery pieces, 6,250 tanks and armoured cars, 7,500 aircraft.

German Army 1 million troops, 10,400 artillery pieces, 1,500 tanks and armoured cars, 3,300 aircraft.

| 16 April 1945 | 4 a.m. First Byelorussian Front attacks from the Küstrin bridgehead.
7.15 a.m. First Ukrainian Front attacks across the River Neisse. |

The Red Army had 600 guns for every kilometre of front line. Altogether they fired 1,236,000 shells.

17 April 1945	First Byelorussian Front led by Zhukov gains the Seelow Heights by evening after heavy fighting.
18 April 1945	First Ukrainian Front led by Koniev crosses the Spree and is ordered towards Berlin from the south.
19 April 1945	Zhukov's Front heads for Berlin from the east.
20 April 1945	Second Byelorussian Front led by Rokossovsky attacks across the Lower Oder northeast of Berlin. Guns of Zhukov's Third Shock Army fire into the city of Berlin. Koniev's first Ukrainian Front reaches German Army Headquarters at Zossen. Hitler's 56th birthday.

Entry into Berlin and Occupation

21 April 1945	First Byelorussian Front enters outer suburbs of Berlin. Goering leaves Berlin.
22 April 1945	First Ukrainian Front enters Berlin, reaching Lankwitz and Marienfelde by evening.
23 April 1945	Red Army occupies Potsdam. 56th Panzer Corps moves into the centre of Berlin. Goering dismissed.
24 April 1945	General Weidling of the 56th Panzer Corps is made Commandant of Berlin. Koniev's and Zhukov's forces encircle Büsse's Ninth Army south-east of Berlin.
25 April 1945	Zhukov's and Koniev's forces complete the encirclement of Berlin. Koniev's forces meet United States forces at Torgau on the Elbe.
26 April 1945	Last Allied air raid on Berlin (no. 363).

Bombs dropped over Berlin in the Second World War: 45,500 tons; 50,000 people killed, 100,000 people injured; 612,000 houses destroyed (roughly 40 per cent of the city).

26 April 1945	Büsse starts the attempted escape of Ninth Army towards Wenck and the West.
28 April 1945	Himmler 'discredited'. SS General Fegelein shot. Hitler marries Eva Braun.
29 April 1945	Hitler writes and dispatches his Last Will and Political Testament.
30 April 1945	Hitler commits suicide (along with Eva Braun). Red Army storms Reichstag.
1 May 1945	Goebbels commits suicide.
2 May 1945	Chancellery 'Group' escape. Bormann commits suicide. Weidling surrenders Berlin to Chuikov (under Zhukov).
8 May 1945	VE-Day.
4 July 1945	Western Allies take up their respective zones of occupation in Berlin.
17 July 1945– 2 August 1945	Potsdam Conference.

Principal Sources and Select Bibliography

The authors gratefully acknowledge the following sources:

Adlon, H., *Hotel Adlon* (Horizon, 1960)

Andreas-Friedrich, R., *Berlin Underground* (Henry Holt, 1947)

Bock, M., Unpublished diary (Copyright: Mrs I. N. Austin)

Brett-Smith, R., *Berlin '45: the grey city* (Hutchinson, 1966)

Büsse, T., *The Last Battle of the 9th German Army* (*Military Science Review*, April 1955)

Byford Jones, W., *Berlin Twilight* (Hutchinson, 1947)

Chuikov, V. I., *The End of the Third Reich* (Grafton Books, 1967)

Dilks, D., ed., *The Diaries of Sir Alexander Cadogan, O.M.* (Cassell, 1971)

Georgen, C., *Berlin 1945, sur les traces du Sturmbataillon de la Division Charlemagne* (*In the Footsteps of the Storm-battalion of the Charlemagne Division*, *Tactiques*, 1986, part 3)

Gross, L., *The Last Jew in Berlin* (Sidgwick and Jackson, 1983)

Grützner, G. and Heise-Schirdewan, R. *Cecilienhof 1945: historische fotos der Potsdamer Konferenz* (*Cecilienhof 1945: historical photos of the Potsdam Conference*, Generaldirektion der Staatlichen Schlösser und Gärten, Potsdam-Sanssouci, 1985)

Horstmann, L., *Nothing for Tears* (Weidenfeld and Nicolson, 1953)

von Kardorff, U., *Diary of a Nightmare* (Hart-Davis, 1965, copyright: Grafton Books)

Kerstan, R., *Blood and Honour* (Lion Publishing, 1980)

Koniev, I. S., *Year of Victory* (Progress Publishers, 1969, copyright: Copyright Agency of the USSR)

Kuby, E., *The Russians and Berlin 1945* (Heinemann, 1956, copyright: Scherz Verlag)

Le Tissier, A. H., ed., *Berlin Soldier* (edited translation and abridgement of Altner, H., *Totentanz Berlin 1947*, *Berlin Bulletin*, 1985 (Copyright: Jonathan Cape, 1988)

Littlejohn, D., *Foreign Legions of the Third Reich* (Bender, 1979)

Lochner, L. P., ed., *The Goebbels Diaries* (Hamish Hamilton, 1948)

Mabire, J., *La Division Nordland: les volontaires Scandinavies sur le Front de l'Est 1941–1945* (*The Nordland Division: the Scandinavian volunteers on the Eastern Front 1941–1945*, Fayard, 1982)

Meissner, H.-O., *Magda Goebbels: a biography* (Sidgwick and Jackson, 1980)

Neustroyev, S. A., *Shturm Raikhstaga* (*Storming the Reichstag*, Voenno-istoricheskii Zhurnal, 1960)

O'Donnell, J. P., *The Berlin Bunker* (Dent, 1979)

Ryan, C., *The Last Battle* (Collins, 1966, copyright: Paul Gitlin Agency)

Speer, A., *Inside the Third Reich: memoirs* (Weidenfeld and Nicolson, 1970)

Stemann, P. E. v., Unpublished diary (copyright: P. E. v. Stemann)

Studnitz, H.-G., *While Berlin Burns* (Weidenfeld and Nicolson, 1964)

Toland, J., *The Last 100 Days* (Barker, 1966, copyright: Random House)

Trevor-Roper, H. R., ed., *The Goebbels Diaries: the last days* (Secker and Warburg, 1978)

Trevor-Roper, H. R., *The Last Days of Hitler* (Macmillan, 1947)

Tully, A., *Berlin: story of a battle* (Simon and Schuster, 1963, copyright: Harold Matson & Co.)

Vosske, H., ed., *Wilhelm Pieck 1876–1960: Bilder und Dokumente aus seinem Leben* (*Wilhelm Pieck 1876–1960: pictures and documents from his life*, Verlag Neues Leben, 1975)

Wendl, E., *Hausfrau at War* (Odhams Press, 1957)

Visitors to Berlin might find the following general maps useful:

Die General Karte, Blatt 5, 1:200,000, published by Mairs Geographischer Verlag, German Democratic Republic

A good street map of East and West Berlin (e.g. Berlin Stadtplan, published by B. V. Reise- und Verkehrsverlag)

These are both available from specialist booksellers in the UK.

INDEX

Index

Academy of Art, Berlin, 111
Adlon, Louis, 109–11
Adolf-Hitler-Platz, 139
Air raids
  22 November 1943, 23, 102
  3 February 1945, 30, 32–3
Alexanderplatz, 97
Allies, Western, 15–16, 45, 50,
  117, 132, 180–1
Altner, Helmuth, 34–7, 58–61,
  118–25, 172–6
Ambassadors
  Anfuso (Italian), 26
  Oshima, Gen. Hiroshi
    (Japanese), 32, 187
American forces, 76, 172–3, 203
Amery, John, 62, 64
Amery, Julian, 62
Amery, Leo, 62
Andreas-Friedrich, Ruth, 94–7
Anti-Fascist Action Group,
  181–2
Arado, 96, 132
Ardennes, 50
Army, German
  9th, 74–8, 117
  12th, 76–8, 117, 172
Army Group Vistula, 38, 49, 54
Army, Soviet
  3rd Guards Tank, 72–3, 144
  4th Guards Tank, 73
  8th Guards, 64–9
Army, Tzarist, 69
Atom Bomb, 195
Attlee, Clement, 192–6
Augsburger Strasse, 106
Augusta-Viktoria Hospital, 126
Auschwitz, 86, 159, 179, 204
Austrians, 139
Autobahn, Fürstenwalde, 120
Axmann, Artur, 168

Babelsberg, 188
Babick, SS Obersturmführer,
  153–5
Battalion, Naval, 128
Battalion, SS 'Death', 122
Battery, 3rd Heavy Flak, 153–5
Baur, Hans, 166–8
Bavaria, 125, 201
Bayerische Strasse, 92
Beelitz, 77
Beeskow, 74–5
Bellevuestrasse, 32
Beltau, Hans, 73
Berlin airlift, 181, 201
Berlin defence rings, 116
Berliner Ring *Autobahn*, 62,
  68–9
Berlin Garrison, 115
Berlin–Oder highway, 68
Berlin Philharmonic Orchestra,
  187
Berlin, surrender of, 171
Berlin Wall, 11–12, 17, 181
Beusselstrasse Station, 133–5
Bevin, Ernest, 193–5
Bindow, 121
Bock, Max, 41–5, 101–5, 179,
  181–5
Boddinstrasse, 203
Borchard, Leo, 187
Bormann, Martin, 41, 117, 150,
  158, 166–8
Boyev, Capt., 136
Brandenburg Gate, 12, 43, 109,
  130–2, 166, 192
Brandt, Ernst, 85–6
Braun, Eva, 105, 129, 156–8,
  191
Brett-Smith, Capt. Richard,
  185–8
British Delegation, 188, 192

Britische Freikorps, 62–4, 117
British General Election, 192–3
Buch Hospital, 158
Buchholz, 77–8
Buckower Forest, 68
Burgdorf, Gen., 129
Büsse, Gen. Theodor, 74–8
Butcher, Oberscharführer, 62
Byelorussian Front, first, 49–50,
    53–4, 64–9
Byford-Jones, Lt.-Col., 196–201
Byrnes, Sec. of State, 192–3

Cadogan, Sir Alexander, 188–93
Cecilienhof, 189, 190, 195
Channukah, the Festival of
    Lights, 92
Charlotte Bridge, 124, 172
Charlottenburger Chaussee, 41,
    44
Checkpoint Charlie, 12
Chuikov, Gen. Vasily Ivanovich,
    64–9, 140–3, 169–71
Churchill, Winston, 15, 188–95
Churekov, Ivan, 158
Clara-Zetkin-Strasse, 12
Cologne, 23
Cordes, Gerhard, 55–8
Corps, German
    3rd, 62
    56th Panzer, 74, 115, 169–71
Corps, Soviet, 5th Mechanized,
    77–8
Cottbus, 51, 70, 76
Crimea, 50
Croatia, 32
Croat Legation, 32–3
Croner, Fritz, 90–3
Croner, Lane, 90–3
Croner, Marlitt, 90–3
Czechoslovakia, 201

Dammsmühle, 40
Diedersdorf, 65
Divisions, German
    9th Parachute, 54
    SS 'Charlemagne' Panzer
        Grenadier, 162–3

SS 'Kurmark' Panzer
    Grenadier, 76–8
SS 'Leibstandarte Adolf Hitler'
    Panzer, 125
SS 'Nordland' Panzer
    Grenadier, 62, 117, 162–8
Division, Soviet, 79th Guards,
    169
Döberitz, 140, 172–3
Dolgelin, 65
Dönitz, Grand Adm., 132,
    150–3, 166
Dorotheenstrasse, 12, 43
Dresden, Destruction of, 33

Eastern Front, 34, 49, 62, 84, 92
Ebertstrasse, 12
Eden, Anthony, 188–92
Eisenhower, Gen. Dwight D., 69,
    180
Elbe river, 16, 50, 76–8, 118, 153,
    159, 172
Elsholz, 77

Falkenhagen, 35, 69
Fasanenstrasse, 102
Fegelein, SS Gen., 144
'Ferdinand' self-propelled guns,
    68
Fieseler Storch, 130
Finow, 74
Flak towers, 21, 43, 118
Focke-Wolf, 190, 130–2
Foreign representatives in Berlin,
    30, 109
Foreign SS volunteers, 62–4,
    117, 128, 163–5
Frankfurt/Oder, 50, 74–6
Freisler, Dr, Pres. of People's
    Court, 32
Fricke, Lt., 120–1
Friedenau, 182
Friedersdorf, 62
Friedrichsfelde, 200
Friedrichstrasse, 12, 118, 166–8
Friedrichstrasse Station, 43, 165
Fritzsche, Hans, 105
Führer's bunker, 74, 117–18,

125, 128–9, 157–8, 161–2, 166

Fürstenwalde, 34, 120

Gartenstadt Staaken, 173
Gas chambers, 33
Gatow, 130–2
Gedächtniskirche (Kaiser Wilhelm Memorial Church), 23, 139, 187
Gestapo, 21, 22, 26, 29, 88–90, 92
Glienicke, 101
Goebbels, children of, 159–62
Goebbels, Josef, 16, 28, 33, 37–8, 41, 51, 81, 105, 117, 137, 150, 158–62
Goebbels, Magda, 41, 132, 158–62
Goering, Hermann, 40, 117, 130, 150, 169, 184
Gorodov, Capt., 135
Goethe Garden, 109–11
Götterdämmerung, 16, 161
Granberg, Herje (Swedish journalist), 28
Greek Government, 192
Greim, Col.-Gen., Robert Ritter von, 130–3
Gritsenko, Col. Yefin, 65
Grünewald, 137–9, 144
Grünewald park, 130
Guderian, Gen., Chief of the General Staff, 33
Guselnikov, Capt., 147
Gusev, Sen.-Lt., Kuzma, 147

Halbe, 77
Hallensee Bridge, 144–6
Halskestrasse, 182
Hamburg, 41
Hanover, 36
Hasenfelde, 118
Hauptgraben–Alte Oder waterways, 53
Havel Lake, 152, 159
Havel, River, 172–3, 185

Headquarters
German General Staff, 72–3, 169
Gestapo, 29, 163–9, 171
Military, 29, 163
Reich Labour Service, 144
Heinrici, Gen., 38–40, 49–51
Herman-Goering-Strasse, 28, 152, 159
Himmler, Heinrich, 28, 41, 49, 117, 132
Himmler's House, *see* Ministry of Interior
Hiroshima, 195
Hitler, Adolf, 15–17, 28, 33, 34, 37–41, 49, 76, 100, 105, 117, 128–9, 130–2, 137, 150–2, 156–61, 166, 179, 181, 191, 201
Hitler's birthday, 106
Hitler Youth, 34, 115–16, 118, 120–5, 127–8, 135, 141, 152, 173, 181, 201–4
Hohenstein, 62
Hohenzollerndamm, 137
Hohenzollernstrasse, 86
Holocaust, 26, 93
Home Guard, *see* Volkssturm
Horstmann, Lali, 82–5
Horstmann, Freddy, 82–5
Hotel
Adlon, 25, 28, 29, 30, 108–11
Am Zoo, 196–7
Bristol, 26, 108
Eden, 25, 108
Esplanade, 28–9, 33, 108
Habel, 108
Kaiserhof, 108
Humboldtshain Park, 118
Hussars, 11th Regiment, 185

Invalidenstrasse, 45–6, 168
Iron Crosses, 144–6
Italian fleet, 192
Italian Front, 25

Japanese Embassy, 187
Jebenstrasse, 137–9

Jehovah's Witness, 45
Jews, 15, 40, 45, 92–3, 179, 200, 204
Johannmeier, Maj. Willi, 152
July 20th Bomb Plot, 22, 26–9, 32, 45
Jungvolk, 34

Kaiser Platz, 185
Kantaria, Meliton, 150
Kantstrasse, 146, 187
Kardorff, Klaus von, 22–5
Kardorff, Ursula von, 22–6
Katukov, Gen., 54
Katyusha rockets, 53, 65, 76, 116
Kellerkinder, 168
Kempka, SS Col. Erich, 159
Kerstan, Reinhold, 201–4
Kerzendorf, 82–5
Ketzin, 175
Kielganstrasse, 32
Kietz, 53
Kiev, 179
Kindlebenstrasse, 101
Kitzbühel, 133
Kladow, 98–100
Klausdorf, 77
Klein Ziethen, 121
Kolonnenstrasse, 141
Koniev, Marshal Ivan Stepanovich, 51, 54, 69–73, 74–7
Königsberg, 50
Königsplatz, 147, 187
Königs Wusterhausen, 40–1, 121
Köpenick, 69
Kosney, Cpl. Herbert, 45–6
Kosney, Kurt, 45
Krampnitzerweg, 101
Krebs, Gen., 129, 161
Kriegk, Dr Otto, 43
Kronprinzenallee, 139
Krukenberg, SS Brigadeführer, Dr Gustav, 162–5
Kummersdorf, 77, 120
Kurfürstendamm, 22, 23, 104, 187
Kurfürstenstrasse, 25
Kursk, 50

Küstrin, 55, 64, 74
Kustrin road, 55–7, 76

Landwehr Canal, 139
Lanke, 159
Lankwitz, 97, 182–4
Latin America, 117
Lehrter Station, 168
Leipziger Platz, 12
Lemke, Capt. Hilde, 144–6
Lenin, 140, 184
Ley, Dr Robert, 43
Lichtenrade, 86–8
Liebknecht, Karl, 198–200
Liedtke, Fritz, 88–90
Lietzen, 36–7, 58–61, 118
Lietzenburger Strasse, 102
Lightning fighter, 21
Lorenz, Heinz, 152–3
Lübben, 70–2
Lüdicke, Helmut, 105–8
Lüdicke, Willy, 105–8
Luftwaffe, 21, 49, 70, 130–3
Lustgarten, 200
Luxemburg, Rosa, 198–200

Magdeburg, 203
Mariendorf, 185
Masalov, Sgt. Nikolai, 141–3
May Day, 104, 115, 169
Meinekestrasse, 43, 102–4, 185
Messerschmidt, 109, 60
Military Police, 120
Ministry
   Foreign, 30–4, 109
   Propaganda, 22, 28, 152
   Interior, 116, 136, 147, 153
Minsk, 179
Moabit, 133–6, 147
Moabit Prison, 45–6, 147
Mohnke, SS Gen., 126
Molotov, 108, 192–3
Moltke the Younger Bridge, 136, 147
Mongolia, 86, 88
Montgomery, SS Unterscharführer, 62
Moscow, 50, 70, 96–7, 198

Müller, SS Gruppenführer
 Heinrich, 45
Müncheberg, 68
Munich, 130
Mustang fighter, 21

Nachtausgabe (newspaper), 43
Nagasaki, 195
National Labour Service, 34
NATO, 12
Neisse river, 49–51, 69–72, 74
Neuenhagen, 64
Neukölln, 88, 163
Neustroyev, Capt. Stepan, 133–6
Nieder-Finow ship elevator, 40
Niederneuendorfer Strasse, 122
Nieplitz Stream, 78
NKVD army, 190
Nollendorfplatz, 105–6
Normandy, 50
Nürnberger Strasse, 106

Oder, Battle of, 38–40, 50–8, 76,
 109
Oder Bruch Valley, 55, 65, 74
Oder–Neisse line, 11, 16, 191
Oder river, 22, 38, 49, 64, 69, 74
Olivaer Platz, 92
Olympic Stadium, 124, 130
Operation Barbarossa, 15, 159
Oranienburg Gate, 165
Oranienburger Strasse, 43
Ordenspalais, 159
Oslo, 73

Palestine, 92
Panzerfaust shells, 55, 57
Pariser Platz, 3, 25
Pasewin, 175
Persia, 190
Pestalozzistrasse, 197
Pfaueninsel, 152
Pichelsdorfer Strasse, 185
Pichelsdorf, 152
Pickford, Mary, 108
Pieck, Wilhelm, 200–1
Pneumonia, 101, 198
Poland, 49, 64, 190–1

Poles, 15, 163
Polevoi, Maj. Boris, 72–3
Political officers, 140–1
'Position 16', 36
'Position 22', 37
Potsdam, 12, 82, 98, 101, 185
Potsdam Bridge, 141–4, 169–71
Potsdam Conference, 181, 188–96
Potsdamer Platz, 12, 28
Pozharski, Gen., 143
Prague, 73
Prelov, Capt., 147
Prenzlau, 38
Press Club, 28
Priesterweg, 94
Pritzsch, Maj. Arnulf, 137–40

Quastenhornweg, 98

Ranke Platz, 102
Rankestrasse, 22, 25
Rauen, 120
Red Army, 21, 22, 49–51, 54, 82
Rechlin, 130
Rechlin Air Base, 166
Reich Chancellery, 104, 109, 118,
 130, 144–5, 166, 191
 Garages, 152
 Garden, 158, 162
 New, 125–8
 Old, 125, 128
Reichssportfeld, 124–5
Reichstag, 116, 118, 128, 135–6,
 147–50, 153–6, 168–9, 191
Reichstag Debating Chamber,
 155
Reitsch, Hanna, 130–3
Reitwein, 53, 54
Reyman, Gen., 38
Ribbentrop, Joachim von, 32, 33,
 105
Ringstrasse, 188, 193
Roseneck, 137
Roskow, 175
Royal Air Force (thousand-bomber
 raid), 21
Ruhleben, 118, 121, 139, 172
Ruhleben Barracks, 121–5, 172

Rukavina, Alfred (Croatian Chargé d'Affaires), 32
Rybalko, Col. Gen., 72

Salzbrunn, 77
Salzkorn, 175
S-Bahn, 116
Schenck, Prof. Ernst-Gunther, 125–9
Schiffbauerdamm, 168
Schillerstrasse, 198
Schleswig-Holstein, 132, 152
Schloss Strasse, 126
Schmargendorf Station, 144–6
Schönefeld aerodrome, 69, 121
Schorfheide, 40
Schulstrasse, 184
Schwanenwerder, 159
Seeckt, von, barracks, 185
Seelow, 54–8
Seelow Heights, 50–1, 58, 65, 115
Semikov, Col. Alexander, 65
Senzig, 121
'Seydlitz' forces, 60–1
Siberia, 159
Siegessäule, 192
Silesia, 191
Silbersteinstrasse, 88
Simonov, Konstantin, 68
Slave-labourers, 135, 147, 179
Sobibor, 179
Sørenson, SS Sturmbannführer Per, 62–4
Sorge, Jutta, 23–5
Soulier, SS Grenadier Pierre, 162–5
Soviet Air Force, 60
Soviet National Anthem, 97
Soviet spies (in USA), 195
Spandau, 21, 122–4, 139, 172–3, 185
Spandauerdamm, 139
Spandau Gaol, 41
Speer, Albert, 22, 37–41
Spree, River, 69–72, 135–6, 147
Spreewald, 51, 74–6
Spremberg, 70
Stadmitte Station, 163–5

Stalingrad, 50, 198
Stalin, Joseph, 15–16, 51, 68–72, 81, 136, 140, 181, 184, 190–5
Stalinplatz, 200
Stankevich, Pte., 135
State Defence Council, 30
State Opera House, 197
Stauffenburg, von, 45
Steglitz, 93, 96, 126, 182
Stemann, Paul E. V., 26–9
Stolzburg, Panzergrenadier, 94–6
Storkow, 76
Stormovik dive-bombers, 70
Strausberg, 62
Stresowplatz, 140
Studnitz, Hans Georg von, 30–4
Stumpfegger, Dr, 168
Sudetenland, 201
Swedish Lutherans, 93
Swiss Legation, 136, 156
Syanov, Sen.-Sgt., 147–50

Tanks
'Joseph Stalins', 55
Sherman, 88
T-34, 55, 64, 146
Tiger, 65, 78, 139
Tiger II, 165
Tauentzienstrasse, 105–6
Teheran Conference, 191
Teltow Canal, 182
Teupitz, 77
Theater des Westens, 187
Treblinka, 86, 179
Truman, Harry S., 188, 191–5
Tsarist Émigrés, 185
Turkey, 190
Tyrlaching, 201–3

Uhlandstrasse, 146
Ukraine, 85, 86
Ukrainian Front, first, 51, 68–73
ULAP Exhibition Hall, 46
Undermann, SS Untersturmführer, 153
United Nations, 192
Unter den Linden, 11, 43, 109, 137, 166, 169

Untermensch, 54, 179

Vaulot, Eugène, 163
Victory Column, 43
Vienna, 36
Volga, 64
Volkssturm, 88, 93, 106, 115,
    120–1, 135, 168, 175
Voss Strasse, 125

Walhallastrasse, 197
Wannsee, 152–3
Warsaw, 49, 179
Wehrmacht, 22, 34, 40, 49, 86, 118,
    135, 172
Weidendamm Bridge, 43, 118,
    165–6
Weidling, Gen., 74–6, 117, 163,
    169–72
Wenck, Gen., 76–8
Wendl family, 98–101
Werewolves, 40, 96
Werftstrasse, 197
Westend, 118
Western Front, 92
Westhafen Canal, 133–6
White Russians, 93
Wilhelmplatz, 159
Wilhelmstrasse, 125

Wilhelmstrasse Station, 166
Wittbrietzen, 77
Wolf's Lair, East Prussia, 28
Wrietzen, 38
Wünsdorf, 77

Yalta, 15–16, 69, 180
Yegorov, Mikhail, 150
Yellow Star of David, 33, 93, 182,
    204
Yermakov, Maj.-Gen., 77–8
Young Communists, 133–5, 141
Yugoslavia, 32

Zachow, 175
Zander, SS Col. Wilhelm, 152–3
Zarn, Rudolph, 84
Zarn, Ulla, 84
Zilch, Luftwaffe NCO Gerhard,
    153–6
Zhukov, Marshal, Georgi
    Konstantinovich, 49–54
Zones of occupation, 11–12, 180
    British, 100–1
    Soviet, 101, 180, 203
Zoo, 23, 43, 102–5, 139, 185
Zoo Bunker, 21, 43, 102, 105, 139,
    146
Zossen, 72–3